BOOKS BY JAY R. LEACH

How Should We Then Live
Behold the Man
The Blood Runs Through It
Drawn Away
Give Me Jesus
A Lamp unto My Feet
Grace that Saves
The Narrow Way
Radical Restoration in the Church
Manifestation of the True Children of God
According to Pattern
Battle Cry
Is there not a Cause?
We Would See Jesus!

WE WOULD SEE JESUS

*Making Christ visible to
a dying world through
grace and truth*

JAY R. LEACH

Trafford rev. 01/15/2020

 www.trafford.com
North America & international
toll-free: 1 888 232 4444 (USA & Canada)
fax: 812 355 4082

And there were certain
Greeks among them that
came up to worship at
the feast the same came to
Phillip ...... saying,
"<u>Sir, we would see Jesus.</u>"

– John 12:20-21

"Now when they saw the boldness of
Peter and John,
and perceived that they were
uneducated and untrained men
they marveled.
And realized that,
"<u>They had been with Jesus.</u>"

– Acts 4:13

CONTENTS

ONE SOLITARY LIFE

He was born in an obscure village, the child of a peasant woman. He grew up in still another village, where He worked in a carpentry shop until He was 30. Then for three years He was an itinerant preacher. He never wrote a book. He never held an office. He never had a family or owned a house. He didn't go to college. He never traveled more than 200 miles from the place He was born. He did none of the things one usually associates with greatness. He had no credentials but Himself. He was only 33 when public opinion turned against Him. His friends deserted Him. He was turned over to His enemies and went through the mockery of a trial. He was nailed to a cross between two thieves when He was dead; He was laid in a borrowed grave through the pity of a friend. Nineteen centuries have come and gone, and today He is the central figure of humanity, the leader of mankind's progress. All the armies that ever marched, and all the navies that ever sailed, all the parliaments that ever sat, all the kings that ever reigned, put together, have not affected the life of man on earth as much as that One Solitary Life. "Do You Know Who He Is?"

By: Dr. James Allen Francis in "The Real Jesus and Other Sermons" 1925

INTRODUCTION

Augustine is considered the "founder of theology" by both Roman Catholic and Protestant theologians. Perhaps the most disastrous change made by him and the early church fathers as they filtered biblical truth through their pagan oriented mindsets – was their redefining of the way of salvation. This has resulted in "repentance" which is foundational to a true salvation experience – being moved by many churches to optional status. In fact, the intellectual Greek mindset changed the wording from "believing in" to "believing that" certain doctrines are true. Accordingly, many of these writers led their readers to believe that salvation comes by "believing that certain doctrines are true."

That one small change in wording has had a mountainous impact, as salvation was redefined through intellectual agreement with a set of doctrines. Instead of "Who do I trust for salvation?" The issue then became "What doctrines must I affirm to be saved?" This type of twisted theology put the American Christian Church into a doctrinal spin that has resulted in centuries of acute doctrinal speculation, trying to precisely define *every* point of doctrine – and accusing those who disagree, of being heretics or heathens.

Satan has in his attempt to destroy the church worked these changes into church doctrine [which in many cases is some individual's or some group's re-interpretation of biblical doctrine]. On many occasions Jesus cautioned his disciples concerning the dangers of the doctrines of men. However, throughout the New Testament writings we find these same warnings over and over again. There is a saying that, *"if you entertain a lie long enough, it becomes truth."* Church history reflects many instances where the doctrines of men have been placed above or even in lieu of biblical doctrinal truth. We are experiencing daily, as our materialistic society puts "self" and "things" above God and His revealed truth. This was the practice from the second century until the days of Constantine; at which time he moved the church from its Jewish origin – opening the door for Greek, paganism, synthesis's secularism and other humanistical and philosophical influences over the centuries to take control of theology using new titles but, it's the same old poison.

Many of these "isms" have come along to contaminate various biblical doctrines [truths] at the local church level to the point where some churches, rather than search the Scriptures – simply become a collection of people, who are developing their very own theology [many individually] based on .what works for them. All due mainly to the prevailing mind-set of "no absolutes" in our all-ready mostly secular-humanistic society. Church, we've got to do better then that! Christians in America today, are engaged in a "truth war" with "demon-possessed culture" for the very soul of this nation. It is quite apparent, we cannot force the "ungodly secular culture" to abide by biblical principles and values. However, being the Church of the Living God, we can *renew* our commitment individually and corporately to God and focus on our own spirituality and standards of conduct as we live daily as "salt and light" in this ever-darkening world.

We cannot stand by *in silence* and watch our families, churches and other institutions being pulverized and crumbling along with the nation. We must counter-attack with meaningful and renewed involvement in our churches, communities and homes. Spirit-guided in so doing, we can work to reclaim our families and churches in new life-changing ways, based on the unchanging "Truth" of God's Word. The writers of the New Testament addressed the churches as the Church of Ephesus, Church of Rome, Church of Galatia, the idea being "one" Church made up of a vast number of believers, yet they live in different parts of the world, so how could they possibly be *one?*

In this book I offer what I see as principal help for countering this devastating theological fiasco that is influencing so many of America's local Black churches in their Christian theology today. My thesis is simple: We must obediently renew the church to the purposes and commands of our Lord and Savior Jesus Christ, Founder and Head, to "make disciples" and "teach them to *obey all* that He commanded [the Bible]!" Presently, in many local Black churches few are willing to accept the challenge to do the teaching. They contend that the new believers have a Bible and the same Holy Spirit we have; "He will guide them into all truth." In the meantime works righteousness, pluralism, departure from the truth, division, and blatant deception are running rampart in many local churches almost at will as "tares" move into key positions.

Additionally, if we are going to be the church of Jesus Christ, we must restore our love [GK. Agape] for God and others in unconditional fellowship [GK. *Koinonia*] centered around shared true biblically-based beliefs and practices, virtues, and values (carefully study Revelation 2:1-7).

`"There can be no deep disappointment where there is no deep love."[1] Likewise, no church can possibly be effective in bringing clarity and commitment to a lost world when it is [voluntarialy], spiritually and biblically illiterate of its own basic principles; which is the case with many of our local churches, this condition is fueled mainly by resistance to change [renewal] coming from unspiritual winskins.

After extensive research on the social world of the first-century church: Another peculiar point concerning early Christianity was the way in which the intimate, close-knit life of the local groups was viewed to be simultaneously "part of a larger, indeed ultimate movement."[2]

Psychologist John Locke would agree. After classifying contemporary society as the first society with attention deficit disorder, Locke writes, "From a physical standpoint, a community is a collection of individuals, but the residents of a true Christian community act like members of something that is much larger than them selves."[3] Amen! Satan is bent on keeping confusion going among the various people groups; which allows him to stealthly move (almost) at will among them in the same manner and purposes he did with Adam and Eve (see Genesis 1-3). From our introduction as slaves, all meaningful gains of African Americans in America were the results of our realizing that as a people, we are involved in something that is much larger than we are! As in the past – only God can deliver us, again! Do you know Him?

Satan, the prince of this world's systems, strives to keep the Church [off balance] from its charge: the local church is to equip and serve our people to be the church to one another. From discipline to benevolence – through equipping our pastors to *shepherd well* – as we continue to push ministry back down to [all] the *members* where it belongs, a living and spiritual organism. There is no substitute for the Church being the true Church [the body of Christ]!

In the divine redemptive plan of God *all* the people of God are called and gifted to play a *primary* role in discipleship; and the loving community of the church is the primary context wherein discipleship takes place. So, you need to declare right now even before reading chapter one; that you are going to be the Church of the Living God [a living and spiritual organism], His ministers of reconciliation. We attempt in this book to show what the reality of a healthy church and each Christian's life looks like – *after* seeing Jesus for themself!

When it comes to the mission of making disciples, as the Lord commanded, much of the African American Church has settled for the mundane substitutes for family and church life. The true Church of Jesus Christ, is experiencing a miraculous move of God to restore the Great Commission of Christ back into the hands of *all* the people of God through love, compassion, and spiritual-giftedness! My prayer is that God will grant us grace, that we allow the Holy Spirit to empower our local churches to accomplish our God assigned missions to the world – by proclamation of the true Gospel of Christ and demonstration of God's presence and power through us. As the people of God, we are commanded to seek first the kingdom of God and *all* these other things will be added (Matthew 6:33). Let us repent and once again, "lift our eyes to Calvary." Where, "God so loved the world, that he gave His only begotten Son, that whoever, believes in Him should not perish, but have everlasting life" (John 3:16).

Jay R. Leach
Fayetteville, North Carolina
December 25, 2019

SECTION I

WHAT JESUS SAID AND DID

Chapter 1

JESUS, KING AND MODEL SERVANT

Jesus said to him, "You shall love the LORD your God with all your heart, with all your soul, and with all your mind. This is the first and great commandment. And the second is like it: *You shall love your neighbor as yourself"* (Matthew 22:37-40).

Jesus came into the world for a purpose; He knew that He was the Messiah. He knew that the Father's will for Him was to die for the sins of the whole world and thereby secure the salvation for whoever would receive it. In John 5:19 we read, "Most assuredly, I say to you, the Son can do nothing of Himself, but what He sees the Father do; for whatever He does, the Son does in a like manner." Jesus never did a thing but what He saw the Father do and what He heard the Father say" (John 8:28, 38).

He also knew that God had called Him to *head* a new people, [New Testament ministers of reconciliation], His body, the organismic Church, and not just to be an individual redeemer. Therefore, His initial act after His baptismal-temptation experiences was to be begin a *fellowship* with four men who would later become *disciples*, traveling and living with Him (see John 1:35).

Jesus cannot give the command to love God without including the command to love our fellowman (Matthew 22:37-40).

Like Jesus, our vertical relationship with God must always be accompanied by our horizontal relationship with the people of God. Immediately, Jesus began to live out God's will and purpose as both the servant and King mirroring God in what He said and did.

Both His *words* and *deeds* revealed His nature – so, it is to be with His true children. When John the Baptist's disciples on a later occasion asked if He was the Christ, Jesus replied, *"Go and tell John the things which you hear and see"* (Matthew 11:4). Emphasis added throughout.

These two expressions, *words* and *deeds* work in tandem, complimenting one another. What Jesus said interpreted what He did – and what He did, interpreted or explained the meaning of much of what He said. Both served to reveal to humanity – what God is like. Jesus made visible the invisible God (see Colossians 1:15) by reflecting three things:

1. The character of God's nature (see Hebrews 1:3).
2. The fact that He was God (see John 1:1; 1 John 5:20; Colossians 2:9).
3. The fact that He had put on flesh (see John 1:14; Philippians 2:5).

When we see both kingship and servant-hood in Jesus, we are to know that God is both Lord and Servant. Jesus said, *"He who has seen Me has seen the Father"* (John 14:9). God has been man's serving Lord from Creation.

Throughout His entire earthly life, we see either His king (Lord) or His servant role being manifested. His very first miracle manifested Him as Lord of creation as He changed water into wine (see John 2:1-11). His first act after that [cleansing the temple] indicated that He had come to initiate a "new dispensation" [His future people living in the present], the new temple that God had promised.

The New Temple

At this time the Jews believed that God's house was the temple where He lived in only one room, but Jesus promised a new temple – the temple of the body (John 2:13-22). God had intended from the very beginning that He would live in the *hearts* of His people, His earthly temple (Genesis 2:7). Therefore, at the beginning of His ministry, Jesus announced the events that would make that possible – His death and His resurrection (John 2:19). Later Jesus stressed the possibility of the "new life" in the kingdom of God:

•   A person must repent and experience a new spiritual birth from above (see John 3:5; 1 Corinthians 5:21).

- The new life experienced must be the life of the Spirit (see John 6:63; 7:37-39; Romans 7:6; I Corinthians 15:45; 2 Corinthians 3:6).
- Jesus taught that the availability of the Holy Spirit would be possible because of His death (see John 3:14, 15).
- God's motivation was behind it all (see John 3:16).

Leaving Judea, the place of His baptism and first miracle, Jesus stressed again that a new day would come:

- When people would worship God in spirit and in truth (John 4:24).
- He promised that He could give that Spirit (John 4:14; John 7:38).
- He showed that He was Lord over life by healing the official's son (see John 4:46).

Meet your King

After His temptation experience with Satan (Matthew 4:1-11), Jesus announced His platform as the expected Messiah during a sermon in His hometown synagogue. He read from Isaiah 61:1-2,

"The Spirit of the Lord GOD is
upon Me,
Because the LORD has anointed
Me
To preach good tidings to the poor;
He has sent Me to heal the
brokenhearted,
To proclaim liberty to the
captives,
And the opening of the prison to
those who are bound;
to proclaim the acceptable year of
the LORD."
(Luke 4:18, 19)

That prophecy in Isaiah referred to the suffering servant-king. Jesus continued, "Today the Scripture has been fulfilled in your hearing" (Luke 4:21).

He was telling them that the King has come and is with them, but the people did not catch on to the activities listed in the Isaiah passage. They did not take the passage literally as God meant it or as Jesus lived it:

- The poor
- The captives
- The blind
- The oppressed

These were the neglected people in Israel. False human-made barriers were constructed to keep these down-trodden people in their place. To the Jewish leadership these people were considered no-bodies or invisible. Sadly, that same spirit was loosed in this country during slavery and is subtly being openly manifested today. Keeping people of color down and in their so-called place is embedded in the very fiber of too much of white America. Subtly the old belief in the superiority of the white race and the moral degradation of African Americans is re-emerging. All the world's systems in this country are geared consciously or unconsciously with that built-in racial bias. The reconciliation that Jesus won at Calvary tore-down racial barriers among Christians. But doesn't that include racial reconciliation? Are local churches obedient to our Lord across this nation? It seems that few are striving to make it happen today. Many churches simply forfeit the Great Commission if reconciliation means assembling ourselves together. Praise God for the remnant. This will be explored at length as we go along in later chapters.

Bridges to God's Grace

There is a huge gap in our society between where increasingly more people are in their lives – and where they desire to be. As tensions continue to rise, even some believers regularly find themselves in a place where God's restorative power seems out of reach. Many people in our society are classified as those old Israelites above were – no-bodies or the invisible. At times these folk try the local church but most come away feeling that:

- The church does not feel like a place where a person can be honest about their real struggles, issues, and sins.
- Certain sins are acceptable to talk about in church, while others are not.
- The church uses shame to motivate people to change.
- Church people come across as fake and unauthentic.

- To accept church, a person must invest ample time and effort in image management or giving the impression that one is doing great and living right even when it is not true.
- The church is constantly asking for money.

Although we may not be able to immediately change the way these people feel; there is much the local church can do. One thing is to make necessary changes and provisions to meet their needs. I repeat, in His death on the cross, Jesus broke down the racial and other barriers that separate people. Satan is behind the toxic attitude and atmosphere in our society today; which has noticeably invaded much of the public square and openly challenges local churches through an angry spirit toward other races. Satan would love for those barriers to be solidified. Praise God there are true Christians in the local churches who are *prayerfully* countering that satanic spirit! Yes, there are growing tensions in this country, but praise God, those who love Christ and truly love this country are growing in grace and the knowledge of our Lord and Savior, Jesus Christ – interceding for all the people and looking forward to His return.

How godly and beautiful it would be if the leadership would prayerfully and actively follow Christ's pattern to keep those barriers down in the local churches; and realize that to do otherwise is blatant disobedience by the substitution of man-made barriers. Certainly, if we would teach and practice the character of Christ with His unconditional love shed abroad in our hearts and the Holy Spirit given to us (Romans 5:5) – our Christian influence as His ministers of reconciliation could change this nation.

A transformed life is God's instrument for effective change. This is not a time to retreat – only good can overcome evil! Therefore, the Church of God is the most influential force on earth for positive change. From the introduction as slaves in this country, through the emancipation of slavery, the Jim Crow era, and the Civil Rights era, the salvation of the African American always was and still is through the redemptive work of Jesus Christ. We saw it manifest in their faith as expressed in their prayers and the songs the "invisible church" sang. Notice their determination: they would slip away to secret places in the so-called bottom [deep woods] to worship God and conduct their prayer meetings – knowing that each time they attended a service they risked up to 200 lashes from the whip and [possible death], if caught [more in Chapter 8].

Seeing Christ in us

Who Christ is in us and who we are in Him are the two most important *realities* of the Kingdom. God taking up residence on earth in the body of Christ is the centerpiece of Scripture. That is of further importance because He has entered *every true believer* [worldwide] as the resident companion of life; thus, extending His Kingdom on earth. Christ in us is the hope of glory (Colossians 1:27).

Christ in His role of God in human flesh, is perfect. He is God on display! People were offered the privilege of seeing God the Father by seeing His Son, Jesus Christ. At the same time, seeing the Kingdom was included because it was present with Christ. Rediscovering Christ and His Church without the rediscovery of the kingdom of God would only be a half-discovery and visa-versa. Two mistakes are commonly made when we consider the kingdom of God:

1. We think of Christ's rule on earth only in future terms.
2. We look for the influence of His power and authority only in the present.

People living half-lives with half-light are not what the Scripture describes as *living* the normal Christian life. Living in clear-view of the Kingdom enables the believer to see life as the Lord intended it. Satan has turned up the heat on the church – for he knows his time is short.

Sadly, many Christians today are saying the same things as the world, mostly conclusions drawn daily from public opinion, newscasts and social media, etc. In his desperation, I believe Satan has loosed an angry spirit in this nation; which is orchastrating the present ugly conduct and behavior witnessed daily throughout the population.

It seems that much of the Black church has moved from half-light for seeing the Kingdom to little or no light. This must be reversed! Another great "spiritual awakening" through preaching and teaching with accompanying demonstration of power, the complete and true gospel of Christ (see Romans 1:16; I Corinthians 15:3-4). His kingdom will counter and derail Satan's long-playing strategy. Demonic activity was unquestioned in the early church. Not only did they know the enemy, but they knew how to defeat him. The church is relevant today that:

- Healing ministry like other gifts are not just for preachers, but given to the church for [building up the body] "through all the members" ministering wherever that Christian may be found in homes, schools, the marketplace or public square. Can God depend on you?

Remember, we are a new future people living in the present – for His glory! As New Testament priests our kingdom involvement is far greater than [self]!

- By building bridges that will connect the spiritually distraught person to the throne of God's grace – a bridge for hurting people who believe they have nowhere to go.
- The church that understands the power of grace and mercy; and refrains from condemnation, can through a ministry of [recovery] and [restoration], offer people the gift of hope and become the place where vision is renewed, and people are healed.
- The church that offers an atmosphere of acceptance and puts into place the unique elements necessary for the process of restoration to begin.
- The church of Jesus Christ provides bridges to grace we all long to experience.

Why the church?

The nature of the church is to be all the people in community who experience Jesus and live out what He said and did, while He was on the earth. For that purpose, the church is called "the body" of Christ. Luke 19:10 says, "The Son of man came to seek and to save that which was lost." Although Jesus certainly came to seek and to save the lost – His broader ministry was about saving, restoring, and recovering all that was lost in the Fall. That is our focus [God's will], that is our purpose. Are you an active-duty member?

"It is the love of Christ that compels us to no longer live for ourselves, but for Him" (2 Corinthians 5:14).

Everything that was lost to us in our sin and rebellion against God has been redeemed at the cross through the shed blood of Jesus; to one day be completely restored. Until that time God invites His followers to join Him in bringing that restoration to the lives of broken and hurting people the world over. Much of the church today is interested in so-called prosperity (how much we receive) – God's concern is in (how much we give). Many African Americans are turning away from the true Church of God, claiming that it is "too narrow." Likewise, many Black churches are striving to attract them by making themselves "too broad" just to accommodate [them]. A very subtle belief called universalism, "all will be saved." No matter the life a person lived here on earth, some preachers are willing to lie [they say] to accommodate the loved ones. If not careful, you will join the universal band by implying they are now in heaven. Lest we forget, "Hell is forever!"

Thy will be done

For years we've heard that America is facing a health crisis. It is estimated that upwards of forty-five million Americans are uninsured. By personal observation, I would say, most people of the world are not really concerned about insurance. They are concerned about health. Insurance would not help in most cases because there are no medical facilities or services available for them. These people want healing! Notice, in the Scripture we read, the people came to Jesus or someone brought the person or persons [even up to multitudes] heard, believed and came to Jesus for healing.

One Sunday morning in my first pastorate, I called the people with needs to come forward for prayer. One lady told me that after living thirty years in New York, she had just returned home to die, she was suffering from stage-four cancer and the doctors had given her up, but she believed God for healing – so did I! I prayed with her, she shouted "I'm healed!" That happened on a beautiful Sunday morning in December (1984).

Today, December 25, 2019, sitting here with this manuscript in my hand to be forwarded to the publisher tomorrow, I reminisced back on that wonderful experience, praise God she is still alert and alive, now in a rest home close in her late 90's now – but still continuously testifying of the Lord's faithfulness to heal. That is just one of the many episodes of God's grace and mercy in divine healing. In fact, two times my own wife received divine healing. I have read and heard many preachers believe that healing and deliverance was ongoing in the early church to authenticate the apostles. I would say that we need to recognize it today to authenticate our local pastors and churches today. Sadly, most churches today do proclamation only.

Think of how the local church can be restored to that New Testament truth. Disease is not a gift from God. It is an intrusion – in a life designed by the Lord for healthy living. Every good and perfect gift comes down from above (James 1:17). Under the Old Covenant, God's people lived with none of the diseases of Egypt. God had promised them, *"You will have none of those diseases"* (Exodus 15:26). Two million people living in good health without the need of a doctor! Divine healing is to be received by faith. But God also uses doctors and medicine as a means to heal. All three are gifts of God's grace – to heal.

It is God's will that we be healed. The Scripture said, *God wants us to prosper and be in health as our souls prosper* (III John 2). Healing is an emergency repair God uses to repair our bodies. Jesus taught His disciples a foundational prayer, *"… your will be done on earth as it is in heaven"* (Mathew 6:10).

All diseases are a contradiction of God's original design. Therefore, just as He taught His disciples to declare the Kingdom is at hand – He desires that we to share His healing with others. While some teach that physical healing was a means of authentication of God's power; which ended with the apostles, others talk the talk but won't walk the walk, because of unbelief. It is imperative that the church awaken to Christ's ways of not only healing the sick, but deliverance from demonic possession and/or attachments. Again, we to must remember doctors and medicine too are good gifts of God to the world.

We can begin by accepting the biblical truth of the priesthood of *all* believers; which we will further explore in Chapter nine. The gist is that we begin by teaching every Christian to allow the life of Christ in them to create a kingdom authority for healing. Rather than health *insurance* – health *assurance* is available to all who will come to Christ for salvation. Daily we hear of more and more people who have no medical insurance – I believe this number will skyrocket before it's all over! Down-sizing due to new technology and other discoveries is putting more and more people of all ages in that category.

At the same time, there are lots of people in our local Black churches who aren't interested in living out loving spiritual organism like this. Eventually those people will probably leave the church because they are not ready for the level of Christian commitment required (see Luke 9:57-62). Jesus admonishes all to count the cost from the start (Luke 14:25-35). We can express the mind of Christ, extend the hand of Christ, and see the power of Christ evidenced in healing [the whole person] today. Jesus said, "this kind goeth not out but by prayer and fasting" (Matthew 17:21) KJV. Let's get back to the New Testament.

If the church would become normal as a healed and functioning spiritual organism, body of Christ, we can offer "The Ministry of Jesus" in the local Black churches as based on Luke 4:18-19; which today remains His agenda. Healing involves both the supernatural and the natural. God made our bodies with healing agents to perform various functions.

The spiritual organism is Spiritually-gifted individually and corporately to build itself up in the most holy faith. Christ our Teacher healed them that needed transformational healing. Notice Luke 9:11 says, "Everyone felt welcomed and wanted." His vision gave them hope! Does all the members of your church share and engage a common vision? We will persue this subject further in Chapters 8 and 9.

Discussion and Reflections: Chapter 1

1. Discuss the four men Jesus began to have fellowship with who later would become disciples.

2. Our vertical relationship with God must always be accompanied by our horizontal relationship with the people of God.

3. Discuss how Jesus's presence on the earth made God visible.

4. Discuss the correlation between the coming of the Holy Spirit and the death of Christ.

5. Discuss the Reformation doctrine of the "priesthood of all believers."

A NEW COMMANDMENT

"A new commandment I give you – that you
love one another" (John 13:34).

Few knew at the beginning of the first century that God *is* love; so, God came in person to *demonstrate* His love (John 1:18). God's coming in the person of Jesus Christ was *"to proclaim the favorable year of the Lord"* (Luke 4:19) and to *pour* His kind of love *(agape)* into the human heart (see Romans 5:5).

Note a few of the many truths:

- This love is expressed in three directions – upward to God, inward to self, and outward to others. Love must be activated in that order, unless one loves and accepts God, He or she will not *love* and *accept* them self. Unless one loves and accepts them self – certainly they will not love and accept others.
- The love discussed in this section is [*agape*]. Agape love is God's unconditional love for others. That kind of love was God's motivation in helping humanity (see John 3:16; Romans 5:8), and it is to be the motivation of His church. Any other kind of love by the Christian individually or corporately fails to act with the same motivation of our Creator.
- The neighbor is anyone with a need as seen in Jesus' parable of the Good Samaritan. To be a neighbor is to meet another's need (see Luke 10:29-37).
- The law is fulfilled by living in God's will and His way; which is His Word. Herein we see God's way of defining the content of love. God knows what's best for His people; therefore, His

commandments are for our good (carefully study Psalm 119 – what a blessing).

- Again, this love is expressed in three directions: Upward to God, inward to self, and outward to others (study carefully John 17:26; Romans 5:5; Galatians 5:22; John 13:34; I Corinthians 13).

By the time Jesus came to earth, the love [intent] of the law had been ignored and abased by the customs and traditions the Jewish scholars had added to the law (see Matthew 15:3). Soon love-intent was muzzled by customs and traditions of men. We suffer the same practices in many of our local Black churches today. Jesus was in no way pleased with these religious and burdensome legalistic and tradition-oriented leaders. He said to them,

> *"But go and learn what this means: I desire mercy not sacrifice'*
> *for I did not come to call the righteous, but sinners to repentance."*
> *"But if you had known what this means, I desire mercy and not*
> *sacrifice,' you would not have condemned the guiltless"* (carefully
> study Matthew 9:13; 12:7).

Jesus taught some applications of that truth:

1. Worship should be preceded by reconciliation with others (see Matthew 5:23, 24).
2. Practicing the commandments without authentic love and care for others is merely a façade (see Matthew 19:16-22).
3. The happy Christian is one who displays mercy toward others (see Matthew 5:7).
4. The persons who overlook the needy condemns themselves (see Luke 16:19-31; Romans 12:6-8).
5. Jesus' instructions to those He sent out included along with preaching and teaching: ministering and meeting physical and spiritual needs (see Matthew 10:5-8; Mark 6:7-13).
6. Witness-evangelism was [and is] to be followed-up with teaching *them* to obey all that Jesus has commanded (see Matthew 28:19, 20).

While the people did not understand that God in Jesus intended to tear down the *spiritual* walls that had separated man from his fellowman – Jesus was not the Christ they expected – nor is He the Christ they wanted!

President Trump and others have in recent times made the phrase "fake news" very familiar. The intent of its usage is very clear. However, "fake biblical theology" is not that easy to spot especially in a voluntary spiritual and biblical-illiterate society such as we are experiencing in this country today. For example, each year many of the sermons, songs, and the pageantry promote the impression concerning the beautiful Christmas story; *"how eagerly the world waited for the coming of the baby Jesus in Bethlehem two-thousand years ago."*

That is "fake theology!" According to the Scriptures, the world did not eagerly wait for the baby Jesus. In fact, the world was so busy doing its own thing that it would not even make room for Him to be born. The past Christmas season was no exception.

Listen to the Christmas story:

> *"She [Mary] gave birth to her firstborn, a son. She wrapped him in cloths and placed him in a manger, because there was no room for them in the inn"* (Luke 2:7).

He had to be born in a stable. The point is, no one would even have noticed the birth – if God had not sent angels to announce it to the shepherds and later; He sent a star to guide the wise men from the east to His location.

The situation certainly is no better, perhaps even worse today: "A few people express sentimental thoughts about the birth of Jesus as they go about their business and pleasures during the Christmas season. But few pay any attention to the real Christ – and they make no room for Him in their hearts and lives."

In fact, each year during the Christmas season from all observations – fewer people pay attention, and even fewer people have room for Jesus. He receives very little or no favorable mention from any of the major networks' fake Christmas specials. The secular news media was more occupied with fake-tracking and reporting on Santa Claus' trip from the north pole. That along with, the Grinch that stole Christmas, overeating, and football!

No room anywhere

Certainly, there were places other than the inn that had no room for Him. To say there was no room for Him in the inn teaches us that – in truth there was no room for Him anywhere. Not only did many important philosophers, along with Caesar Augustus, and the other Gentile elite have no room for Him, even the various schools of learning had no room for Him – at first, the coming of Christ was unknown to such people. However, when it was made known they laughed at the gospel of Christ; and many continue to laugh and joke today as few look for Him. Hollywood has no shame toward its innuendos, fictitious plots and accusations concerning His life on earth.

The case was different for ancient Israel. Israel had her well-known prophets and prophecies. The prophets could even tell where the Christ child would be born. Even though He was born less than 12 miles from the palace of King Herod, who killed thousands of babies trying to stop Him. He inquired of the chief priests and scribes where He would be born, and he even conversed with the wise men who went on and found Him and worshipped Him and returned home another way, deceiving King Herod who waited in the palace just a few miles away. Although the king's wise men could tell him where Christ would be born – not one of them was concerned enough to make the short journey to greet and worship Him.

Today we seldom find any regard or room for Christ:

- among politicians
- among the schools of learning
- among philosophers
- among the world's scientists
- among the most learned religious leaders
- among religious families
- among well-to-do people
- among poor people

Rejected of people

Let's look again at some "fake theology," many of us would argue the point, that "though it is true that there was no place for Christ among the wise, the mighty, and other elite of this world – but surly there is a place for Him among the poor common folks, such as ourselves."

"We would welcome Him!" We pride ourselves by thinking that common people are more charitable, compassionate, and more religious – wrong! Neither did they make room for Christ. The Bible teaches us,

> *"We all, like sheep, have gone astray,*
> *each of us has turned to his [or her] own way;*
> *and the Lord has laid on him*
> *the iniquity of us all."*
> (Isaiah 53:6, emphasis added)

It is not a poor/ rich, good/ bad thing. Most of us are so filled body, soul, and spirit with our own personal interests that there is little interest in Christ. And there is little time for Him! Considering our possessions and pleasures it seems, there is no room for Jesus Christ, the Savior except in the stable. As a young teenager, I remember the controversy in many of the local Black churches over "X-mas" replacing "Christmas" on TV, commercial business window displays and in the newspaper advertisements of various toy stores. Their fears are certainly being fulfilled in our consumer and material-driven society today.

Until you have opened the doors of your heart and invited Jesus to reign in your life – you are no different than the masses who slept comfortably in their warm beds while Mary gave birth to the "Lamb of God" that takes away the sins of the world in a cold and uncomfortable stable. Do you have room for Christ?

If you don't, I plead with you, receive Him now! "Make room for Him! We are warned in Hebrews 3:7-8, "Today, if you hear His voice, do not harden your hearts ...." "Now is the accepted time, now is the day of salvation" (2 Corinthians 6:2).

The world cares for its own

Jesus foretold those who are His, *"If you belonged to the world, it would love you as its own. Yet because you are not of the world, but I chose you out of the world, therefore the world hates you"* (John 15:19).

Jesus said to His disciples, *"In this world you will have trouble. But take heart! I have overcome the world"* (John 16:33).

Though the world hates *you* and has no room for you; since the day you accepted Christ as your personal Savior – Jesus will have room for you! He said,

> *"Do not let your hearts be troubled. Trust in God; trust also in Me. In My Father's house are many mansions; if it were not so, I*

would have told you. I go to prepare a place for you. And if I go to prepare a place for you, I will come again and receive you to Myself that where I am, there you may also be" (John 14:1-3).

The question of God's whereabouts may be asked concerning all the hideous crimes committed toward the helpless, and atrocities of slavery in the history of this country, disasters, evil upsets and forget not the injustices we suffer as African Americans making the headlines daily! God was and is in the world reconciling it unto Himself. The Scripture says, *"For when we were still without strength, in due time Christ died for the ungodly. For scarcely for a righteous man will one die; yet perhaps for a good man someone would even dare to die. But God demonstrates His own love toward us, in that while we were sinners, Christ died for us. Much more then, having now been justified by His blood, we shall be saved from wrath through Him. For if when we were enemies we were reconciled to God through the death of His Son, much more, having been reconciled, we shall be saved by His life. And not only that, but we also rejoice in God through our Lord Jesus Christ, through whom we have now received the reconciliation"*(Romans 5:6-11).

Paul emphasizes that as uncommon as such a sacrifice is – His point is that we were neither of these persons the *righteous* or *good* – yet Christ sacrificed Himself for us (see v.7).

The Gospel of Jesus Christ

Through His death, burial, and resurrection, Jesus is the [only] way to the Father's house (see 1 Corinthians 15:1-5). Jesus, our Example, said we would do greater things. Of course, He was speaking of His collective body, [spiritual organism], the Church. While Jesus' work was confined to Palestine, like the disciples of old we can witness everywhere [as God's mail carriers of the "Good News"], we see the conversion of thousands – because as Jesus promised, we are transformed and empowered by the Holy Spirit.[4] A transformed life is God's deterrent against the prince of this world and his complete agenda today.

Many people are screaming out today concerning all the sin and evil in the world, along with increases in deaths from dangerous hurricanes [one after another], deadly fires, droughts, floods, and diluted leadership, "Where is God in all of this?" The question was asked in every quarter after 9/11, "Where was God?"

The Scriptures show: "He was in the same place He was when His Son, His only Son was crucified on the cross in our place." The Bible says,

> *"For God so loved the world, that He gave His only begotten Son, that whosoever believes in Him shall not perish, but have everlasting life"* (John 3:16).

> *"Therefore, just as through one man sin entered the world, and death through sin, and thus death spread to all men, because all sinned ...."* (Romans 5:12).

Jesus puts His words into action

Through the years, witness-evangelism has been the lifeline of the local Christian Church (through various forms). Those who have accepted Jesus as Lord of all consider His gospel to be *exportable* and themselves to be *expendable* in getting the gospel to the whole world. Once they are converted, and baptized, disciple [teach them the Bible], and encourage them to fully surrender their lives to the Lord. He can use them to reach others. Once they are stabilized send them out as ministers of reconciliation to the streets, the nation, and the world.

Although Christians maintain a loving trust for their Lord, they remain anxious about propagating the gospel; which means more than life itself – possessing a militant spirit that makes *living* Christianity an aggressive and judgmental force in the affairs of humanity.

From centuries past to this present hour; God has always had a person or group of people so responsive to His *will* and *purpose* that they become open channels through which His love and power can be relayed to and unreached world offering reconciliation. Over time however, the established order [flesh] can become so mechanically efficient, to the point of blocking this work of the Holy Spirit and His ministries.

At that point a *new channel* would be cut to allow a full penetration of the Holy Spirit!

This means that the Lord God is going to keep His redemptive power flowing to a lost world – even if He must establish a new outlet for that purpose. Today the local Black church's choice is to evangelize or fossilize!

Those churches that are able instruments in the hands of the Holy Spirit give a cutting-edge to God's redemptive plan for humanity. Additionally, they have been captivated by certain Christlike ideals. For simplification I have separated the section into three parts:

1. Christ led of the Spirit
2. The true Spirit-led disciple
3. The Spirit-led church

Christ led of the Holy Spirit

Jesus immediately began to *live out* the promises of His inaugural sermon. He cast out an unclean demon (see Luke 4:31-37) and touched a sick person to heal her (see Luke 4:38, 39). In these actions He showed:

1. His kingship [Lord over nature]
2. His servant-hood [He ministered to the needs of others]

He ministered to the needs of people. He tore down walls of partition others would not dare touch, and people of all walks of life came to Him. Throughout His life, Jesus met both the physical needs and the spiritual needs of people. Christendom's ideas, customs and traditions have obscured the mission of the body of Christ [spiritual organism] to the point that much of the church today like Israel in the past has chosen fear and ethnical segregation of people; therefore, building social-economic, political, and other partitions [walls]. We will cover this more in Chapter 8, "Lest We Forget."

When the people began to observe and understand Jesus' motivation; they were filled with anger and tried to kill Him. God's purpose of love will always be opposed by the prejudices of hatred. Here we can clearly see the difference between the kingdom of God and the kingdom of the world. When you consider the church scene across America each Sunday morning at 11 a.m. it is easy to understand why Dr. Martin Luther King Jr. pinned it as the most segregated hour in America.

My wife and I have made many friends [of various races and nationalities] as we worked alongside and shared with missionaries [three years in Panama and two years in the Republic of South Korea] from various Christian denominations in the United States; while assigned there in the military.

However, when we returned to the United States and visited some of our white friends or they visited us, the love and fellowship was present between us, but sadly we were merely tolerated in some; and seldom welcomed to minister together in many of the local churches [both black and white] due to racial prejudice [the man-made partitions are still up]. In fact, it seems a spirit of anger and distrust is consuming the American people today; as shown daily in partisan politics; which makes the scene much more volatile.

I believe that racial prejudice [of the flesh] will rapidly increase as more and more as people in the churches chose to walk after the flesh, rather than walk after the Spirit in obedience. Additionally, carnality seems to be "the accepted norm" in the larger portion of our local churches today. Most churches today love making converts, but they are not making sure they grow in depth and maturity – which is not complete unless we have the sacrificial love of Christ in our hearts. Christ stated in the Great Commission, *"teaching them to observe [obey] all that I have commanded you."* Emphasis added. Though Paul's first priority was to preach the gospel and plant churches; he spent nearly three years in Ephesus teaching that church the whole counsel of God from the Scriptures (Acts 19-20). Jesus, our Example, continued His ministry showing that He is the kind of Lord who used:

- His lordship to serve the needs of other people.
- His privilege was coupled with purpose.
- His exaltation was with humility.
- His power with pity.
- His superiority with sacrifice.

Jesus broke customs and ritual traditions of men to meet the needs of people:

- He permitted His disciples to pick grain on the Sabbath (see Luke 6:1-5; Mark 2:23-28; Mathew 12:1-8).
- He Himself worked on the Sabbath to help others (Matthew 12:9-14; Mark 3:1-6; Luke 6:6-11; John 5:1-9).
- His disciples did not keep all the religious practices just because it had always been done that way (Matthew 15:1; Mark 7:1).
- He touched a leper (Matthew 8:1-4; Mark 1:40; Luke 5:12-16).
- He touched material that a dead person had touched (Luke 7:11-17), both of which made Him religiously "unclean" according to the traditions of men.

He forgave the "unforgivable" of His day:

- A woman rejected by religious leaders (Luke 7:36-50).
- A woman caught in adultery (John 8:1-11).

- The people who denied Him, and His own executioners (Luke 23:34).
- When Jesus forgives – He forgets (Hebrews 8:12).

His ministry of care was not restricted to His own group or not necessarily to those who followed Him:

- He helped a lonely widow in her grief (Luke 7:11-17).
- He helped a man everyone ostracized (Matthew 8:28-34).
- He helped a woman of a despised race (Matthew 15:21-28).
- He helped a convicted criminal (Luke 23:39-43).

John closes his gospel with, "the world itself could not contain all the books that could be written about the life of Christ" (see John 21:25).

The Spirit-led disciple

While there is an open-denial of disciples in name or title today, there are those persons who are blood-washed, Spirit-filled instruments doing a cutting-edge witness-evangelism; and have been captivated and matured by certain convictions of biblical truth and promises. The promised Holy Spirit has two things to do in this disciple, just as He did with Christ:

1. At Jordan, He *baptized* Christ with mighty power for mighty deeds. Jordan was His preparation for Calvary. On the cross there were no mighty deeds – yet Calvary did more for the world than all the mighty deeds in Galilee.
2. Perhaps we think too much of the "mighty deeds," which may mean the "greater works" than the *"death and fellowship"* which means "fruit!"

You might work all your life and only accomplish so much, even with mighty deeds – but if you are willing to die with Christ, the mortification of the fruit will be so great that; your seed shall be like the sand of the seashore. There is a limit to "work," even as Christ's works were limited to certain places when He was on earth – but there is no limit to the "fruit" that come out of His death!

We become united with Christ in the likeness of His death. When the graft is put in the tree, first a cut is made and afterward the insertion of the branch the two are bound together with a cord. Why? So that the *life* in the tree might go into the graft, and both tree and graft have one life. Likewise, when God takes the knife and cuts you off, to graft you into Christ's death, His life-sap begins to flow into you – Oh! What fruit of life, joy, peace, longsuffering, and kindness is loosed on the world! The fruit comes from Him, through your life. And what do you do? *Abide in His death.* *"Knowing this,"* that our "old man" was crucified with Him." This is God's declaration of the meaning of Calvary.

The apostle declares that when Jesus Christ hung there, bearing in His own body the sins of the whole world, our "old man" – the first Adam and creation – was crucified with Him. It was Christ Himself who explained His cross to Paul and not man (see Galatians 1:12); showing him that when He hung there the old Creation hung there and died with Him. Here then, is the foundation victory over sin for the believer.

It is you securing your place in Christ's death, and consenting to be grafted into it, "counting yourself dead to sin" while the Holy Spirit does the work of deliverance in you. This is the only way of victory over Satan, for it is through sin known or unknown – that he holds us, and it is only as we take our stand on the truth declared in Romans 6, when the devil attacks with his deceptions and temptations to sin, or when you want deliverance from sin; that you can say, *"On the ground of my death with Christ, I am now dead to that sin, and it shall not reign."* Then the Holy Spirit applies the *power* of Christ's death breaking the connection with sin – even the desire for it. Therefore, among true believers the most prominent traits are the following:

1. They are committed whole-heartedly to basic biblical convictions. To them truth is not relative. Instead they consider themselves the *new channel* agents of absolutes which are worthy of our unconditional support.
2. Their souls are held by a deep sense of destiny.
3. They are aware of being called by the Holy Spirit.
4. They have a clear-cut detachment from the world and its prevailing beliefs and practices.
5. They are clearly more sensitive to what the Lord has said in His Word about them – than what the world has to say. Thus, acknowledging that Christ is the answer to *all* the ills in the world!
6. They are filled with compassion for those who have not found the way. They condemn the practices of sin, but they are full of love for the sinner.
7. They feel that the coming of Christ is imminent – which places an urgency in their appeal. They insist on "rapture readiness" as the only proper preparation.
8. They are acutely aware of their own personal responsibility and accountability to God. They feel that choices determine

destiny – right choices could mean eternal rewards and wrong choices eternal punishment.

9. They exalt Christ as the only way of salvation. His atonement is the only source of *any person's* release from the penalty and guilt of sin. Thus, Christianity is a rescue or recovery operation rather than one of achievement.

10. They are persuaded that the good news of the gospel must be shared. They share beyond denominational lines.

11. They are Bible-centered in their proclamation and demonstration, basing the authority of their challenge on the Holy Spirit and the Word of God working in tandem.

12. They honor the Holy Spirit resident in them.

To them, the most effective witness-evangelizing for Jesus Christ is one to whom Christian character is not mere moral or legal correctness [ethical respectability], but the possession and manifestation of the nine graces of Galatians 5:22, 23, [the Fruit of the Spirit]:

Character of the believer's inward state

- Love
- Joy
- Peace

Character in the believer's expression toward others

- Longsuffering
- Gentleness
- Goodness

Character in the believer's expression toward God

- Faith
- Meekness
- Temperance

Together they manifest a moral portrait of Christlikeness in those believers who are truly yielded to Him.

Witness-evangelism remains the common heritage and mission of all Christians. That is God's way!

Witness-evangelize like so many commands of our Lord is being totally ignored within many local Black churches today. The traditional "Ya'll come" and the Sunday morning 11 a.m. Service's "Invitation to Discipleship" seem to be the extent of much church evangelism today. Please church be reminded that the outstanding feature of witness-evangelism and discipleship has been two-fold:

1. An emphasis on the power of the gospel of Jesus Christ.
2. A life of victorious service through the *power of the Holy Spirit.*

A note of warning

So far as the local Black churches fail to bring the gospel of Christ to the knowledge of the unsaved – they disobey the last command of our Lord. That church then,

*   Declines in spiritual life
*   Forfeits their commission
*   Risks the removal of their candlestick out of its place

Many local churches are suffering from these maladies. Jesus Himself lists their strengths, then a restoration remedy for personal and corporate deliverance in Revelation 2:1-5:

> *"To the angel of the church of Ephesus write, these things says, He who holds the seven stars in His right hand, who walks in the midst of the seven golden lampstands: "I know your 1) works, 2) your patience, 3) and that you cannot bear those who are evil. And 4) you have tested those who say they are apostles and are not, and have found them liars, and 5) you have persevered and have patience, and 6) have labored for My name's sake and 7) have not become weary"* (vv. 1-3). Emphasis added.

> *"Nevertheless, I have this against you, that you have left your first love"* (v. 4). [Christ's condemnation]. Here Jesus assessed the church's weakness and provides a clear path to restoration.

> *"Remember therefore from where you have fallen; repent and do the first works,"* (v. 5a).

*"Or else I will come to you and remove your lampstand from
its place – unless you repent"* (v. 5b). [Christ's warning of
judgment]

In this verse judgment is threatened. The Lord Jesus had a cause for the
case against the angel of the church of Ephesus. The church *had left its first
love;* this charge is very serious. The Lord never forgets His joy in the first
love of His people. Thus, says the Lord:

> *"I remember you,*
> *The kindness of your youth,*
> *The love of your betrothal,*
> *When you went after Me in the*
> *wilderness,*
> *In a land not sown.*
> *Israel was holiness to the Lord,*
> *The first fruits of His increase.*
> *All that devour him will offend;*
> *Disaster will come upon them says, the Lord."*
> Jerimiah 2:1-3

The Lord never forgot Judah's first love; neither does the Lord Jesus
forget the first love of His Church. The first commandment is, "You shall
love the Lord your God with all your heart, with all your soul, and with all
your mind" (Matthew 22:37). Love is the center of the soul – the very *essence*
of the new birth experience.

The Lord is saying to the Church of Ephesus, "Remember the heights
of love you once demonstrated and the moral elevation you once possessed.
And then check yourself and see how far short you have fallen – and repent.
Check your heart and judge yourself or I will be forced to judge you. I will
judge you quickly unless you repent and return to your first love and your
first works.

Christ is speaking to applicable local Christian churches [both large and
small] across the United States and around the World today saying, "Repent
or I will judge you," for like Ephesus you have left your first love and the
only remedy for you is to repent and return. If you don't, I will come unto
you quickly, and will remove your candlestick out of his place, except you
repent (Revelation 2:5).

The removal of the lampstand as a *light bearer* has to do with the whole
church. The lamps which once shone so brightly in the part of the world
these churches were located especially Ephesus – have been taken out of
their place, and the land today is engulfed with great darkness. Islam is the
religion in the seven cities where these churches were located. So, we see the
lampstand *has been removed.*

The same holds true for the churches in America, unless we repent, remember, and return to our first love our lampstand [the Holy Spirit and the Word of God] will be removed. We have been blessed and highly favored of God because of our faith in God and love for Jesus Christ. Unfaithfulness on the part of an individual or a church must be judged; and will be judged by a holy God.

When we read or hear talk about the average Black church today, few if any of the concerns are about spiritual matters. Because growth is a spiritual work, perhaps we can better understand why one church grows while another church struggles. On any Sunday in any town or city, USA, one church may be thriving, that is growing spiritually and numerically – and just down the street, another church often in the same denomination has not grown in years.

The second church like many others has begun the long slow *process* of decline that could eventually lead to death, unless measures are instituted to stop the process. Many people think that health and growth of a church mainly depends on demographics or methodology, but here we have two churches in the same setting, with the same approach, yet one is thriving, and the other is dying. Why? Several reasons:

- One reason a church may experience decline is because Jesus is displeased with the way the church has handled past challenges.
- Another is that the church is disobedient of the Great Commandment and Great Commissions. The church fails to "teach them to obey all..."
- Many local churches have divorced the Holy Spirit; His gifts and ministries. Prayer meeting is almost gone also; just as Jesus taught His disciples to pray – likewise it is expected of us.
- Some believe the Holy Spirit and the apostolic ministries [Ephesians 4:11] ceased after Pentecost. Many of these churches operate strictly through science and reason rather than by the Spirit.

Today, congregations are realizing that God uses different methods and models to reach different kinds of people. Yes, it is even alright to be traditional or institutional if God is using your church in reaching your community for Christ effectively. We must remember, every model presented here is just a model. Models are tools, but too often they become rules.

Unless the Christian Church in America repents and returns to its first love and work, Jesus, the Head of the Church will evaluate us and call us to repentance; as we lose our proper focus (see Revelation 2:5, 16, 21-22; 3:3, 19-20).

The Nicolaitans are alive and well in the churches

Now we turn to another concern of Christ in His evaluation of the church of Ephesus in the text, in verse 6, Jesus gave the Church of Ephesus a favorable mention in their hatred of the deeds of the Nicolaitans, which Jesus said He also hates. The word comes from *nikao,* which means "to conquer" and *laos,* means "the people" (the laity).[5]

The deeds of the Nicolaitans hated by the Church of Ephesus was the setting up of certain men *to rule over* the ordinary believers in the church, probably the beginning of the priestly order which continues in the Roman Catholic and some other denominations. God never intended His church to be divided into priests and laiety.

> *No man has a right to be "lord over the people of God* (I Peter 5:3). *"There is one God and one Mediator between God and men, the man Jesus Christ"* (1 Timothy 2:5):

- Under grace every born-again believer is a [New Testament believer-priest] (1 Peter 2:9).
- The Scripture shows that every true believer-priest is invited to enter *boldly* into the holy place (carefully study Hebrews 10:19-25).
- God appoints under shepherds to care for the flock, to feed the sheep and keep out the wolves.
- God does not appoint church bosses, or special men and women to pray for us or listen to our confession of sins.
- The Scripture says, "Therefore if the Son makes you free, you shall be free in deed" (John 8:36).
- For as many as are led by the Spirit of God, these are thee sons of God (Romans 8:14).

We are to confess our sin to God through our Mediator the Lord Jesus Christ.

Have you ever wondered what Jesus Christ thinks of these man-made set-ups today, for example:

- The members are commanded to sign a pledge card, sign a document, or sign a resolution.
- The members are required to submit a current financial statement annually and immediately submit any changes in income to the financial secretary.

- They are commanded to faithfully bring all their tithes into the "storehouse" meaning their local church before they can be considered for any position of responsibility: deacon, Sunday school teacher, choir director, member of the choir, ushers, or member in the pew.
- Activities of secret lodges and fraternal organizations are assimilated into church life as Christian activities.

Those people who lord it over God's people belong to the same sect that the spiritually-minded believers at Ephesus hated:

- They did not hate the persons ……….. but they hated their deeds.
- God loves all people regardless of how sinful they are, and certainly *true* believers should love all, regardless of their wickedness.

We do not love their sins, but we love *them* because Jesus died for them.

Tolerating corruption

When corruption is tolerated in the church, it spreads rapidly, notice:

- The Church of Ephesus was commended by Christ for hating the sins of the Nicolaitans – but the Church of Pergamos assimilated and kept the sins of the Nicolaitans.
- Ephesus was troubled only with their deeds and practices – but by the time the deeds and practices reached Pergamos, they had become doctrine (Revelation 2:15).
- Ephesus would not put up with the Nicolaitans, but Pergamos held the corrupters to her bosom and permitted them to corrupt and poison the sources of purity and morality in the church there.
- Folks, the Nicolaitans are alive and well today in the local churches; and they are still peddling their poisonous counsel, [tolerate immorality, idolatry, and heresies, change the truth] in the name of a satanic substitute *progressive religious* Christianity. In this case linking the sins of Jezebel. Remember, "Nicolaitans" mean *"to conquer the people."*
- Praise God, His cutting-edge Spirit-filled disciples are there to keep the doctrine pure.

Jesus declares that if we acknowledge our weakness and zealously repent, committing ourselves to overcome it – He will give His personal blessing.

A Spirit-led Church

Ignoring the King's final instructions would not make sense, especially when He holds all authority in heaven and earth. Before ascending into heaven Jesus told His disciples, "You shall receive power after the Holy Spirit has come upon you; and you shall be My witnesses both in Jerusalem, and in all Judea and Samaria, and the uttermost part of the earth" (Acts 1:8).

For Jesus' followers with their Jewish background, the concept of "receiving power" and the "Spirit coming upon" people were not a mystery. They could remember how the seventy received of the Spirit. Then they had the sacred Scriptures and the familiar adventures of Israel's famous heroes such as Gideon, Samson and David, whose lives were dramatically transformed when the Holy Spirit came upon them. Samuel the prophet, anointed David with oil, "and the Spirit of the Lord came mightily upon David from that day forward" (1 Samuel 16:13).

Elisha knew without a doubt that if he were to replace Elijah, he *must have* the same Spirit that rested on Elijah – without that powerful anointing it *would be impossible!* No doubt, Peter and the other apostles must have realized that if they were to carry on Jesus' mission, they would need that same power.

The Scriptures make plain how bashful Peter, who denied His Lord, was amazingly transformed by the coming of the Holy Spirit upon Him. Notice,

- His fears disappeared
- He became bold
- Fearless in proclaiming the gospel accompanied by demonstration

Praise God, for godly pastors who insist that this is a necessary experience. Alfred North Whitehead defined: "Experience is first doing something; then doing something that makes a difference; and finally knowing what difference it makes."[6] Thus, each member would be set free from his or her inhibitions and reluctance to stand strong and fearless and witness the gospel of Jesus Christ to others.

Personally, I had missed many opportunities to bear witness of Christ and be public about my commitment to Him during my early years after graduating from High School and entering the US Army. I believed with all my heart that Jesus was the Son of God; that my sins were forgiven, and I had eternal life because of Christ's finished work on Calvary – but, even after being born and raised in a Christian home [all my life dad was a pastor], but desiring and pursuing a military career [my three favorite uncles were World War II combat veterans, my three older cousins served in the Korean War, my brother and I served in combat in the Vietnam War – I was little more than a carnal Christian for the next five years; which were my formative years in the military [call me "Gung HO!"], rising in the ranks very quickly. Later I realized that it was all in God's plan for my life. I married the love of my life, Magdalene in 1963. We will celebrate our 57th Wedding Anniversary January 20, 2020, if it's the Lord's will. I spent 1967-68 in the Vietnam.

Of course, everything changed drastically after returning from Vietnam, to my [baptized in the Spirit] wife and our five-year-old daughter. I was assigned to Fort Knox, Kentucky, where my wife and I joined a small Pentecostal [Baptist] Church in Vine Grove, Kentucky. Rev. Kelly, our pastor called it "holy boldness." Oh! What a blessing! Thereafter, my wife and I walked in bold witness-evangelism for Christ in the military. From that assignment until retirement in June 1984 and beyond, God directed our steps and seemingly our duty assignments. Each duty station presented my wife and I vast experiences and opportunities to inhance ministry in the various local Christian communities – that we have been privileged to be a part of for the past 35 years as pastor.

Earlier I shared with you our experiences working with missionaries overseas. Additionally, I was privileged to pastor three Missionary Baptist churches in Southeastern North Carolina during the past thirty years. However, my wife and I planted the Bread of Life Ministries, an equipping ministry which include planting churches and non-traditional Bible Institutes in 1998. We carry a personal burden for those in church settings where the Great Commission is ignored or not fully carried out mainly in the: *"teaching them to **obey all things** whatsoever I have commanded you"* (Matthew 28:19-20) KJV. Emphasis added. By choosing to disregard this command, many local African American churches; no matter whether traditional, institutional, or contemporary alike seem to be truthfully, "making practical atheists" instead of "disciples."

Over the years, this disobedience to Christ's command has accelerated the decline of spirituality in the churches; which has promoted open rebellion against doctrinal purity and morality – both are foundational pillars of truth.

Things must change [Restoration]

The gathered church [Hebrews10:25] is the place where the presence of the Holy Spirit is evident. According to the Scripture, we are supposed to be a Spirit-filled community,

> *"Speaking to one another in psalms and hymns and spiritual songs, singing and making melody"* to the Lord with all our hearts (Ephesians 5:19).

> *"For the promise is for you and your children and for all who are far off, as many as the Lord our God will call to Himself"* (Acts 2:39).

The Scripture says, the manifestation of the Spirit is for the common good (1 Corinthians 10:8). Spiritual and structural changes must be made. Space must be provided for the Holy Spirit to freely do His work in us. Many clear biblical truths and practices rooted in His presence are clearly missing in many of our Black churches. There is need for *Spirit-led restoration* of biblical teaching and practical training in the churches, not merely personal renewal or even revival, but *structural restoration*.

Foundational doctrine and current issues must be addressed. Things have got to be changed; this is evident in the increasingly high number of Christians especially the millennials, who are leaving the traditional institutional churches. Amid the current confusion men and women are stepping into pastoral positions with little or no theological teaching or practical training.

In too many of the Black storefront churches there are those who are hailed for making the journey from the streets to the pulpit with a powerful deliverance testimony, but the majority lack proper theological and doctrinal preparation needed for building up the body to maturity [disciples]. After founding the Bread of Life Bible Institute [non-tradational] in 1998 and equipping people for ministry over the years – my wife and I without a doubt have concluded that bi-vocational pastors should at least be required to complete at least a Bible College level pastoral ministry degree. Its amazing how every indeavor begins with a basic course accept the local Black church. There is an anti-educational spirit over many small traditional churches, especially in rural areas that leads them to believe they can't afford change. People like my wife and I are referred to as foreigners in the Baptist denomination we came out in, because they believe we are usurping the pastor-teacher gift of Ephesians 4:11. Yet, most of these churches are proclamation only churches; undoubtedly because Bible teaching and practical Christian training were not a priority in the founders' traditional instructions for their church.

Black churches should begin to welcome [the restoration] presence of the Holy Spirit and His ministries and replace man-made methodologies and non-spiritual forms of godliness. When a community of believers becomes filled with the Spirit – their church life will be transformed from the flesh of Romans 7 to the Spirit of Romans 8.

The presence of the Holy Spirit *can change everything*, not only in the life of each individual but in the total corporate experience as well. As we witness the presence of God, we begin to understand that we are fully accepted sons and daughters by grace. Remember, He is the Spirit of Truth, change is now possible:

- Change takes time.
- Change can only be executed properly where people have happily yielded themselves to it.
- It cannot be forced upon the unwilling.
- Hearts must be won and prepared by the preaching and teaching of the true gospel of Jesus Christ.
- We have the example of the men who joined David's growing Army who said, *"We are yours."*
- These new candidates had come to love and trust David.
- They gave David their unadulterated allegiance.

God wants and expects His pastors to relate to their congregation as friends [not bosses or enemies]. When people know they are loved, even after receiving words that hurt, the Scripture says, because they believe that *"faithful are the wounds of a friend"* (Proverbs 27:6).

One of the goals of parents is to create within their children the ability to make wise decisions. Sadly, some parents and many church leaders fail in their endeavors because they are overbearing with their children or members, while others are too weak:

- They give commands instead of counsel
- They give orders instead of training
- They give scolding instead of corrections
- They talk at people, rather than talk to them

In the end, what they have accomplished is insecurity and low self-esteem in their children. I have found that many people coming from authoritative positions especially in the U.S. Military, former police officers, security personal without proper biblical teaching and training many times fall into these dangers. Jesus said to His disciples,

---

*"The kings of the Gentiles exercise lordship over them, and those who exercise lordship over them, are called benefactors.' But **not so** among you ...."* (Luke 22: 25-26). Emphasis added.

Leadership in the church does not exalt, it serves. It shows respect for others. True church leaders will labor for others, just as a servant would. In a nutshell, the Lord's view of greatness is the exact opposite of the world's view. Pastors, your leadership is essential in guiding and preparing your people for heaven. Love for the church and a desire to bring people to Jesus will reinforce and renew your leadership.

> *"All authority has been given to Me in heaven and on earth. Go therefore and make disciples of all nations, baptizing them in the name of the Father, and of the Son and of the Holy Spirit, teaching them to observe all things that I have commanded you; and lo, I am with you always even to the end of the age"* (Matthew 28:18-20).

This passage of Scripture reveals that the Great Commission rests on the authority of Christ, therefore, every human being needs to hear His gospel. A number of local churches in this country has abandoned God's redemptive and evangelistic plan for all the world – and have restricted themselves to in-house evangelism, programing and tracts.

"Making disciples" involves three steps: 1) go/ preach the gospel, 2) baptizing, and 3) teaching. As mentioned earlier, the lack of biblical teaching especially for the youth and millennia has opened a revolving door in the American Black Christian churches as the motherly or maternal characteristics inherited from earlier centuries of Christianity have all but disappeared. The Bible clearly *teaches* that people have always needed maternal care.

Note Moses' argument in Numbers 11:12 revealing the people's need as he complains to God, "Why have you afflicted your servant? And why have I not found favor in your sight, that you have laid the burden of all these people on me? Did I conceive all these people? Did I beget them, that you should say to me, carry them in your bosom, as a guardian carries a nursing infant-child; to the land which You swore to their forefathers?"

When Jesus came along, it is no surprise that He laments the spiritual condition of God's people with spiritual imagery. "O Jerusalem, Jerusalem, you who kill the prophets and stone those sent to you, how often have I longed to gather your children together, as a hen gathers her chicks under her wings" (Matthew 23:37).

Then too, Paul says of the church in Thessalonica: "We were among you, like a mother caring for her little children" (I Thess. 2:7); and to the churches in Galatia he writes, "My dear children, for whom I am again in the pains of childbirth until Christ is formed in you" (Galatians 4:19).

The Word of God is clear, Christians need maternal care to grow-up, but it teaches us that the church is the one who provides that care. The members of the church are "her children." In Ephesians 4:11-16 Paul wrote that God created the church and gave gifted men and women to serve in it; therefore, we are no longer infants, but grown-ups in every way to be mature adult disciples (4:14-15).

To take infants and transform them into mature adults is a parental responsibility and since 3:14-15 identifies God as the Father of this family of believers – this points to the local church as the mother. She then, nurtures and helps God's children to mature in the faith. How does the church provide the nurture, care and transformation for spiritual growth to adulthood (a disciple)? Prayerfully I hope you are beginning to accept the idea that the church is your spiritual mother. God works through the local church to help transform us into finished disciples nourishing us with:

- Comfort in times of difficulties
- Feeds them on the Word and the Lord's Supper
- Mentorship
- Godly examples
- Discipline as we stray
- Growth toward Christlikeness [biblical maturity]

The local church provides maternal care for all of us helping us to grow to become more like Christ. Nothing can be more honorable or have greater eternal significance than serving our Lord and Savior, Jesus Christ in His Church. Certainly, there can be no greater responsibility. Sadly, though the church is the agent for spiritual growth [sanctification], she must deal with the fact that there are those who participate in church regularly, but do not seem to be growing. Undoubtedly some do not grow because:

- The church does not function in a manner whereby it can provide the benefits that God intends His church to provide.
- Many attend the church, but never engage.
- Many religiously attend church services weekly, be involved in programs and other church activities, but they have never had a personal encounter with Christ.

- Growth is slow and sometimes it seems to have ceased.
- The church spends so much time dealing with the usual such as prayer meeting, Bible-study, and visiting the sick – sometimes the repetition causes us to miss the cumulative effect it could have in transforming people.

Foundational truths we all should grasp

1. The church is the only institution that Christ promised to build and bless (Matthew 16:18).
2. The church is the gathering place for true worshippers (Philippians 3:3).
3. The church is the most precious assembly on earth – Christ purchased it with His own blood (Acts 20:28; 1 Cor. 6:19; Eph. 5:25; Col. 1:20; I Peter 1:18; Rev. 1:5).
4. The church is the earthly expression of the heavenly reality (Matt. 6:10; 18:18).
5. The church will ultimately triumph both locally and universally (Matt. 16:18; Phil. 1:6).
6. The church is the realm of spiritual fellowship (Heb. 10:22-25; I John 1:3, 6-7).
7. The church is the proclaimer and protector of divine truth (I Timothy 3:15; Titus 2:1, 15).
8. The church is the chief place for spiritual growth and edification (Acts 20:32; Eph. 4:11-16; 2 Tim. 3:16, 17; I Peter 2:1; 2 Peter 3:18).
9. The church is the launching pad for world witness-evangelism ((Mk. 16:15; Titus 2:11).
10. The church is the environment where strong spiritual leadership develops and matures (2 Tim. 2:2).

Understanding these ten truths builds a foundation for effective church ministry. Unless spiritual people devote their lives to these realities and biblically and spiritually lead the local churches the next generation will be extremely blemished. Forget not, the gospel of Jesus Christ is only one generation away from distinction!

The way forward

The most important way forward is for believers to follow God's call on their lives. God knows His churches' needs, and He has heard their cry. He is calling for the spiritually-fruitful and spiritually-gifted, to spear-head His recovery/restoration service as theology educators, [our churches need a practical infusion of true truth]! Just as He called Moses to lead Israel from bondage; we are to lead people out of darkness to the light of Christ. As noted earlier, normal theological education with Master of Divinity and Doctoral Degrees through classic classroom instruction *are not* necessarily the answer.

There are numerous models for theological education, leadership training, and pastoral preparation. Some of the most effective are adaptations of generations-old training models found in early church cultures such as:

- Bible Colleges and ministry offered in denominational schools
- "Watch and do" learning
- The master apprentice model
- And the on-the-job training

Theology educators should avoid the trap of thinking that they *must train* believers the same way in which they received their training. **An understanding of the content is more important than the style of teaching used to convey it.** The greatest model of sound doctrine, effective teaching, and clear biblical application can be found in the pastoral ministries of my father the Rev. Curtis A. Leach and his generation. They were called the Great Generation not because of the World Wars only, but because they were great kingdom builders for Christ.

Many of them had little formal theological training, but they learned the depths of their theology and scriptural application on their knees praying, in their home libraries studying, and in mentoring relationships. Their view of ministry can be seen in this profile:

- The basic qualification of personal holiness
- Spiritual giftedness coupled with single-minded learning in the interpretation of Scripture
- A spirit of prayerfulness
- A deep love for God and the care for the people of God
- The ability to unfold the mysteries of the gospel
- All in the context of total dependence on the Lord
- They sought to marry learning to their spirituality

How did all of this come about? They met monthly at church level, quarterly at Association level, and semi-annual at convention level. The training did not have to mirror the high literacy of academia. The younger learned from the older – their goal, to understand God's Word within a theologically sound framework and be able to communicate that truth to others (2 Timothy 2:2).

There is a tremendous increase in the number of theologically shallow Black churches and poorly equipped pastors which cannot continue; too much is at stake today. We can begin to plug the drain by prayerfully selecting and training the right people who will be accepted.

Discussion and Reflection: Chapter 2

1. From this chapter discuss the revealed truths concerning the kind of love Christ came to pour into the human heart. How does the fact hit you that the gospel of Christ is always only one generation away from distinction?

2. Discuss the parable of the Good Samaritan: Who is my neighbor? What is my responsibility to my neighbor?

3. Discuss: One purpose for Jesus' coming was to tear down the walls that separate man from his fellowman.

4. Discuss the enthusiasm shown or not shown among the people at the First Advent of Christ. What is the attitude of the people today concerning His Second Coming?

5. How does God view His divided church today? Does the Word of God support the priests and laity model? Explain the church as, our mother.

Chapter 3

THE COMPASSION OF CHRIST

*"When He [Jesus] saw the multitudes, He was moved with
compassion for them, because they were weary and scattered, like
sheep having no shepherd"* (Matthew 9:36). Emphasis added.

Jesus' compassion was clearly demonstrated by the tremendous emphasis
He placed on healing the sick and delivering people from tormenting evil
spirits. It was an integral part of His witness-evangelism and discipleship
methodology; which He also used to train His disciples (Matthew 10:8).
Jesus' miraculous feeding of the five thousand as recorded in the gospels, also
demonstrates His compassion and concern for human need.

Repeatedly, Jesus' compassionate heart is the motivational trigger
that activates His power. For example, in Matthew 14:14 He saw a great
multitude and feeling compassion for them, He healed all that were sick.
God's mercy was perfectly demonstrated when Jesus healed the sick. Many
people backed away from one person suffering from leprosy, but Jesus, moved
with compassion…. stretched forth His hand and touched him (Mark 1:41).

The power to heal was present and moved by compassion, Jesus gave
men and women a demonstration of God's awesome grace and mercy. He
made God visible to the world. When I was personally healed in answer to
prayer – the pain left my body. I began to weep not simply because the pain
was gone but for His amazing grace and mercy toward me. I often see people
begin to weep when they are healed. Jesus' personal touch and tender mercy
become manifest in the lives of those healed. What has the Lord done for
you? Give Him praise and glory!

To be like Jesus

The Scripture says that God's primary purpose for our existence is that we glorify Him in His Son being "conformed to the image of His Son" (Romans 8:29). We hear the voice of "unbelief" saying that's impossible. "Pride" chimes in, "There is a better way," or "the price is too high." Ask the average person even in the church, their primary purpose would probably be, survival! Trust in God is lacking today, even after hearing His promises preached to us Sunday after Sunday. As I stated earlier, little happens in many of our local churches that requires the supernatural.

However, when my faith stands tall and responds with, "I chose to live by the principles Jesus modeled for me as the Son of man here on Earth in the way He related to the Father." I can become like Him; but only the Holy Spirit can produce that miracle in me as I:

- yield to Him daily,
- allow His full control, and
- obey His leading
- then Christlikeness can emerge in us

We can see Jesus

There is a drought for truth in the land today stemming from a lack of the spiritual and biblical knowledge of the truth of Christ. The earthly life of Jesus is unique in human history as the *pattern* for all Christians. The culture has so naturalized heaven that many are believing that going there is like – deciding to take a trip to New York. Just "do it" "my way." Certainly, this situation deserves more than a simple glance.

In fact, we must:

- Study it thoroughly from God's Word
- Understand it
- Apply the same principles to your own lives
- Spend time consistently alone with the Lord
- Worship Him and hear His voice
- Wholly and joyfully obey Him

The beauty of this life is – we do become like Him:

*"But we all, with unveiled faces, beholding as in a mirror the glory
of the Lord, are being transformed into the same image from glory
to glory, just as by the Spirit of the Lord"* (1 Corinthians 3:18).

It's important that we get this; all believers in the New Covenant have
absolutely nothing blocking their vision of Christ and His glory as revealed
in the Scripture:

- Paul uses a mirror here, not so much on the reflective capabilities of
  the mirror as it is the intimacy of it.
- Just as we did in our childhood, you can put a mirror right up to
  your face and get an unobstructed view.
- Though the vision is unobstructed and intimate, believers do not see
  a perfect representation of God's glory now but will one day.
- Believers are continually being transformed into Christlikeness (see
  Roman 8:29; Philippians 3:12-14; 1 John 3:2).

The goal of the true believer is to be like Christ!

Jesus Christ relinquished all rights to function as the Son of God to
fulfill the purpose of being sent to Earth as the Son of man. To do that, He
laid aside His deity – but retained the nature of His deity. We should be
aware of the five reasons He came – and commit them to heart:

- He came to reveal the Father (Hebrews 1:3).
- He was born to die on the cross to make atonement for the sins of
  the whole world (1:1-2:23).
- He came to destroy the works of the devil (1 John 3:8).
- He came to model how we are to live free from guilt and the
  penalty of sin (1 Peter 2:21).
- He came to be our life (Colossians 1:27; Galatians 2:20).

Let's get it right

When Jesus was taken down from the cross He was buried in the tomb,
burial being the final act declaring death to be past tense. At conversion we
are commanded to be baptized in the name of the father, the Son and the
Holy Spirit – and there our burial takes place – not an effort to kill the old
man [sinful nature] but as a declaration that our old man has died *together*
with Christ (Romans 6:4; Colossians 2:12).

We do not bury people to kill them – but we bury them because they have died!

To the measure we are joined to Jesus; we are partakers in His death. Similarly, we must receive the truth that we were crucified with Him (Galatians 2:20). The Bible says that both have taken place as a matter of fact (Romans 5:17-21).

The gospel sets us free from sin; that is the good news! Notice also:

1. It delivers us from condemnation.
2. It gives us righteousness as a gift.
3. It releases us from the power of sin and makes us slaves of righteousness.
4. The Holy Spirit uses us as channels through which God can impart life.

A walk of faith

Now that we clearly understand our ground of victory – the Christian life becomes a walk of faith. We fight the good fight of faith. When Abraham was promised that he would father a son; his age and other factors would suggest the impossibility of such an event. But instead of contesting it, he became fully convinced that what God had promised He was able to perform (Romans 4:21).

Abraham grew strong in faith – giving glory to God. When the Scripture promises us freedom from sin, we are prone to gravitate to prior failures and thus turn a deaf ear to the life-giving Word of God. Faith comes by hearing and hearing by the Word of God. If God has promised it:

• He can perform it in us and through us.
• He can write His laws on our hearts therefore, freeing us from the power of temptation.

We walk by faith and not by sight. God oversees time, so any delay in the full completion of this promise in daily life does not defuse the promise any more than the extended delay in Isaac's birth. When Abraham fell short in his early experience it did not disqualify him from fulfillment later. He was *restored* to the promise.

> We must learn to confess our sins and receive forgiveness
> for failure – but do not abandon the goal of the promised
> freedom (see 1 John 1:9).

Many tend to think of failure as inevitable and settle for constant confession as the norm. It is essential that we let the Word of God working in us by the Holy Spirit reveal the truth of the matter to us. It is paramount that we go on believing God until we experience full realization.

To develop us as men and women of faith, God will delay answers to our prayers and the fulfillment of promises He has spoken to us to test us to see whether we trust His character when we cannot find Him. In the Book of Job this strategy was on full display for Job as He waited on God who came through mightily for him in the end.

> *My brethren take the prophets, who spoke in the name of the
> Lord, as an example of suffering and patience. Indeed, we count
> them blessed who endure. You have heard of the perseverance of
> Job and seen the end intended by the Lord – that the Lord is very
> compassionate and merciful* (James 5:11-12).

James also discloses that sometimes God allows some of His close disciples to suffer, in order to mentor others in how to go through unexplainable difficult trials triumphantly. He did that not only with Job but also with the apostle Paul (carefully study Acts 27). The only way we will come through the severity of those kinds of tests is:

To study, in this case God's justice from His Word – as well as all His other attributes. Jesus spent untold hours *teaching* life-changing truths to the multitudes and even continued *teaching* His *disciples* in much greater depth. He spent countless hours revealing more and more truth about His Father God and proving in numerous ways that the Father had sent Him. Notice in Luke 24:7, Jesus said,

> *"The Son of Man must be delivered into the hands of sinful men,
> and be crucified, and the third day arise again."*

He clearly stated the Father's purpose in sending Him to Earth – to redeem mankind. Give Him praise and glory!

A solemn warning

It is totally unimaginable the high price to having a *sustained in-depth* and *anointed* Bible – teaching ministry. Only those who have paid the price will clearly understand what I mean. Our messages take 45 minutes to an hour, sometimes several times in a day, but the listeners have no idea of the many hours or days spent in preparation and prayer; that God has required of the teacher before the message could be delivered with authority.

Notice the solemn warning to those who are called by God to teach His Word:

> *"Let not many of you become teachers,*
> *knowing that*
> *we shall*
> *receive a stricter judgment"* (James 3:1).

The very next verse explains that we are accountable to God – in relation to our lives matching up with our words.

> *"For we all stumble in many things. If anyone does not stumble in word, he is a perfect man, able to bridle the whole body"* (v. 2).

James does not give the warning of judgment to others without applying it to himself.

Teachers called of God

As teachers called of God, we will stand before the judgment seat of Christ, the Master Teacher, and be judged more strictly than others. The teachers' greater influence translates into greater responsibility. This judgment is not speaking of eternal separation from God but suggests a through judgment before Christ.

The teachers' greater influence translates into greater responsibility!

Also consider the following Scriptures:

> *Whoever therefore breaks one of the least of these commandments, and teaches men so, he shall be called least in the kingdom of heaven; but*

whoever does and teaches them, he shall be called great in the kingdom of heaven (Matthew 5:19).

But why do you judge your brother? Or why do you show contempt for your brother? For we shall all bow before the judgment seat of Christ. For it is written:

> *"As I live, says the LORD,*
> *Every knee shall bow to Me,*
> *And every tongue shall confess*
> *To God."*

So, then each of us shall give account of himself to God. Therefore, let us not judge one another anymore, but rather resolve this, not to put a stumbling block or a cause to fall in our brother's way (Romans 14:10-13).

All believers are accountable to their Master, Jesus Christ, for they will appear before Him. Every believer will be evaluated to determine his or her reward (study carefully 1 Corinthians 3:11-15; 2 Corinthians 5:9, 30).

Jesus' promise

Jesus promised, *"Most assuredly, I say to you, he who believes in Me, the works that I do he will do also; and greater works than these will he do, because I go to My Father"* (John 14:12).

Because He is now exalted at the right hand of the Father with all authority, He can continue to fulfill these great works through His church. In His promise Jesus did not leave these "greater works" to the paid professionals only, but to the whole church [*all* members are ministers of reconciliation]. Church is not for spectators:

- The work of Christ is tremendously hindered or brought to naught in numerous local Black churches today by the many unanointed wineskin leaders' resistance to change [at all echelons].
- There are many unemployed old and new anointed wineskin believers in our Black churches [from the traditional to the contemporary], who because they are not *ordained;* feel that all they can do is stand silently on the sidelines as a spectator. Such churches have forms of godliness but deny the power – the Holy Spirit.

Listen to Peter's summary of Jesus' earthly ministry in Acts 10:38:

"God anointed Jesus of Nazareth with the Holy Spirit and with power, who went about doing good and healing all who were oppressed by the devil, for God was with Him."

God empowered Him for war! Jesus was hostile toward sin, sickness and death regarding them as His enemies. Notice in the Scripture, when He came upon a funeral – He raised the dead. The sick who sought Him were healed. Jesus claimed that the Father, dwelling in Him did the work (John 14:10).

If Jesus, who was God manifested in the flesh, worked in such a manner spending so much of His time busily healing, why would we think for a moment that God the Father and God the Son have changed their minds about our doing greater works?

Jesus affirmed faith in Him wherever He found it. The little frail lady for instance, who was pleased to remain hidden in the crowd, but Jesus found her and affirmed her, *"Your faith has made you whole"* (Matthew 9:22). He celebrated the opportunity to make public the faith that she had when she touched the hem of His garment.

Jesus showed the same compassion and enthusiasm when he marveled at the faith of the centurion who invited Him to simply *"say the word"* and not come to his home. Jesus expressed real appreciation for the fact that the Gentiles were beginning to put their trust in Him; and He was saddened that no such faith manifested in His own home town. Faith clearly plays a very important part in the release of healing. I have observed faith growing in many throughout the Bread of Life Ministries – where people are consistently being healed and delivered.

In fact, for a season a fellow minister, Pastor Alfred Green and I would on occasion team up in revivals and other services. I preached and gave the invitation appeal to the unsaved (Romans 10:9-10); to the believers (1 John 1:9) and the sick (1 Peter 2:24). Green ministered to the sick, while I ministered to the others. The Holy Spirit blessed mightily in each service.

A particular healing comes to mind. In one Sunday morning service during the gospel appeal a deacon from one of the other local churches came forth for healing. He had been released from the hospital after the doctors had given him up with a terminal illness. He made preparation for his approaching death, by turning his affairs and construction business over to his sons and was now prayerfully just waiting to die.

Green spoke in a low tone to the man, anointed him with oil and prayed the prayer of faith. The brother fell backwards to the floor like a dead man. Soon he stirred and got up – totally healed. Today, more than fifteen years later he is still testifying and praising God for his healing and his business is thriving – to God be the glory!

Let the church say, Amen!

The apostles were not alone in performing signs. Stephen and Philip, who were called to fulfill a role of caring for the poor widows, performed signs in the name of Jesus (see Acts 8:12-13; 6:7). The ministry which Jesus began has continued through His followers to this day.

The Book of Acts has no ending as the other books of the New Testament, because Christ continues His work today through the Holy Spirit in His followers. In that sense the book continues to be written today. When my wife and I joined the Charismatic Movement in the mid-sixties, for a while there seemed to be two streams of the movement in the churches.

1. One stream promoted Christianity as a private and personal [religious] experience which in no-way interfered with your normal church-going [in organization].
2. The second stream realized God's presence and power along with a refreshing vitality in the churches: The Holy Spirit and the transforming Word that demand a new mindset [in spiritual organism].

The presence and power of the Holy Spirit is manifested for the common good of all (see 1 Corinthians 10:8). Unlike the first stream, if others are to benefit, in spiritual organism there must be a love-sharing of the spiritual gifts in a public context, not exclusively in private or to only a select few.

A spiritual change must come

We are expected to be a Spirit-filled community (Acts 1:8; Ephesians 5:18). Worship is expressed in a variety of ways and with the participation of *everyone* (1 Corinthians 14:26). Emphasis added throughout.

However, major organizational and structural changes will have to be made in most of America's Black churches to accommodate the Holy Spirit and the Word freely working among them. Probably beginning with a renewed mind. The manifest presence of the Holy Spirit is non-negotiable:

- Notice, the tabernacle in the wilderness, in all its beauty was not complete until Exodus 40:34-35: *"Then the cloud covered the tabernacle of meeting and the glory of the Lord filled the tabernacle. And Moses was not able to enter the tabernacle of meeting, because the cloud rested above it and the glory of the Lord filled the tabernacle.*
- Likewise, in 2 Chronicles 7:1: *When Solomon had finished praying, fire came down from heaven and consumed the burnt offering and the sacrifices; and the glory of the Lord filled the temple. And the priests could not enter the house of the Lord, because the glory of the Lord had filled the Lord's house.*
- Thirdly, the Day of Pentecost Acts 2:1-2: *".... And suddenly there came a sound from heaven, as a rushing mighty wind, and filled the whole room where they were sitting.*

The coming of the ministry of the Holy Spirit

There is much confusion in the church concerning the Holy Spirit. In fact, many Christians and some denominations have become so confused, that they no longer care to know Him. Yet, as I stated earlier; much is written about Him today and a renewed spiritual interest in the Holy Spirit and His ministries is sweeping the world, praise God! Could this be the time of restitution promised before Christ returns? Carefully study Acts (1:6 and 3:21).

It is the privilege of every Christian to experience what the apostolic church experienced. For the Scripture says, "...... and you shall receive the gift of the Holy Ghost. The promise is unto you, and unto your children, and to all that are afar off" (Acts 2:39).

Prior to the Protestant Reformation, Roman Catholics were taught that only the priests and hierarchy glorified God. The priestly vocation stood as the only or best means of honoring God. But a new view came with the Reformation. The Reformers taught that **all** of life should be lived *Coram Deo* – "before the face of God." Not only were priests and ministry sacred vocations, but every Christian and every vocation – clerk, janitor, cook, CEO, and so on is a calling to glorify God. Consequently, every Christian needs to learn how to honor God in their ordinary everyday pursuits. Boys and girls, men and women must be taught and assisted to bring their entire lives under the lordship of Jesus Christ.

In many of our local churches today, the philosophy of ministry separates Sunday from Monday through Saturday. Christianity becomes a one-day-a-week event rather than a Spirit-controlled life and biblical worldview lived [24/7]. As stated earlier, we want to teach people to yield their family, employment, finances, dating, politics, sex, and cultural being to the rule of Jesus Christ through His Spirit and His Word. They are to be taught the value of knowing how to study the Bible for themselves. Anything less robs Christians of the benefits of a renewed mind, knowledge of the truth, and God's will for them. I've had so many people come to me for counsel with problems and other concerns that have their lives and their families turned upside down – simply because they don't know what the Word of God has to say concerning the matter!

When Jesus gave us the Great Commission, He did not merely say, "Teach them everything I have commanded you." That's not accurate. Jesus says, <u>"Teach them to *obey* everything I have commanded you."</u>

Many Christians and churches have deleted "obedience" from their spiritual notebook thinking that its too narrow and optional. Such persons do not have a good grasp on the basics of the Bible and discipleship. Knowing this, discipleship efforts in the Black Church must emphasize faith-powered and grace-motivated *obedience* to all that Jesus commands. Otherwise, the church will continue to see stagnation and peripheral spiritual "living." Many Christians seems to have forgotten that the Lord chastens those who are His (see Hebrews 12:6; Revelation 3:19). True discipleship requires transferring learning into obedience!

The people are denied a gold mine of blessings that comes from learning and meditating on the many promises of God. Have you ever considered the many blessings of the Jews who are not Christ followers, but are devoted to God's Word? They have received success just as God has promised? For example, how important is your body to God?

- To the believer, the Scripture says, "the body is the temple of the Holy Spirit."
- To the unsaved and to a growing number of Christians, a summary of the tremendous amount of money spent annually in this country for care of the human body for natural reasons – would probably dwarf the nation's social welfare or healthcare costs. Who would have dreamed that care of finger and toe nails, gym fees, body sculpture, wrinkles, footwear, and so many other accessories spent on the body [the natural temple of meism] would demand so much attention today? In fact, the cost for care of the body receives a higher love and priority than childcare and the family meals in the home – in too many cases.

The world's order of importance is *the* body, soul, and spirit; while God's order for the child of God is *the* spirit, soul and body.

Notice, I did not say that attention to the body is wrong, but spirituality works from the inside out [from the spirit through the soul to the body] from the heart in other words. People often say, "I am willing to die for Christ," and that is very honorable I'm sure, but let me humbly say:

- God does not necessarily want you or me to die for Jesus in this Dispensation of Grace.
- He wants us to *live* for Him! He wants each of us to be *"a living sacrifice."*
- He wants us to be a holy temple [His dwelling place].
- And He desires that whatever we do whether we eat, or drink, or whatsoever we do – God wants us to do it for His glory (see 1 Corinthians 10:31).
- Under the old covenant, the sacrificial animals were slain. But since the one Sacrifice [Christ] once for all time – has been accomplished on Calvary, there is no further need for *dead* sacrifices.

What God wants is that we *present* ourselves to Him a living sacrifice – putting ourselves into His hands for His pleasure. The living sacrifice contrasts with the legal sacrifice. Therefore, the apostle Paul is pleading for *spiritual sacrifices* in the name of Jesus.

- Every outgoing act of a Christian's heart in grateful praise and prompted by the love of Christ, is itself a sacrifice to God, a sweet-smelling savor – worship (Hebrews 13:15-16).

In 1 Peter 2:5, the apostle explains metaphorically that God is building a *spiritual house* putting all believers in place integrating each one with the others, and each believer with the life of Christ. Further, we are a holy priesthood.

The Scriptures have noted that Old Testament priests and New Testament-priests have many similar characteristics:

- Priesthood is an elect privilege (see Exodus 28:1; John 15:16).
- Priests are cleansed of sin (see Leviticus 8:6-36 and Titus 2:14).
- Priests are clothed for service (see 5:5; Exodus 28:42; Leviticus 8:7; Psalm 132:9, 16).
- Priests are anointed for service (see Leviticus 8:12, 30; 1 John 2:20, 27).

- Priests are prepared for service (see Leviticus 8:33; 9:4, 23; Galatians 1:16; 1 Timothy 3:6).
- Priests are ordained to obedience (see v. 4; Leviticus 10:1).
- Priests are to honor the Word of God (see v. 2; Malachi 2:7).
- Priests are to walk with God (see Malachi 2:6; Galatians 5:16, 25).
- Priests are to impact sinners (see Malachi 2:6; Galatian 6:1).
- Priests are messengers of God (Malachi 2:7; Matthew 28:19, 20).

The early Church could grow and become full of bonified New Testament believer-priests because it was made up of thousands of men and women whose level of spiritual experience and biblical knowledge together would make novices of many seminary graduates today. The obedience of Christ's disciples who could [all] go everywhere and preach the gospel of Christ to every creature – challenges us to engage in the same endeavor (Acts 8:1, 4).

The spiritually-equipped local New Testament African American churches that preach the whole counsel of God, can be confident that as the Lord was working with the early Church, He will also work with us!

Discussion and Reflection: Chapter 3

1. Discuss Jesus' compassionate heart as He demonstrated God's grace and mercy in healing the sick and meeting other needs (see Matthew 10:8).

2. According to the Scriptures, what is God's primary purpose for our existence (see Romans 8:29).

3. Discuss Jesus' modeling how we are to live free from guilt and penalty of sin (see 1 Peter 2:21).

4. Discuss the solemn warning, God gives to those who are called by Him to teach His Word (see James 3:1,2).

5. Every believer is accountable to their Master, Jesus Christ and will appear before Him for evaluation to determine their reward (carefully study 1 Corinthians 3:11-15; 2 Corinthians 5:9, 30).

Chapter 4

A BURDEN FOR THE LOST

"But to each one of us grace was given according to the measure of Christ's gift" (Ephesians 4:7).

The more I study Jesus' life, the more I am appalled at how far the Black Church has moved away from God's blueprint given in His Word. The local church, the body of Christ, the redemption of mankind, and a biblical worldview are basic study requirements for all Christians. The need for Church renewal is apparent, simply by taking stock of the number of true believers easily moving from church to church and some even leave their denomination, as many churches depart from the faith once delivered to the saints (Jude 3). Many are turning to what they call power empowerment, at the same time turning from the power of God unto salvation [the gospel of Christ]; this condition is very threatening, especially for the millennials and younger people. New generations are questioning the shallow and more often then not, syncretistic versions of Christianity that their parents believe.

I believe the flame of the *lampstand*[7] is being removed at an increasingly alarming rate. More and more Black churches are choosing for various reasons to turn away from the ministry and power of the Holy Spirit – to some blended form based on earthly philosophies, ungodly persuasions, imagination, greed and prosperity, and some are even turning to the O.T. law.

Paul knew that in our day, we would encounter the same deceptions. "For such men are false apostles, decietful workers, disguising themselves as apostles of Christ. And no wonder, for even Satan disguisises himself as an angel of light. So it is no surprise if his servants, also, disguises themselves as servants of righteousness. Their end will correspond to their deeds" (2 Corinthians 11:13-15).

In a day where media and the movies promote pluralism; a condition many of us had to put up with most of our lives. We heard the Sunday sermon preached by our pastors and then, listened to contradictions for the next five days from our school teachers in public school, barbers and other areas of the marketplace. However, many local Black churches have embraced a word that no longer means the same as it did many years ago: the word is *inclusivism*. Countering inclusivism is another word *exclusivism*.

- *Inclusivism* – adherents teach that since Jesus knew that everyone would not have a chance to hear the gospel, He included all religions in His work. Additionally, that every religion has value in its own right. This view cuts the very jugular vain of Christianity if permitted.
- *Exclusivism* – adherents teaches that there is no other Savior than Jesus Christ alone and you must be born again. Further, we believe that persons without the new birth by faith in Christ, are separated from God and will spend eternity in hell. Those Black churches with this perspective believe in the exclusivity of the gospel of Jesus Christ and proclaim it and fulfill the Great Commission to rescue the perishing and bring glory to God.

My wife and I travel a lot in ministry and in many cities and towns, we are seeing church buildings with their steeple still intact being purchased and used for storage warehouses, thrift shops and other secular purposes. Sometimes on the same block we notice former office or retail space being converted to a church or Para-ministry. To me this shows that the people want to experience the presence and power of God, the Holy Spirit – not the skits, programs, entertainment and syncretic Christianity so popular today in many institutional Black churches. People want truth! Jesus is truth!

Certainly, some of us remember when the steeple held the tallest tower [point] in the community, marking the churches' locations. The warmth, peace and tranquility of the old church is no longer a guarantee upon entering today. Many problems that confront the Black church today could be quickly resolved if the churches would faithfully and obediently "teach the new believers and some old ones to *obey* all that Jesus has commanded:

- Studying and obeying the *revealed* truth of God's Word in what it signifies for the new believers, before water baptism, thoroughly teach the new converts: 1) Romans 1-6, and 2) Romans 7-8 afterward. Take if slow.
- Prayerfully and actively pursuing recovery of their burden for the lost and recommit to actively obeying the Great Commissions [Praise God!].

- Teaching the people the value of believing the promises of God and teaching them the significance of personal daily prayer and Bible study for their own spiritual growth, enrichment, and problem-solving.
- Pursue the prodigals.

One main hinderance that always seem to come quickly into view happens when biblically-based counsel suggests theological and structural changes, that go against long-standing church traditions, programs and policies – at times the session is over at that point – due to those famous seven last words of a dying church, "We have never done it like that!" Then there are those who think *truth* is too narrow! The Word of God admonishes all Christian churches to "hear what the Spirit is saying to the churches" (see Revelation 2:29).

What I have written so far is in no way a boast, but to try and provide an example and a bit of persuasion to those who have problems with changing their ministry models and methods:

- Churches must discern methodology influenced and guided by ethical respectability, and political correctness – in contrast to true Holy Spirit-led leaders who through new wineskins of technology and innovation practice follow and obey what the Spirit is saying to the churches.
- For centuries, witness-evangelism and discipleship training have been the lifeline for many Christian churches in America.

Those believers who have accepted Jesus as Savior and Lord of all – consider His gospel to be *exportable* and themselves to be *expendable* in getting the gospel to the whole world. It is imperative that the Christian:

- Maintain a loving trust for his or her Lord.
- Remain anxious and engaged with the propagation of the gospel of Jesus Christ.
- Possess a militant spirit that makes true Christianity an aggressive and judgmental force in the affairs of humankind.

Further, we are reminded that the church is a Spiritual entity and not some social club, fraternal organization, or secret society in the city or town to be manipulated by the local culture and politicians.

Satan will gladly use people connected with the church, so that he or his demons can manipulate them to gripe and complain about the church. More and more I hear such ungodly admissions from Christians as:

- The blood sacrifice was Old Testament only!
- Satan is the prince of this world, and he is in charge?
- Jesus, who?
- Truth is relative and so is morality.
- There are more than one-way to heaven.
- We all serve the same God.
- Let the kids grow up and let them decide for themselves.
- "Not my child!"
- There are many definitions under the sun for "born again."
- Salvation without repentance.
- We have never done it like that.
- That's all there is.
- That's just the way it is.

These lies and excuses are sometime transmitted from "jest" or just plain voluntary spiritual and biblical ignorance. Such thinking reflects the gains made through political correctness, progressive liberalism, and secular culture planted through secular humanism's agenda dominating the public educational systems and society at large. But today, the greater threats are "loss of the gospel" and "eternal life," as happened during the dark ages of the church. Sadly, in many churches, false prophets and teachers are teaching and preaching a false, and distorted gospel – of which much of their congregations are for the most part unaware. In many messages we hear today, what is said may be true, but what is not said becomes the problem. It is imperative that we remember, loss of the gospel includes loss of the power to save.

The fault lies mainly among those of us who have been called to stand and preach and teach the true Gospel of Christ and further His kingdom agenda on earth.

Because a thing has been practiced in the church for many generations – does not mean it is right. Likewise, because it has not been practiced for generations does not mean it is wrong!

Rather than stand and declare the whole counsel of God, many have laid aside the Great Commandment and the Great Commission and succumbed to a form of godliness that results as churches turn inward to their own false doctrines and self-formulated mission statements and organizational policies fostered by strict adherence to customs and traditions of men. All supported by entertaining programs and other gimmicks, publicized through a public relations website beckoning, "You all come *see* us!"

This inward turn has not only fueled an exodus from the pews, but forfeits our God-given mission – unless such churches repent and return to the Lord; sadly, their lampstands will no doubt be removed.

We have changed our moral code to fit our behavior instead of changing our behavior to harmonize with God's moral code.– Evangelist Billy Graham

---

The church outside

The post office operation provides a great metaphor of the *Bible-believing* New Testament Church. Can you imagine the chaos if everyone had to go to the post office to pick up their mail? Well, long ago that problem was solved through the establishment of a system of individual mailboxes. Rather than all the people coming to the post office for their mail – the post office carries the mail out to the people. We have read much concerning the decline in church influence and people-involvement. I'm sure that the gadgetry and latest ideas of fixing the problem from the inside of the church building have all played out. The command from our Lord was to "go" and as you go "make disciples."

Like the post office, the local church's [entire membership] is commanded to take the gospel of Christ out to the people everywhere. Jesus came into the world to make God who is Spirit visible to the world. How successful at doing His mission would He have been; if He had spent all His time down on the porch of the temple?

As stated in other sections throughout this book, Christ wants *all* of the church membership deployed as soul-winners. Jesus said, "You are *witnesses* of these things" (Luke 24:48). "You also must *testify*" (John 15:27). "You will be My witnesses" (Acts 1:8). Much of Paul's ministry was witnessing (Acts 22:15-16; 26:16, 22).

One very important tool for witnessing is the true believer's personal testimony. This may be shared to the saved as well as the unsaved. Testimony to non-Christians is a very powerful form of witnessing. The church must teach her people that their testimony should follow these rules:

- Your testimony must relate personally to Jesus Christ. Tell of His goodness, guidance, love, blessings and answers to prayers.

- Your testimony is to bring glory to God, not yourself. Testify in a manner that the person remembers what Jesus did – not you.
- Your testimony must be humble, so God can work though you. Humble is the way. You must not let pride enter, if so you will be of no use to God.
- Your testimony must be adjusted to the situation. Save some for another time. Your own testimony humbly given can bring life to your Bible expertise.
- Watch for opportunities to weave your testimony into conversations inoffensively.
- Your testimony can help to create opportunities for others to testify.
- Your testimony must be relevant and up-to-date.
- Your testimony can form some of special appeal.

Seeing Him who is invisible

Therefore, as Christians our mission is like Christ's mission when He was on earth, just as He made God visible to the world (see John 24:9-10). Christ expects each true believer to witness both by life and lips. Witnessing is primarily to Christ, but also to the Father and to – Bible truth. So, His body, the church [corporately and individually] is to make Him [Christ] visible to the world. Like the Greeks, people want *to see* Jesus! Right now, Christ is seated at the right hand of the Father in heaven. But the Word of God tells us that He is present here in His body, the Church.

The Spirit-filled Church is God's way of making His *Invisible* Son visible to the world – incarnate in us (see I Cor. 6:9-20). When that happens, we have access to spiritual gifts, abilities and insights previously unavailable. Just as Phillip and the others were able to see the *invisible* Father by watching and observing Jesus, the unbelieving world can now look at the Christian Church [the body of Christ] and see the *invisible* Christ Jesus made *visible*.

The song writer said,

> "This little light of mine I'm going to let it shine. "Everywhere I go I'm going to let my little light shine." "Hide it under a bushel, No!"

This is one of those old church songs, each member can make personal: "sing" and "do!"

- "All in my home, I'm going to let it shine"
- "All in my neighborhood, I'm going to let it shine"

- "All on my job, I'm going to let it shine"
- "All in my school, I'm going to let it shine"
- "All in my walk, I'm going to let it shine"
- "All in my talk, I'm going to let it shine"

Jesus made God the Father visible; by being full of grace and truth. The church is *called* and *empowered* by the Holy Spirit to make the ascended Christ visible in the world today by being full of grace and truth:

> *He raised us up together and made us sit together in the heavenly places in Christ Jesus, that in the ages to come He might show the exceeding riches of His grace in His kindness toward us in Christ Jesus. For by grace you have been saved through faith, and that not of yourselves; it is the gift of God, not of works, lest anyone should boast"* (Ephesians 2:6-9).

> *Grace and peace be multiplied to you in the knowledge of God and of Jesus our Lord, as His divine power has given to us all things that pertain to life and godliness, through the knowledge of Him who called us by glory and virtue, by which have been given to us exceedingly great and precious promises, that through these you may be partakers of the divine nature, having escaped the corruption that is in the world through lust"* (2 Peter 1:1-3).

The genuine Christian is secure in his or her salvation and will persevere, and grow; having received everything necessary to sustain eternal life through Christ's power. He or she lives reverently, loyally, and obediently to the praise and glory of God!

Show some genuine love

One of the slang names I hear some young men call each other today is "dog." The Jews called the Gentiles dogs, during Christ's days on the earth. Isn't it something that after the resurrection of Christ and the coming of the Holy Spirit – Nero, the Roman Emperor had the apostle Paul beheaded?

Today people name their dogs, Nero. Even the dog Nero knows whether your love is real or phony. They can sense it and be stand-offish until you show some genuine love. Why would a Christian whose love perhaps is nil or has grown cold, think they can fake it?

The life of a Christian is a life of love; anything less is easily spotted because you are marked by Christlike love [agape], the hallmark of every Christian (1 John 3:10, 14; 4:8):

- Every Christian is commanded by Christ to love one another.
- Every Christian is to love the lost with a love like Christ's love.
- Christ's love is infinite ours is finite, His love is perfect, ours is truly imperfect.
- Yet our love like Christ's must be personal, practical, holy, and self-sacrificing.

Love – God's seal

Though you may possess other abilities; to be a Christian you cannot fake authentic [unconditional] love. Unless we love God and others [including the lost] with a Christlike love [agape], we have missed the all-essential standard.[8] The Scripture promises, that if we love one another, God will abide in us and His love will be perfected in us. What more could we possibly want than that? We certainly don't live up to this statement. And that is so tragic, because there is a serious warning in this passage that states, "those who don't love don't know God." If this is true, and it is, then what does this say about the local churches?

Spiritual leaders at every level in the church are to demonstrate this truth more than anyone else. Those in leadership are to be models of love. This love of God *in* Christ can be modeled in only one way and that is by being filled with this river of love and then letting it flow out of you in the church and the world for which Christ died.

As Christians we must *remember,* if this fullness of divine supernatural love is not constantly streaming out from all of us, and especially those in pastoral ministry; then we are misrepresenting Jesus Christ. The only true ambassador of Christ is the ambassador of love (2 Corinthians 5:20).

A warning: He or she who does not pour out love *slanders* the God of love they claim to represent. I venture to say, love is the main ingredient in all Christian service; especially to the lost.

The importance of loving one another is the emphasized standard throughout the Scripture (see Romans 12:9-10; 1 Corinthians 13; 1 Peter 4:8), sadly, many local churches are missing out on some extraordinary blessings because of a lack of love.

Love is the fragrance, the glory, and the power for all Christian living.

One important way we love God is in our love for others, especially through our burden for the lost. The more you transmit and express His love to others, the more He can flood you with His love. Then you will more fully be able to share the love He expresses to you. Notice the characteristics of such love:

1. **It suffers long** – is patient (1 Thessalonians 5:`14)
2. **It is kind** – gentle especially with those who hurt (Ephesians 4:32)
3. **It does not envy** – is not jealous of what others have (Proverbs 23:17)
4. **It does not parade itself** – but puts itself on display (John 3:30)
5. **It is not puffed up** – arrogant, or proud (Galatians 6:3)
6. **It does not act rudely** – mean-spiritedly, insulting others (Ecclesiastes 5:2)
7. **It does not seek its own** – way, or act pushy (1 Corinthians 19:11)
8. **It is not provoked** – or angered (Proverbs 19:11)
9. **It thinks no evil** – does not keep score on others (Hebrews 10:17)
10. **It rejoices not in iniquity** – takes no pleasure when others fall into sin (Mark 3:5)
11. **It rejoices in the truth** – is joyful when righteousness prevails (2 John 4).
12. **It bears all things** – handles the burdensome (Galatians 6:2)
13. **It believes all things** – trusts in God no matter what (Proverbs 3:5)
14. **It hopes all things** – keeps looking up, does not despair (Philippians 3:13).
15. **It endures all things** – puts up with everything; does not wear out (Galatians 6:9).
16. **It never fails** – the only thing it cannot do is fail (1 Corinthians 16:14).

How to receive a passion for the lost

A great start is for you by faith to believe that God, the Holy Spirit, will give you a passion for the lost if you ask for it. Not everyone is called to be a Billy Graham. But every Christian is called to bear fruit – both the fruit of the Spirit and the fruit of souls.

There is no greater joy than to lead a person to a life transforming experience with Jesus Christ. The more you taste this joy, the more you will want God to make you a soul-winner. How is this accomplished?

1. The passionate commitment to Jesus Christ is the foundation of soul-winning.
2. Make it part of your daily prayer to ask God to help you lead people to Christ.
3. Ask God to make you sensitive to the needs of others.
4. Humble is the way.

Your prayer life clearly reveals your spirituality. Your soul-winning ministry demands spiritual power. The Holy Spirit is the *source* of all power, and He is given in answer to prayer.

> *"If you then, though you are evil, know how to give good gifts to your children, how much more will your Father in heaven give the Holy Spirit to those who ask Him"* (Luke 11:13).

This tremendous promise is not for some specially chosen group, notice Jesus immediately after He had given the great promise, He said,

> *"Ask and it shall be given to you; seek and you will find; knock and the door will be opened to you."* He added, *"For everyone who ask receives; he who seeks finds; and to him who knocks, the door will be opened"* (Luke 11:9-10). Emphasis added.

Spiritual ministry is dependent upon the Spirit. Please understand, that is God's way and His way is not optional! You can never minister effectively in your own strength [flesh] – therefore *unless* we are filled with the Spirit; daily anointed; led and empowered by the Holy Spirit – we don't measure up!

Our greatest need then, if we want to see the conviction of sin among the unsaved is the powerful presence of Christ through the Holy Spirit (see John14:16-18). Remember also, our preaching, teaching, or witnessing unless anointed and empowered by the Spirit may hinder rather than bless.

"Preach, preach and sometimes use words." Francis of Assisi 1225 A.D.

Truth applied by the Holy Spirit changes lives (see 2 Corinthians 3:6). Sadly, most people depend more on their study, work, and planning than on prayer ministry which is the main channel for the flow of the Holy Spirit in your life.

> "Where there is "much prayer – there is much power!"
> "Where there is little prayer – there is little power!"

The local church and prayer ministry

A New Testament spiritual leader in any capacity small or great has got to be God-made – and he or she is made during prayer ministry. Power in prayer has a direct relation to time spent in prayer. Sometime ago I read about a visitor who came up to Pastor Charles Spurgeon and asked him about the effectiveness of the great preaching ministry of the Metropolitan Tabernacle in London. He simply led the man over to the door which led to the basement, opened it and the man was able to see a group of men and women on their knees praying. Glory to God!

Many local Black churches have practically given up on mid-week prayer ministry because only a small fraction of the membership will show up, this is happening in the larger congregations as well as the small ones. We are so numbers oriented that we forget Jesus' words, "Where two or three are gathered together in My name there am I in the midst of them" (Matthew 18:20). That is the smallest form of the local church. Certainly, numbers are a factor, but this promise came straight from the Head of the church, Jesus Christ.

> Prayer ministry prepares you for every aspect of your Christian duty and work. Do nothing without it!

Any task assigned to an individual Christian in the local Black church is too big for him or her alone. No matter how great or how menial we may think the task is, it must drive us to prayer. As I stated earlier, many churches are folding today as more and more of them turn to proclamation only.

- Research shows that the decline in churches across America has been consumerate with the decline in corporate prayer.
- To many today, the Black churches' cooperate prayer meeting is considered antiquated and unnecessary today? God forbid!
- Failing churches don't realize that healthy churches prioritize prayer as a vital part of their corporate life.

Some of these churches may be spared through spiritual-innovation and Scripture-led changes in methodology and structure. Over the past fifty years one of the most popular changes is from the mid-week church prayer meeting and Bible study to the forming of "small groups," "Home teams" or some variation of these teams to carry out this mission. Much prayer ministry, planning and training must accompany building a new structure, especially in the area of spiritual leadership, which we put in place to shepherd small groups of men and women. The church must move from an inward focus and work toward moving to an outward focus. As stated in another section, the Bible clearly states that as pastors, we will be held accountable for how we lead, love, prepare the people for heaven and protect those whom the Lord has placed in our care.

If we are asking people to be willing to share in the joys and sorrows of our communal lives – then the people who are put in place to strengthen, encourage and lead these groups must be spiritually mature, grounded in the faith, and the truth of God's Word, trustworthy disciples. The bar must be high for them. Remember, the prayers of our foreparents, who risked 200 lashes from the whip, just for assembling with the saints to pray together. During slavery, the Jim Crow era in the South and certainly the Civil Rights Movement were all bathed in much prayer. Our people looked to God for deliverance – and He has never forsakened or failed us. However, more and more African Americans are sucombing to the extreme progressive humanism [no God] in society today. At the same time, many are preaching a false message of unconditional favor of God. Unless this nation confess, repents, return to God and keep His Word, the judgment of God is surely imminent. Preachers are saying, "God understands and agrees with pre-marital sexual relations." This "god" they continue, has the attributes of love, mercy, and forgiveness *without* justice meaning the absence of judgment and punishment for sin. Sadly, such people have been blinded by the devil and little do they realize, just how far they have strayed from the truth [unchanging standards] of a Holy God. No nation, government, person or persons have the right to change or lower God's standards.

Sadly, it seems that the majority of the African American community moved away from God as our Source after the death of Dr. Martin Luther King Jr. and the end of the Civil Rights Movement. What a mess we have made since those days, first by moving away from Almighty God and His Word to lean on our own understanding [using our own natural wisdom and intellect]! It's like trying to dig a ditch with a teaspoon. In other words, when the leadership leaves the war, by whatever means – the revolution dies! Many of our foundational institutions have been blasted from their mooring:

- Marriage and the family
- The Black Church

- Education [all levels]
- Economics
- Politics
- The village versus Individualism
- Reaching back to bring our brothers and sisters along
- Racial clarity

Remember the saying, "A family that prays together – stays together?"

God called the church a body because He wants us to understand how integral we are in the lives of one another. How we chose to function with one another will determine if our *one body* will be healthy and fruitful or just another accident waiting to happen. Two gospel traits when put into practice, can bring life and purpose back to the members of many dying churches. These two factors are, Spirit-guided humility and Spirit-guided unity:

Spirit-guided Humility

In Romans 12:3, Paul states concerning the body of Christ, *"For by the grace given to me I say to everyone among you not to think of himself more highly than he ought to think, but to think soberly and according to the measure of faith that God has given."* Humble is the way. Paul reminds us that when we begin to think about what our purpose is in the body, *pride* will be afforded an opportunity to strike. *Humility must prevail in our hearts* – Filled with the Holy Spirit, the body is to remain healthy and be fruitful. In 1 Corinthians 12, Paul says that:

- Every member of the body is of equal value to the body.
- It is absurd to think that one body part is more important than another.

Paul equates body parts to spiritual gifts – and each part of the body of Christ has been given a gift or gifts to be used to build up and make the body function properly. For example, the gift of teaching could be like an arm. As you faithfully teach, God uses that gift to keep the church body healthy, just as a healthy arm serves its role in the human body. Serve the body of Christ faithfully with your spiritual gifts and be watchful to encourage and help others serve with their gifts.

Unity of the Spirit

There is unity in the human body. Though it is made up of many diverse parts, it moves in one direction and works together to accomplish its mission. This is one of the most vital actions necessary to be healthy. Spiritual unity will sustain a body of believers through even the most difficult times. Unity is the building block for spiritual growth. This unity is no human product. It is supernatural; and its origin is from above. This unity is planted in the hearts of all believers, for this unity is the unity of the Spirit (Ephesians 4:3).

What does the unity of the Spirit mean to us? It is the duty of every believer to work hard to keep that unity, *recognize it as real, and act upon it* without a sectarian spirit (see John 17:20-26). The Holy Spirit dwells in the hearts of all true believers, and yet this Spirit is one. Because He is one and because He dwells in each one of us – He *makes* all of us one. Even as He Himself is one; He is in all of us; we are one even as He is one. Because the Spirit dwells in all true believers who now live or have ever lived; and though we may have numerous differences, we have one fundamental likeness: *The Spirit of God dwells in each one of us.* Those who have this Spiritual unity are our brothers and sisters in Christ – and there is no division. Why?

- Our unity is in all believers and therefore makes us one – making it *impossible* for there to be division between true believers. We may disagree on occasion, but are all agreeable in Christ.
- If you have the Spirit of Christ in you, and I have the Spirit of Christ in me; then we both belong to the same church.
- We are united by one Spirit and that Spirit dwells in both of us.
- The only division possible between believers is time and distance. For example, we are in the same church and town; however, a job change may cause you to move a hundred miles away – we are still one, we are both indwelt by the same Spirit and we are still both in Christ. Our division is only in time and distance.
- Paul told the believers in Ephesus to *"keep the unity of the Spirit."* He did not say, "Get the unity of the Spirit." We already have it. So, we need simply to keep it. God never told us to *become* one with other believers. We don't need to create unity, but just maintain what we already have. Paul addressed the church *of* Ephesus. The local churches of Ephesus in Christ Jesus are one; so are the churches in Christ of any city or town, USA.

We are one *in* Christ by the Holy Spirit. In order to break this unity, the believer would have to rid him or herself of the Holy Spirit. Certainly, we can *destroy the effectiveness* of our unity with one another. When we have done this, the expression of the church is lost. When this happens, we have not only failed to preserve Christian unity; we have destroyed the fruit of our oneness. Sadly, today there is little outward sign of this beautiful unity we [all] have as children of God.

We cannot insist on *any* unity among believers except the unity of the Holy Spirit who dwells within us and has made us one in Christ. All who have this unity are in the church. All other actions work together toward this one. The more the others are practiced, the more there will be unity among the believers. The Holy Spirit brings unity to a body of believers. Societal barriers and racial bias cannot affect true Christian unity; which can only exist among true Christians. Much of the disunity we see in churches today are secular imports from the outside, meet a true Christian from any race or language loving unity will win out. Sadly, we walk the same streets suffering the same pains of circumstances, yet we don't know each other due to ethnic, and other societal pressures – but not so with true children of God! Paul explains,

> *"I therefore, a prisoner for the Lord, urge you to walk in a manner worthy of the calling to which you have been called, with all humility and gentleness, with patience, bearing with one another in love, eager to maintain the unity of the Spirit in the bond of peace. There is one body and one Spirit – just as you were called to one hope that belongs to your call – one Lord, one faith, one baptism, one God and Father of all, who is over all and through all and in all. But grace was given to each one of us according to the measure of Christ's gift"* (Ephesians 4:1-7).

Christ gave the Holy Spirit to the believers as a guide after He ascended back to the Father. It is He who guides, empowers, enables, gives and unifies life Himself through regular prayer. We must be eager to maintain unity and be willing to boldly defend it. The gospel is our defensive and offensive weapon [the power of God unto salvation], (see Romans 1:16).

The devil knows that a local church without Christian unity is the least effective for advancing the kingdom of God on earth. Sins like slander, deception, adultery and unfaithfulness fuel the enemy's agenda in the local churches. Pastors, teachers, and other spiritual leaders must maintain vigilance to keep the church doctrinally pure. How? In the text above Paul made clear what those believers have; who possess this sevenfold unity of God and man:

1. One body – the church
2. One Spirit – the Holy Spirit
3. One hope – the Christian calling
4. One Lord – the Lord Jesus Christ
5. One faith – the gospel form of doctrine
6. One baptism – a baptism into the body of Christ (see 1 Corinthians 12:13; Galatians 3:27; Colossians 2:12; Romans 6:3-7)
7. One God – the Father of all

Through these seven components [or the lack of them] in the believer, we can know whether or not the individual has the unity of the Spirit. These seven components are the common heritage of all of God's people. Either we have them or we don't, if not and we are knowingly living as if we do means, as stated in an earlier chapter; this person has bought into Satan's deceptive lie, that there is more than *one* way to heaven.

Don't be fooled, you are not an accident, you are part of a brilliant plan that started before the world began and continues beyond it. Jokes about God's Church, God's people, and self-depreciation [God's temple] are as wicked as slandering God. We are belittling something that God planned and crafted Himself. He chose *us* before the foundation of the world and knew us before He made us:

> *"Before I formed you in the womb*
> *I knew you;*
> *Before you were born I sanctified you;*
> *I ordained you a prophet*
> *To the nations."*
> *Jeremiah 1:5*

And drew up callings for us before we were created:

> *"For we are His workmanship, created in Christ Jesus for good works, which God prepared beforehand that we should walk in them"* (Eph. 2:10).

That thought should bring the peace of God to our often-over-stressed souls. Think about it, I'm sure you feel honored as I do to be chosen as part of God's eternal plan for His Church. The Scripture is very clear; there is a real connection between our unity and the believability of our message, the gospel of Jesus Christ.

If we are seriously concerned and have a passion for the lost, then we must be equally seriously concerned about pursuing unity!

This unity "oneness" of the Spirit is why Paul used a human body analogy for the unity of the Church of the Living God. If your inclusion in His church excites you, it may help you to know that there are beings in heaven that observe the church in wonder.

> *"To me, though I am the very least of all the saints,*
> *this grace was given,*
> *to preach to the Gentiles the unchangeable riches of Christ,*
> *and to bring light for everyone*
> *which is the plan of the mystery hidden for ages in God,*
> *who created all things,*
> *so that through the church*
> *the manifold wisdom of God*
> *might be made known to the rulers and authorities*
> *in the heavenly places."*
> Ephesians 3:8–10

Think about what this is saying, God wanted to show heavenly beings His incomparable wisdom – He created the church! I believe especially today, we have a sacred responsibility to function as His church displaying the love, humility, unity of the Spirit in such a way that the rulers in heavenly places can marvel at God's wisdom. They ought to see a oneness in us that displays God's brilliant plan. What would it be like, if we followed God's plan for the church and in so doing allowed the church to be *pruned down* to only those who wanted to obey His command to "love one another as I have loved you?" (John 15:12)

Spirit-guided unity

Jesus said that the world would see the unity and love we share in the church; and believe in Him through that. Therefore, nothing can separate us from one another. When Jesus was approaching the cross, He prayed a very challenging prayer for His disciples:

> *"I do not pray for those alone, but also for those who will believe*
> *in Me through their word; that they may be one, as You, Father,*

are in Me, and I in You; that they also may be one in Us, that the world may believe that You sent Me. And the glory which You gave Me I have given them, that they may be one just as we are one: I in them, and You in Me; that they may be made perfect in one, and that the world may know that You have sent Me, and have loved them as You have loved Me" (John 17:20-23).

Jesus' prayer in the present tense of the verb "to be" indicates that Jesus was praying for those the Father had given Him, but also for the *unity* of future believers that takes place through *sanctification*. That is what Jesus commanded, (see 13:34, 35).

- His followers had to love each other so that the world may believe in the reality of Jesus' love. The loving relationship of believers to each other is the greatest witness to Jesus Christ.
- The revelation of Jesus Christ through His disciples is the means to unity. Such unity begins with *belief* and *correct thinking* about Jesus and God the Father – with doctrine. Correct belief must bear fruit!
- that is a life that demonstrates God's love and produces the *unity* between all believers.
- The mutual indwelling of the Father *in* the Son and the Son *in* the church through the Holy Spirit is also the means to *unity*, the ultimate expression of God's love (see 13:15; Romans 8:17).

If we are to be true and faithful servants of the Lord Jesus Christ, we must follow the example He set before us and deliver the message He gave, without adding to or taking away from it. He gave us the example of love and humility, and we who are His servants should never be ashamed or too proud to follow His example. Give Him praise and glory!

Discussion and Reflections: Chapter 4

1. Discuss the Lord's intention that His gospel is to be *exportable* and His people are to be *expendable* in getting the gospel to the whole world.

2. The church is God's way of making His *Invisible Son* visible to the world.

3. Discuss Christ's expectations of the Christian's love for the lost.

4. Your prayer life clearly reveals your spirituality.

5. Discuss the absurdity of a gifted person to think he or she is more important than all the other gifts – in conjunction with the unity of the Spirit.

SECTION II

WE WOULD
SEE JESUS

Chapter 5

TRUE CHRISTIAN FELLOWSHIP

*"That which was from the beginning, which we have heard, which
we have seen with our eyes, which we have looked upon, and our
hands have handled, concerning the Word of life – the life was
manifested, and we have seen, and bear witness, and declare to
you that eternal life which was with the Father and was manifested
to us – that which we have seen and heard we declare to you, that
you also may have fellowship with us; and truly our fellowship is
with the Father and with His Son Jesus Christ. And these things
we write to you, that your joy may be full"* (1 John 1:1-4).

Fellowship as practiced in a number of local Black churches in this country
may consist of coffee and doughnuts, exchanges of fundraiser programs,
or something else from the creative minds of humanity. However biblical
Christian fellowship goes much deeper. When the apostle John spoke of
fellowship as used in this passage, he does not mean social relations but
translates the Greek word *"kimonos"* to denote "a partaker" or "partner.[9]
To walk in the light (v. 7), is to live in the fellowship with the Father and
the Son.

Sin interrupts fellowship:

- Confession restores fellowship (1:9)
- Immediate confession keeps the fellowship unbroken (1:7)

True Christian fellowship

A main goal for John writing here is to create "joy" in the reader through proclaiming the reality of the gospel to produce a fellowship in eternal life. Fellowship has to do with our communion with Christ – not our union with Christ, which is sonship. Our daily fellowship changes; but our sonship remains the same.

In his gospel, John tells us how to be saved, justification (John 20:31), Christ, [*the Word made flesh*] died for us; therefore, the penalty for sin is taken care of when the sinner turns and trusts Christ. But the power of sin over the believer's daily life is an altogether different matter. In his first epistle, John explains and emphasizes, [sanctification], Christ [*the Word made real in us*] now lives in us through the Holy Spirit; therefore, we may have victory over sin and know how to get forgiveness if we do sin (1 John 2:1-2).

That we may have joy (1:4)

A Christian can have no real joy except in a proper relationship with God and others. John expresses his purpose in writing, "that your joy may be full." Joy is the realization of something good despite circumstances. However broken fellowship negates joy (v. 3). The only source of joy is in the Lord – abiding in Him. Abiding in the Lord is habitual obedience (John 15:4-7). Jesus' life of obedience is the Christian's pattern. Those who claim to be Christians ought to live as He did. The idea being to settle down in Christ or resting in Him. It is evidenced by a life modeled after Christ with these things:

- Trusting in the Lord
- Abiding
- Obeying
- Uninterrupted communion

Walk in the Light

An authentic Christian habitually walks in the light [grace and truth]; not in darkness [falsehood and sin]. If there is no control in a person who claims to be a Christian, John makes it clear – this person has never been saved. Today as in John's day, false teachers deny the existence or importance of sin.

Those who deny the reality of sin demonstrate their lack of true salvation.

Today false teachers have stepped up their efforts to pervert the fundamentals of the faith. It's so sad seeing so many Christians deceived into accepting their progressive-false Christianity. To counter this deception, John repeatedly emphasized the basics of true Christianity:

- The need for a proper view of the gospel
- The need for repentance
- The need for obedience
- The need for love
- The need for a proper view of Christ
- The need for a sanctified life and lifestyle

The true believer's habitual lifestyle of righteousness stands out in sharp *contrast* to those progressive-false teachers who practice sin (see vv. 4, 6). Since Christ died on the cross to transform sinners, those truly born from above, have replaced the habit of sin with the habit of righteous living.

II Corinthians 5:14 explains, it is the love of Christ that compels us to no longer live for ourselves – but for Him.

Dead to sin and alive to God

The apostle Paul says, *"Do not present your members as instruments of unrighteousness to sin but present yourselves to God as being alive from the dead, and your members as instruments of righteousness to God. For sin shall not have dominion over you for you are not under law but under grace"* (Romans 6:13, 14).

Before sin can have power over a believer, it must first pass through the individual's will. Therefore,

- Do not let sin therefore reign as king in your mortal body, causing you to be subject to its lustful cravings.
- Do not yield your members to the enemy to be used in unrighteous acts, which serve as weapons against your spiritual victory.
- Instead, surrender your members, even your whole body to God as living – risen from the deadness of sin.

- Surrender every member of your body to God to be used as weapons against sin, so that you can enjoy your spiritual birthright and complete victory over sin through the power of God.

To make a reality of the righteous life above requires a renewed or transformed mind (Romans 12:1-2). We often hear the pastor or evangelist giving the invitation to the unsaved and he or she speaks of saving souls. Each of us is a tricotomy consisting of a spirit, soul, and body. The soul comprises the will, the mind, and the emotions [feelings]; therefore, whoever or whatever controls our soul controls us. Unless a person is born again from *above* – he or she is lost.

The world operates mainly by feelings [emotions] today. Therefore. the will and the mind being subject to feelings produce what we see in our sin-filled populance – impulsive and depraved human conduct and behavior. The only hope is the redemptive work of Jesus Christ, our Savior! Continue reading.

Romans 6:14 can be understood and accepted only by the believer who accepts the truth that Christ is "the end of the law for righteousness" (Romans 10:4). The wages of sin is death – both physical and eternal. "The sting of death is sin; and the strength of sin is the law. But thanks be to God, which gives us the victory through our Lord and Savior, Jesus Christ (I Corinthians 15:56, 57).

Victory over death, hell, and the grave is brought about by the complete and utter abolition of the law .... Which is "done away with in Christ" (II Corinthians 3:14; Ephesians 2:15). This gospel in its power and beauty can never be fully realized until that point is settled.

Writing to the Galatian believers, Paul said: For as many as are of the works of the law are under the curse: for it is written, cursed is every one that continues not in all things which are written in the book of the law to do them. But that no man is justified by the law in the sight of God, it is evident: for, *the just shall live by faith*. And the law is not of faith: but the man that does them shall live in them.

And the law is not of faith: but the man that does them shall live in them.

Christ has redeemed us from the curse of the law, being made a curse for us:

For it is written, cursed is every one that hangs on a tree. The argument in verses 1-14 of Romans 6 is that the believer is not *led* into a sin life, because he or she is saved by grace and – no longer under the law. Therefore, "we are more than conquerors through Him that loved us." The believer, having died to sin, is alive unto God; and God is working in Him, both to will and to do His good pleasure (Philippians 2:13).

Set apart unto God

The church today *desperately* needs to emphasize, <u>practical holiness</u> in the life of every believer – that is every Christian (who is truly born again from above) and living the life of righteousness described in Romans 5. Paul teaches:

- In verses 6-11, "substitution" – Christ died on the cross for us.
- In verses 12-21 "identification" – believers are in Christ and can live victorious sanctified "set apart" lives over sin.
- Give Christ all the "honor, praise and glory!"

To be set apart does not necessarily say anything about the nature of a thing – only its position with reference to God. For example, the wood, metal, and other materials used in the construction and service of the tabernacle were not of themselves "holy," but they were set apart exclusively for God's use. In John 17:19 Jesus says that He sanctified Himself. What He means is simply that He set Himself apart to serve God and, through His atonement, was able to set believers apart to the glory of God.

It is essential that we thoroughly understand what all of this means, as not only our eternal destination depends on it – but the local churches' survival depend on it. In Scripture sanctification is three-fold:

1. Positional – the believer is seated with Christ in heaven (John 17:16).
2. Practical – the believer has day-by-day victory over sin and grows in holiness [sanctified] and in likeness to Christ (1 John 5:4).
3. Perfect – "We shall be like Him for we shall see Him as He is" (1 John 3:1-2).

It is imperative that we keep the message of Romans 6 with that of chapter 7 otherwise, we will be confused as we miss blessings; as our prayers go unanswered, and we begin to experience a yo-yo lifestyle – incapable in our obedience and energy of the flesh to glorify God.

> The sinner can only sin, but a Christian can both live holy
> and sin – but, not at the same time.

In his book *The Normal Christian Life,* Watchman Nee describes these two possibilities in the life of the Christian. Sins are the direct result of a sin nature in us. Further he states that "sin" in us is the factory – and the product produced by that factory is "sins." The idea is, Christ "bombed" the factory [at Calvary] knocking out the old sin nature and its production capabilities.[10] In its stead is the new divine nature which produces Christlikeness.

I heard Dr. Billy Graham illustrate this condition of the human nature in a sermon with a story of a man who owned two dogs, one black and the other white. Each Saturday afternoon he took his two dogs down to the village square where he would let them fight. He took bets predicting which dog would win and he always won the bets. Later a friend asked him how he always knew which dog would win? His answer, the one I feed always wins.

Like many Christians, I struggled with this condition for years; wherein I had a set of rules and regulations that I obeyed religiously in the flesh; in this book I call works righteousness. The most deceitful life a Christian can continue to live is to appear so sanctified and so spiritual when their flesh is in constant war with God.

O how far from the real thing! Only when the Holy Spirit directs our lives from within and we obey out of a heart of love is there ever God-honored Christian living. Perhaps you are living this life experience yourself. To know the dilemma study carefully Romans 7:13-25.

After my defeating experience with the Law, from the Scripture I gleaned two principles operating in the life of the *believer*:

1. The law of sin and death *in Adam* – is the old nature operating when the believer wants to do good, evil is present. Even the good we would do is tainted with evil (v. 21).

2. The law of the Spirit of life *in Christ* – this law or (principle) counteracts the law of sin and death. It is not by submitting to outward laws that we grow in *holiness* and serve the Lord in an acceptable manner – but by surrendering to the indwelling Spirit of God (see 8:2). This teaching is so important and essential for the local churches today. Many families are presently raising their first generation of children to grow up without any knowledge of the church or having never heard the gospel of Jesus Christ and His finished work!

No "good thing" in the flesh

So, here we see the difference between the victory of Romans 6 and that of chapter 7. The believer gains victory over the evil things of the flesh – that he or she ceases to deliberately do (Romans 6). In Chapter 7 the believer triumphs over the "good things" the flesh would do in obedience to law.

But God will not accept the flesh – for in our flesh there is no good thing. *"The flesh profits nothing!"* (John 6:63).

Even after reading and hearing these truths repeatedly, many Christians set up laws for their lives and seek to discipline their flesh into obedience, when God clearly says, *"The carnal mind is not subject to the law of God, neither can be"* (Romans 8:7). You may be asking at this juncture, "How do I apply all this to my life?" I'm glad you asked:

In our new position before God – as dead to the law, we are not expected to obey God in our own strength. God has not brought us unto some "Christian law" that we must obey to be holy." This truth can be liberating for many Christians and local churches – if they would simply allow the Holy Spirit to have His designated place at work within them. God has given us His Holy Spirit who *enables* us to fulfill the demands of God's holiness. But there is something else. Shouldn't we be producing *fruit* for the Lord? But how – you may ask?

1. Accept the truths of Romans 7 – that we are indeed failures, no matter how well-meaning we may be.
2. Realize that the minute we start doing works in our own strength, we discover that we are failures in ourselves [period].
3. Acknowledge the truth, that the Law is good, but we are carnal, and then turn and allow the Holy Spirit to work out God's will in your life.

I pray that the Lord enables us to "reckon" ourselves dead to sin (chapter 6), and dead to the Law (chapter 7), that we might through the indwelling Spirit, and divine nature overcome the flesh and enjoy the blessed peace of no condemnation and the liberty of a fruitful Christian life; as we'll see in the next segment.

It is in chapter 8 that Paul presents some relief "there is therefore now no condemnation" (vv. 1,2). Our condemnation was met by the Blood of Jesus, through which we found peace with God in salvation (Romans 5:1, 9). But knowing that, I still may be experiencing defeat and inward condemnation as was the situation Romans 7 reveals. Victory can be ours once we come into the knowledge of *life in Christ* and this becomes my experience as I learn to walk in the Spirit. Before I realized that Christ is my life, I worked under a constant condemning sense of limitation and defeat. "I cannot do this – I cannot please God "in the flesh" (Romans 8:8).

But there is no "I cannot" *in Christ:* "for those who walk not after the flesh, but after the Spirit" (v.1). Praise God! Now it's: *"I can do all things through Christ who strengthens me"*(Philippians 4:13). Paul says, here is how you get there? *"The law of the Spirit of life in Christ Jesus has made me free from the law of sin and death"*(v, 2).

The law could not do anything about sin. It had no power to put sin to death in a person's life. But God accomplished what the law could not do by sending His own Son. Jesus came in the likeness of sinful flesh taking on human nature, susceptible to temptation – but He never gave in. He never sinned. He fulfilled the law. The true believer receives the righteous standard of the law, love (see Romans 13:8-10).

By no means is this received by the law but by being in Christ and walking in the Spirit:

> But God demonstrates His own love toward us, in that while we
> were still sinners, Christ died for us. Much more then, having now
> been justified by His blood, we shall be saved from wrath through
> Him. For if when we were enemies we were reconciled to God
> through the death of His Son, much more, having been reconciled,
> we shall be saved by His life (Romans 5:9, 10).

The condition of salvation, meaning deliverance from wrath and from the power of sin is outward confession: *That if you confess with your mouth the Lord Jesus and believe in your heart that God has raised Him from the dead, you will be saved. For with the heart one believes unto righteousness and with the mouth confession is made unto salvation* (Romans 10:9-10). What a precious promise! Receive it now.

DISCUSSION AND REFLECTIONS: CHAPTER 5

1. Contrast the difference between fellowship and communion with Christ; and union and sonship with Christ.

2. Discuss the Christian's habitual walk in the light. What does John have to say about one who habitually walks in darkness?

3. Discuss the significance of Romans 6:14 and 1 Corinthians 15:56, 57 about death and sin.

4. In Scripture sanctification is three-fold. Briefly explain them below:

5. Discuss the futility of Christians settings up their own laws for their lives and seeking to discipline their flesh into obedience.

Chapter 6

WE WOULD SEE JESUS

"And there were certain Greeks among them that came up to worship at the feast.' The same came therefore to Philip, which was of Bethsaida of Galilee, and desired him, saying Sir, we would see Jesus" (John 12:20).

Jesus "came to His own, and His own received Him not." This national rejection was about to be made public by the Jews delivering Him up to the Romans to be crucified. As prophesied in Luke 2:25-35, Jesus would visit the Gentiles following the rejection by His own people, *"to take out of them a people for His name"* (Acts 15:14).

It is very striking that these Greeks came *to meet Jesus* at this time. We could say they are a *"first fruit,"* so to speak of a coming harvest, and pointed to those "other sheep" which the Good Shepherd must bring (John 10:16). It is also interesting that Gentiles were among the first to show an interest in Jesus at His birth [the wise men came from the east to worship Him and present gifts]; so now these Greeks came to Him shortly before He was crucified.

The Scripture does not tell us why these Greeks sought Philip and not any of the other disciples, nor how they knew Philip was a disciple. They probably heard enough of the truth from Old Testament Scripture to know that a Redeemer was coming, and I believe they sought Jesus as the One who was to come. Philip serves as the connection point and leads the Greeks to where Jesus is teaching.

Twice in the Gospel of John we find Philip bringing other people to Jesus sharing the "good news" he had found. Jesus did not receive the Greeks that day because *in the flesh* He had come into the world as King of the Jews, and it was necessary that He be crucified before Gentiles could be brought into the fold. By not receiving these Greeks into His presence, they would be taught that:

- Salvation was not through His perfect life or through His wonderful works, but by *faith* in the crucified Savior.
- They needed to look upon Him as the Lamb of God "slain from the foundation of the world," rather than as the Messiah of Israel.

It was through His death that He broke down the "middle wall of petition," and now both Jews and Gentiles are members of the body of Christ, the New Testament Church:

> *"Therefore, remember that you, once Gentiles in the flesh — who are called Uncircumcision by what is called the Circumcision made in the flesh by hands — that at that time you were without Christ, being aliens from the commonwealth of Israel and strangers from the covenants of promise, having no hope and without God in the world. But now in Christ Jesus you who once were far off have been brought near by the blood of Jesus. For He Himself is our peace, who has made both one, and has broken down the middle wall of separation, having abolished in His flesh the enmity, that is, the law of commandments contained in ordinances, so as to create in Himself one new man from the two, thus, making peace, and that He might reconcile them both to God in one body through the cross, thereby putting to death the enmity. And He came and preached peace to you who were afar off and to those who were near. For through Him we both have access by one Spirit to the Father"* (Ephesians 2:11-18).

The apostle Paul gave the bleak condition of the Gentiles/ the unsaved:

- They were without Christ
- They had no hope
- God had not reached out to them
- They were aliens from the commonwealth of Israel
- They were strangers from the covenants of promise
- They were without God in the world

Reconciled to God

Paul emphasizes the truth that all believers are united in Christ because the church is the one body of Christ. He described how God formed this new body from Jews and Gentiles with Christ as the Head. Through Jesus' death God reconciled sinful people to Himself. This reconciliation with God has its effects on earth from three points of view in verses 11-22:

1. From a *Historical view* – Before Christ, God dealt with humanity through the Jewish nation. Since Christ, God has been moving around the world including both Jews and Gentiles, who are willing to follow Christ. He makes them part of a new people, His new creation.
2. From an *individual view* – Both nations are made up of individual Jews in the Jewish nation and individual Gentiles in the Gentile nations. God now deals on the individual level in both nations.
3. From a *new creation* – God now deals with a new nation of people, a new body of people who make up the true citizens of His Kingdom. These citizens are "born again from above" individuals from all the nations of the world who now approach God through Christ.

God makes a **"new man"** out of the now saved individual and promises that he or she will become a member of God's new body and new nation – His true church (1 Corinthians 10:32). It is these believers – those who believe in Christ – who are to constitute the true *family of God* and to inhabit the *new heavens and earth* which God is to create in the future (2 Peter 3:10-13; Revelation 21:11).

Wouldn't it be grand if we could all do evangelism, like Philip, taking people to meet Jesus face-to-face? When our friends, family members, neighbors and co-workers have questions about Jesus, we could just bring them, their questions and all to Jesus. Wouldn't it be wonderful to say to them, "I don't know the answer to that question ...... but I know who does, let's go ask Jesus? Don't we have the same access to Jesus that Philip had?

Seeing Him who is invisible

Unlike Philip we don't have Jesus standing in front of us. Jesus is now in heaven seated at the right hand of the throne of God (Ephesians 1:20-21), so He is no longer physically present on earth. Now He like the Father is invisible to us.

Like Philip we want to take people to meet Jesus, but it's hopeless now. Keep reading, in Ephesians 1:22-23: *"And He put all things under His feet and gave Him to be head over all things to the church, which is His body, the fullness of Him who fills all in all."*

The Church here does not refer to any one local church [Black or White], but to [all true believers worldwide]. The Bible tells us that in some mysterious way, Jesus is present here on earth through the Church – which is His body. In a like manner our bodies are the way our invisible thoughts are visibly communicated to this world. I can't emphasize this enough. The church – Jesus' body is God's way of making His invisible Son visible to us on the earth again! Just as Philip was able to see the invisible Father by watching and observing Jesus, a sceptic and unbelieving world can look at the church and see the invisible Jesus Christ made visible. The church is *called* and *empowered* to make Christ visible in the world today by being full of grace and truth. Ephesians 2:6-9 say,

> *"God raised us up together and made us sit together in the heavenly places in Christ Jesus, that in the ages to come He might show the exceeding riches of His grace in His kindness toward us in Christ Jesus. For by grace you have been saved through faith, and that not of yourselves, it is the gift of God, not of works, lest anyone should boast."*

Christians have always been saved by grace – the grace of God is the source of salvation, and faith is the conduit, not the cause, God alone saves. Salvation never originates in the efforts of people – it always arises out of His lovingkindness. Truly, "salvation is of the Lord" (Jonah 2:9). Yes, God has poured out His grace on us so that we might in turn, be *living demonstrations* of His grace to others. In other words, when people see the grace of God in us – they will see Jesus in us – just like the people saw God in the fullness of Jesus' grace. Jesus said,

> *"If you love Me, keep My commandments.*
> *and I will pray the Father, and He*
> *will give you another Helper, that*
> *He may abide with you forever*
> *The Spirit of truth,*
> *whom the world cannot receive,*
> *because it neither sees Him*
> *nor knows Him;*
> *but you know Him, for He dwells with you*
> *and will be in you.*
> *I will not leave you orphans;*

I will come to you."
John 14:15–18

These verses indicate some distinction between the ministry of the Holy Spirit to believers before and after Pentecost. Notably, the Holy Spirit has been with all who have ever believed throughout redemptive history as the Source of truth, faith, and life, Jesus is saying something new is coming in His ministry. That something new is the Holy Spirit dwelling with His children and in them. In John 7:37–39 we see that this new unique ministry would be like *"rivers of living water."* This verse confirms the fact that "any person" of any race and generation from the fulfillment of this prophecy can experience this "river of living water." Praise God!

Discussion and Refections: Chapter 6

1. Why did Jesus visit the Gentiles following the rejection by His own people?

2. Discuss the effect the three points of view concerning reconciliation with God on earth.

3. Discuss how God formed a new body from Jews and Gentiles with Christ as the Head.

4. Through Jesus' death God reconciled sinful people to Himself.

5. What people are to inhabit the new heavens and earth?

Chapter 7

THE REFORMATION
AND BEYOND

*"........... for the equipping of the saints for the work of ministry,
for the edifying of the body of Christ"* (Ephesians 4:12).

A little study of church history would quickly reveal that the American Church and Christians therein have been deeply influenced by the upheavals, struggles and new forms of church life that arose in the sixteenth century Protestant Reformation and even some borrowed pre-Reformation forms. Certainly, the great assertions: 1) justification by faith alone; 2) the priesthood of all believers; 3) and the Scripture is the final authority are biblical truths; yet they have been widely ignored for various reasons until recent Church history. One of the most neglected, but crucial for the church today is "the priesthood of all believers."

Although many new denominations and new forms have emerged since the Reformation – even in some of the new, the old hang-ups as listed below are still practiced in many local churches today:

- lay and clergy
- whether so-called lay or ordained
- male or female
- the hierarchical of the few
- homogeneity [birds of a feather flock together]

Despite God's intention, and spiritual gifts for all believers' ministry – the old wineskins above remain the choice of most of the local protestant churches in America today. In view of the critical situation, the question is, "can our present structures and patterns really inhibit God's will in the way we are doing the Christian worship, work, and evangelism of the church?"

In the past 50 or 60 years, serious signs of resistance to change have been extremely visible in the life of traditional institutional churches in America. While there is much evidence of Spiritual renewal and growth in Christianity in some areas of the country, it is still true that mainline denominations along with other foundational institutions have lost much of their influence. Many local churches, have turned inward to institutionalism – their ministry is accomplished through the set apart, "top-down" leadership in the body. It was the institutionalism of the Roman Catholic Church, [the depository of Christianity for eleven hundred years], that the Reformation came against with the intention of change.

What they faced

The rigid hierarchy of medieval Roman Catholicism represented by the three-fold offices of bishop, presbyter, and deacon were developed during the second and third centuries of the church. Church history records that these positions of status and honor were then stratified which created a seedbed for corruption. As a result, during the Middle Ages [Dark ages for the church]; the church gained power equal to and often above the state. This dominance over the people evolved into a theology that said that Christ had delegated the right to the church – giving the hierarchy of priests the power to:

- Dispense or withhold grace.
- Priests as the exclusive celebrants of the Lord's supper.
- The bishops or pastors were priests who exclusively presided at the altar as consecrated celebrants.
- It was generally accepted that there were two kinds of people – clergy and laity.
- Ordination was interpreted as a kind of second baptism that lifted the clergy into a superior stage of Christian achievement.
- Clerical robes symbolized their elevated status.

The Reformation's concept of ministry [a new wineskin]

The clerical order was in place when Martin Luther rediscovered the evangelistic gospel. The discovery of the doctrine of justification by faith was so shockingly revealing that it was considered "new wine" bursting old wineskins and creating new wineskins. Luther's rediscovered gospel:

1. Put all Christians on an equal footing.
2. A person is made right with God through a personal response to the saving grace of Christ.
3. The rediscovery of the gospel marked a radical shift from the institutional church's being the dispenser of grace – to the proclamation of the gospel as the means of salvation.

The doctrine of justification by faith would have a marked effect on the *view* and *practice* of ministry:

- Under Roman Catholicism, ministry was conceived in hierarchical terms because receiving grace and being within the realm of the church was the same thing. *There was no grace apart from the church.* This made those in leadership the dispensers of grace – and church order was their call.
- By contrast the Reformation linked the reception of grace with the gospel message and the individual's response to Christ. Being made right with God is not mediated through the institution of the church – but directly through Jesus Christ. Neither priests, pastors, bishops nor popes can represent a person before God. Only Jesus Christ can do that alone.
- The hierarchical concept of ministry is therefore, undermined by the gospel. With the reclamation of the gospel came a rediscovery of preaching.

To the Reformation, the true church was distinguished by two qualities: The rightly divided and proclaimed Word of God, and the Lord's Supper righty administered.

- The proclamation of the gospel with demonstration inspired by Spirit and Word of God, through the priesthood of *all* believers.
- The power of God to save based solely on the completed work of Jesus Christ as proclaimed in the gospels.
- The total rejection of the church as the repository of God's grace.

The Doctrine of the Priesthood of all believers

It's a known fact, if you try to mix water and oil together soon, you'll realize, they don't mix very well. One will separate and rise to the top while the other sinks below. Likewise, when you attempt to mix spiritual organism, the body of Christ, with the institutional definition of church they don't mix very well, simply because they are two different theologies. The frustration of this mixture began in the Reformation and continues to this day.

If the doctrine of the priesthood of all believers is ever to reach fruition in the church; the spiritual organism or body model of ministry alone must be engaged as only one people [all the people] and one ministry – not two people [clergy and laity]; which eventually leads to two ministries. Therefore, the kind of theological lens we use in this matter will affect the kind of church we produce.

If ministry is to be returned to the people of God, we must have a bottom-up spiritual organism view of the church. The apostle Paul makes it clear that there must be *order* within the organism. In I Corinthians 13 and 14, he outlines principles of order to govern the disorder created by the Corinthians' abuse and mismanagement of *spiritual gifts*. If we would be eager to please God, we would also have a deep desire to *become mature*.

The Christian community in Corinth had evolved into an entertainment center to show off their spiritual gifts and building themselves up rather than seizing the opportunity to edify the body to the glory of God. The church became more of a performance-oriented club than a bastion for Christ and the truth of His Word. Paul reminded them that, "unless the gifts are motivated by love – they are nothing" (see 1 Corinthians 13:2-3).

The call to maturity

Paul's call to maturity is in a context that highlights our abiding call to still be like children. He writes, "Brethren, do not be children *in understanding; however, in malice be babes, but in understanding be mature"* (1 Corinthians 14:20).

In the fourteenth chapter, he continues to deal with problems that arose pertaining to their worship services. If ever a church struggled with both an unbecoming lack of *maturity* and a deep need to become more like children, it was the church at Corinth. This church was rocked with schism and scandal, *all routed in pride*. Paul had to deal with a group for Apollos, a group for Peter, and even a group for Paul, all Christians defining their identity not in terms of following Christ but in following a favorite teacher. Additionally, the Corinthians thought themselves so mature, tolerant, and graceful; that they prided themselves with being able to cope with a man who was having an affair with his step-mother as a sign of their maturity. In his rebuke Paul, rightly points out – that this was something that even the pagans would not do. Yet, many of our churches are bowing to culture and making the same mistake; which always negates spirituality.

That same spirit showed itself in their prideful pursuit of spiritual gifts in the church. Many people saw their gifts as signs of God's favor and spiritual superiority for those who had them. Again, in chapter 13, Paul reminds them that none of the things they were scrambling for meant anything without love. In his recommendations for correction, we find the same incidents repeated in many local Black churches today. Notice:

- Some were speaking in tongues without interpretation; despite the fact, that he had previously addressed the value of speaking in tongues with interpretation into a meaningful message (see 1 Corinthians 14:27).
- Secondly, he addressed a problem related to governing prophecy. To restore order Paul wrote, "Let two or three prophets speak, and let the others weigh what is said. If a revelation is made to another sitting by, let the first be silent. For you can all prophesy one by one, so that all may learn, and all be encouraged; and the spirit of the prophet is subject to the prophet. For God is not a God of confusion but peace" (see 1 Corinthians 14:29-33). He concluded with, "All things should be done decently and in order" (1 Corinthians 14:40).

This is precisely the kind of *immaturity* that Paul is warning against. Because we live in an *egalitarian* age, we consider our own thoughts ought to be given the same weight as the wisdom of the centuries. We no longer honor the fathers gone before, and we think too highly of ourselves. A mature understanding is one that realizes how deceitful our own hearts are.

If you have come up with an idea that has been rejected by the church as error for two thousand years, how likely is it that you are correct and the rest of the church throughout history is wrong? – One wise theologian

---

Maturity in a sense means, holding to the great truths of Scriptures held down through the ages. Therefore, despite the absolute attention we must pay to the church as spiritual organism, there is a legitimate need for a certain amount of order particularly the institutional elements of policy, and structure. The church's authority is derived from Christ, the Head, who indwells [all] His people [believer-priests]. Maturity remembers the repeated wisdom of Paul, that when we add anything to the Head's work, we take away from Christ's work. However, if we cling to the Spirit and the truths of God's Word; which is maturing us to discipleship [through the process of sanctification] – in the end we bear much fruit.

The Priesthood of Believers

Isn't it ironic that the Church of Corinth which seemed to be so dysfunctional – yet within the Holy Spirit and His spiritual gifts were operating among the members (carefully study I Cor. 12-14). The goal of making mature, obedient disciples who are integrated into the Spiritual organism [the body of Christ] is a high impossible ideal, apart from God. This is why Jesus promised to fulfill the ministry task:

> "But you shall receive power, after the Holy Ghost has come upon you; And you shall be My witnesses both in Jerusalem, and all Judea, and Samaria, and unto the utter most parts of the world" (Acts 1:8).

Believers are constantly exposed temptations in a world system energized by Satan and his demons. Their efforts are designed to discredit the church and destroy its credibility. One of their main strategies is to find Christians whose lives are not consistent with the Word of God, then expose them to unbelievers just to show how hypocritical the church is.

In spite of Satan's devices and the effort on the part of some theologians to squash the biblical doctrine of the priesthood of believers (see I Peter 2:5), as New Testament believer-priests, a new creation in Christ Jesus, in transition. We are called to press into God through Christ to overcome the many worldly sinful distractions; and be able to co-labor with Him to accomplish His plans and purposes. The Word of God says, And have made us kings and priests to our God; and we shall reign in the earth (Revelation 5:10).

In an earlier chapter we covered the similar characteristics between the Old Testament priests and the New Testament believer-priests, the reality revealed is that every priest offers sacrifices to the Lord to include thanksgiving, praise, worship, unceasing prayer and intercession. God issued a call to intercession as part of the restoration of the priesthood of all believers to His Church. The main privilege of a priest – is access to God.

For much of the church in this country the importance of intercession seems to be some sort of joke today, but it can't be overestimated. Yet, Satan has been successful in his attempt to convince many Christians that prayer is useless. A look at the Gospels reveals that it was just the opposite with Jesus. Many times He spent all night in fervent prayer prior to ministering to the multitudes. In fact, He spent His last night before being crucified, in the Garden of Gethsemane praying.

Once the blinders are stripped from the believer's eyes and he or she sees Jesus, in the glory of His Presence, their attitudes toward prayer changes. As they have entered the life in the Kingdom, intercession, or standing in the gap for others is not a complicated task. It is a joy! The type of sacrifices we offer today and our reasons for offering them – still proves it is profitable to study the Old Testament priesthood. Throughout the study of OT patterns, we should be mindful and remember that *every believer* is called to be a priest unto our Lord today. We need to understand that the duties of prayer ministry are no longer confined to the faithful few – but there is no greater duty any believer can perform than prayer. Paul admonishes in Ephesians 6:18, "praying always [all times] with all prayer and supplication in the Spirit." Then in I Thessalonians 5:17, we are told to "pray without ceasing." He uses a different Greek term for each passage. In Ephesians 6:18, "pray at all times," he uses the GK word *kairos* which has to do with a specific time [my dental appointment is at 3 PM today, an appointed time] verse 13 a time. In I Thessalonians 5:17, "pray without ceasing" is the GK word *kronos* which means [I am going to pray about these times we are living in].

Intercessory prayer

I believe the missing component in the lives of most Christians and most churches alike is intercessory prayer. I'm talking about fervent biblical prayer. It's the kind Paul and James wrote of. Jesus said that prayer has a direct impact on *spiritual warfare*. Prayer is the necessary means by which we as believers are able to withstand and overcome the attacks of the devil. For example, in Mark 9:14-29, the disciples were attempting to cast out a demon, but it wouldn't bulge. They came and asked Jesus what the problem was. He said to them, *"This kind can come out by nothing but prayer and fasting."* (v. 29) "This kind" in Jesus' reply, indicates that some demons are more powerful and obstinate, and therefore more resistant to being cast out, than others. Then, sometimes we can become overconfident from earlier successes (see Mark 6:13). The disciples' success at casting out evil spirits from people – demonstrates Christ's power over the supernatural world (see v.7). This indicates that there are evil spirits that are not compelled to respond by any other means than prayer and fasting. Also, Jesus once told Peter that Satan had asked to sift him like wheat. *"But I have prayed for you,"* Jesus said to him (Luke 22:31-32). Prayer helps in the deliverance of people who are presently expiricing spiritual attack.

The early church also experienced the power of prayer. After Jesus had ascended and the disciples were waiting for further instructions, what did they do?

- Acts 1:14 tells us, they *"were continually devoting themselves ..... to prayer."* Italics added throughout.
- Prayer was also what they were doing when Pentecost happened (see Acts 2:42).
- Just before the major miracle of the church, Peter and John were going to the temple to pray (Acts 3:1).
- As Peter and John returned from being flogged, they explained the privilege of suffering in the name of Jesus. They prayed as the believers gathered around them. The room in which they were gathered shook, the Holy Spirit came upon them, and they *all* began to speak with great boldness (Acts 4:31). The rest of the Book of Acts follows this same pattern. Whenever God's supernatural power is evident by signs, wonders and transformed lives – we can be assured that someone somewhere has been praying. When we commit to intercessory prayer – lives are changed. Remember, the Book of Acts does not have an ending as the other NT books – it is still being written!

Power falls where prayer prevails!

The Third Great Awakening

Clearly Christ wants His church to hear and understand what the Holy Spirit is saying to the churches today (Revelation 2:7). Thankfully, He is still speaking today! Often we preachers speak of how the devil has stepped up his game in these lasts days. The Scripture speaks of his present-day activities. However, much more worthy to speak of is the incredible new era the church has now entered – the Day of the saints. In spite of the resistance to change found in many of the traditional institutional churches, those churches that are hearing the Spirit are beginning to do some brand new things in some new ways. The devil and his demons will now face a New Testament church they have never encountered before.

A worldwide revival is rolling through America and the world, once encountered you will notice that it is bigger than anything we've seen before. These are exciting days because it's a time for the whole church to participate. The church will be functioning in Kingdom of God governing authority, with every member ministering. It will be based upon the foundation of the apostles and prophets, and the ministry of all believers – no place for spectators. There has never been a move of God like this one [Third Great Awakening]. I am excited because the African American church can really glorify God in spirit and in truth. We will see in the next chapter, that it was during an earlier Great Awakening the Black church truly took on her own persona.

During slavery, the Jim Crow, and the Civil Rights era the Black Churches were on their knees and God came to their rescue. In the next two chapters, our focus is on the Lord *not* forgetting us. A strong and vibrant church was our heritage – but many of us individually and corporately have forsaken God and His church, deceived by the spirit of the age to selfishly think that the Bible way is too narrow and the world has a better offer.

This should be our brightest hour rather than as many perceive it to be our darkest hour. Christ is still the answer to our problems. If the gospel is hid from our people today it's our own fault. The anti-Christ spirit has hindered many today, but God is going to steamroll demons and strongholds that were *perpetuated* intentionally on plantations for control purposes. The trauma of those days continue to take a toll on all African Americans in this country. Folks we left, but we have not arrived. Let's try Jesus, you'll find that, "He's alright!"

Discussion and Reflections Chapter 7

1. Discuss the three biblical Reformation truths rediscovered, but widely ignored for various reasons until recent history.

2. Discuss how the mainline denominations along with other foundational institutions have lost their influence after turning inward to institutionalisms.

3. Discuss the hierarchy of the bishop, presbyter, and deacon developed in the Roman Catholic Church during the second and third centuries, created a seedbed of corruption during the Middle ages.

4. Discuss the rediscovery of the Gospel of Christ marked by a radical shift from the institutional church's being the dispenser of grace to the proclamation of the gospel as the means of salvation.

5. If ministry is to be returned to the people of God, we must have a bottom-up view of the church.

SECTION III

REPENT AND RETURN

Chapter 8

LEST WE FORGET

"Remember the former things of old, for I am God and there is no other; I am God, and there is none like Me, declaring the end from the beginning, and from ancient times things that are not yet done, saying, My counsel shall stand, and I will do all My pleasure" (Isaiah 46:9-10).

"Do not remove the ancient land marks which your fathers have set" (Proverbs 28:22).

Anything that man can imagine only becomes impotent idols unfit for comparison with the God of Israel (see Isaiah 40:18-20). God urged Israel to remember:

- The history of all the fulfilled prophecies
- The miraculous deliverance from Egypt
- The miraculous crossing of the Red Sea
- The providential blessings Israel has experienced

"Are these not ample evidences that I alone am God?"

IF WE FORGET OR NEGLECT THE ERRORS OF THE PAST, WE ARE DESTINED TO REPEAT THEM!

God's appeal to the reason of the people

In every generation we seem to hear God saying, *"Come now, and let us reason together."* Although these are a rebellious people, God still reasons with them. Once more the piece of man-manufactured helplessness called, and idol is placed before their thoughts. What can it do for them? They cry unto it, but it cannot answer, nor save them in times of trouble. Is God to be compared with that thing?

Again, the positive argument is brought forward. God alone has the power of prediction. "From the very beginning of a period of history He can announce the far-off issues; which are incalculable to human eyes." At this point in time, World history and Church history at any moment are not a mere play of passion and chance, but all things are working together to a *foreseen end*. One day I clearly heard a notable preacher on TV admonish the crowd with these words and I quote, "God said forget the past and move forward into your destiny." "Lest we forget or ignore our errors of the past – we are destined to repeat them!"

False trusts

The United States of America like Israel of old has been borne in the arms of God from its very infancy by His faithfulness, power, tender mercy, and kindness in the past; which could continue to the furthest future. However, like the Babylonians, we make mistakes which result in serious consequences. We never know if God has a Nebuchadnezzar warming up in the bull pen to take down this country or any other country – but truly this is not the time to put our faith in man and false trusts.

Many times, people put their hope and trust in national leadership, or even some other nations, but the condition of this world is far beyond man's natural abilities. Men put their trust in that which proves to be delusive and even burdensome:

- Unholy alliances
- Unwise friendships
- Ill gained wealth
- Exalted positions which they don't have the ability nor strength to fill
- High honors which they have no grace to carry
- Learning in one direction, but unbalanced by knowledge in the other direction

You see men who thought to bless themselves with these "idols," expected to get rich and be sustained by them. Instead they are staggering under their weight, blinded and misled by them. Instead of their gods carrying them, they must carry their gods. A prime example was when cotton was "god" during the years of slavery in this country. The true and Living God always has the last word!

A deadly cancer

A deadly cancer spread throughout the United States of so-called Christian white America. How could a democracy infused with Christian principles from its birth, continue to sanction the enslavement of millions of human beings?

- The practice of slavery began in America on August 20, 1619, when a Dutch frigate off-loaded 20 Negro slaves at Jamestown, Virginia.[11]
- By 1830 the number of slaves had increased to about two million. For them the webs of the struggle were very basic to human existence, and extremely religious in character; in fact, all sides turned to the Bible to interpret their experiences.[12]

Out of necessity the white masters stripped the slaves of everything – including their African gods. The uprooting of Negroes and their transportation to this country had a tramatic effect on their whole existence. The slave holders deprived the slaves of their African culture breaking up their social organization; which in turn took away their sense of place in the world.[13]

Many slaves committed suicide during the Atlantic crossing. Approximately 3 million Blacks died in Africa and the Middle Passage slave trade.[14] Once in their new abode others submitted to their fate, and in their confusion sought meaning for their hideous existence.

The break with the African Homeland

The development of the social and cultural life of the Negro in the United States was atrocious, beginning with the slave traders and the way they treated the negroes once they captured them; mostly in certain areas of West Africa. Another lucrative source for the slave trade came from intertribal wars; where the captives were young and vigorous males. It was determined that the young slaves were not likely candidates for bearing the cultural heritage of a people. This standard was in accordance with the demands of the slave markets in the New World.

Another slam against the slaves by the white slave owners was their preventing the slaves from transmitting their African social heritage through dehumanization. Their methods began with the manner in which the slaves were treated while being held by the slave-traders prior to their being shipped to the New World and right up to their eventual purchase.

The captives were packed all together into makeshift concentration encampments without regard to age, gender, family ties or tribal affiliations. Even the transport vessels for the voyage across the Atlantic Ocean [middle passage] were designed to further promote the dehumanization of the slaves; as they were packed into holds of the ships again, with absolutely no regard to gender, age differences, family ties or tribal differences.[15]

In the New World the process of dehumanization and stripping of their heritage was completed:

- The size of the plantation had a great influence on the amount of or lack of contact between the slaves and the whites. The larger plantations provided some limited opportunity for slaves to maintain or re-establish their old ways.[16]
- Newly imported Negroes from Africa were usually "broken in" to plantation life and the ways of the new environment by older slaves.
- The slaves were required to learn the language of their masters for communication purposes. At the same time any attempt by the slaves to preserve their native language was forbidden.
- If slaves who spoke the same language were accidentally thrown together, it was the policy of the slave masters to separate them immediately.
- There was a general restriction on any assembly of five or more slaves without the presence of a white man. This was especially enforced at their gathering for religious purposes.

Christianity among the slaves

Historical records show that both Islam and Christianity played an important role in enslavement in Africa. The Arab-controlled Trans-Sahara slave trade helped to institutionalize slave trading on the continent. Christianity gave the slave a center for his or her life in their new environment. In the beginning many slave owners strongly opposed teaching the Bible to slaves for fear they would find some ideas of human equality; which might incite them to riot.

Therefore, slaves were forbidden by the masters to attend church, or in many cases, even to pray, and they risked floggings [up to 200 stripes of the whip] for sneaking off to attend secret prayer meetings and to worship God. At the same time, other masters were persuaded that those who learned the Bible were more willing to accept the control of their masters:

- From the Bible the slave learned about the white man's God and His way with men.

- Even though slaves were permitted to marry, the law did not recognize slave marriages. As a result, there was no conscious effort on the part of a master to keep marriages nor slave families together. Often children below the age of thirteen were separated from their parents and sold, never to be reunited. "Under the chattel principle, every advance into enslaved society – every reliance on another, every child, friend, or lover, every social relation held within it the threat of its own dissolution.[17] Though married all of the women and girls were personal property and subject to the slave masters' sexual whims. Rape was an inevitable aspect of slave life for many Black women, who had no social or legal power to resist. The white man would never be prosecuted.

- In her autobiography *Incidents in the Life of a Slave Girl,* Harriet Jacobs relates the moral agony of choosing between being raped by her enslaver or a more willing but no less unequal sexual relationship with a free white man. Raised by a Christian grandmother who exhibited constant concern for Jacob's safety and sexual virtue, the young slave girl agonized over her decision, unsure of how to respond to her sexual partners. For years she had done her best to avoid the lecherous tentacles of her enslaver, Dr. Flint. To her white female readers, she implored, "But, O, ye happy women, whose purity has been sheltered from childhood, who have been free to choose the objects of your affection, whose homes are protected by law. Do not judge the poor desolate slave girl to severely!"[18]

- Again, any member of a slave family could be sold at any time to another master in another city, county, or state. At the marriage ceremonies preachers often joined couples with, *"until death or distance do you part."*[19]

- Slavery permitted unchecked dominance and promised unlimited fulfillment of unrestrained desire. Slaves were considered commodities therefore, the owners had the legal right to rape one's human property. From the beginning of slavery in the Americas, white men had believed that when it came to enslaved women, purchase promised privilege. Male slave masters justified themselves by saying that African American women were more sexual, less moral, less beautiful, and less delicate. Such claims excused rape, the rejection of children, the sale of lovers [remember marriage was not recognized by law among slaves] and forcing black women to labor in jobs for which white women were considered too delicate.

- Black and white abolitionists identified family separation and the exposure of enslaved women to sexual abuse as two of the most devastating impacts of the domestic slave trade. White American Christians during this period turned a blind eye to the separation of families, the scarring of bodies, and the generational trauma of slavery.

- Since all other forms of organized social life were forbidden among the slaves, and having no priesthood, the Negro preacher became the important figure in the "invisible institution" – of the slave church.

- His own experience of the "invisible institution" was recalled by former slave Wash Wilson:

"When de niggers go round singing 'Steal Away to Jesus,'
dat mean dere gwine be a 'ligious meetin' dat night.
De masters .... Didn't like dem
'ligious meetin's so us natcherly slips off at
night, down in de bottoms or somewhere
sometimes us sing and pray all night."

- Preachers licensed by the church and hired by the master were supplemented by slave preachers licensed only by the Holy Spirit. Text from the Bible, which most slaves could not read, were explicated by the verses from the spirituals.

- The key to an understanding of the "invisible institution" may be found in the typical remarks of an ex-slave who wrote: "Our preachers were usually plantation folks just like the rest of us. Some man who had a little education and had been taught something about the Bible would be our preacher. The colored folks had their code of religion, not nearly so complicated as the white man's religion, but more closely observed.

- Slaves frequently were moved to hold their own religious meetings out of disgust for the so-called gospel preached by their master's preacher: "The preacher came, and he'd just say, "Serve your masters. Don't steal your master's turkeys. Don't do this or that …...." When we had our meetings of this kind, we held them in our own way and were not interfered with by the white folks."[20]

- According to Fredrick Douglas, the abolitionist orator who escaped from slavery, the preacher was one of the slave notables. The preacher seems to have achieved his authority because of personal qualities. The authority was given greater weight when the slave who had been called to preach was licensed by the Methodist or Baptist church.[21]
- Because of the local autonomy of Baptist churches in contrast to the centralized hierarchy of the Methodist church, the Negro preacher was free to exercise his gifts and to direct followers.
- Two qualifications which the Negro preacher among the slaves needed to possess were some knowledge of the Bible and the ability to sing. No matter how imperfect or distorted his knowledge of the Bible might be, the fact that he was acquainted with the source of sacred knowledge, which was in a sense the exclusive possession of his white masters, gave him prestige in matters concerning the supernatural and the religious among the slaves.
- As one white minister put it, the religious instruction to the slaves required *preaching* **rather than** *instruction in the Christian faith.* Preaching meant dramatizing the stories of the Bible and the ways of God to man. These slave preachers were noted for the imagery of their sermons.
- Although the masters were unwilling to tolerate any form of organized activities among the slaves, different members of the "congregations" played various roles according to their talents and abilities:

  1. Ability to sing
  2. Ability to influence other slaves to get converted
  3. Ability to influence other slaves to attend religious services

- Reflecting the revival spirit of the time – the Negro preacher was "called" to his office – in most cases through some experience that indicated, that God had chosen him to be a spiritual leader.
- By this means the preacher came to display his personal qualities and achieve a position of dominance. In time, he learned to dramatize biblical stories for Negroes and to interpret many characters and events in terms of the slave's experiences. The dominant events were the birth of Moses and the oppressive slavery experience of the Hebrews in Egypt. However, first among the biblical characters was Jesus Christ.
- Constantly supplying the fuel for the Negro sermons and spirituals were stories of the Creation; the passage of the Red Sea;

the destruction of Pharaoh's army in the Red Sea; The desert wandering; and crossing the Jordan river into the Promised land.

- The recognition the whites allowed the Negro "congregations" was only as a segment of the white organizations. White control of these segments was never eased. Therefore, there was always tension, because the slaves preferred their own preachers and wanted to conduct their religious services according to their own way of worshipping.

- Additional tension was always present because there were some free Negroes in the churches which were established as a segment of the white church organizations. The Negro church never emerged as an independent institution except under the Negroes who were free before the Civil War.

There seemed little hope for deliverance here on earth, during the dark days of bondage so, emancipation came to be linked with death, when Jesus would remove their shackles and release them into another and happier world. Peter Randolph, a slave in Prince George County, Virginia, until he was freed in 1847, described the *secret prayer meetings* he had attended as a slave. Not being allowed to hold meetings on the plantation, "he wrote," the slaves assembled in the swamp, out of reach of the patrols. They have an understanding among themselves as to the time and place … This is often done by those first arriving breaking boughs from the trees and bending them in the direction of the meeting spot. "After arriving and greeting each other, there was preaching, praying and singing until feeling the spirit, which resulted in many falling to the ground under the influence. They risked up to (200 lashes of the whip if caught). For years all manner of people and circumstances conspired against the slaves *ever* hearing the true gospel, and especially their responding to it in freedom and joy. One of the largest obstacles facing the slaves was white supremacy and sheer prejudice.[22]

Later the slaves were brought into the religious practices of their white masters. These strategies as well as all the others discussed above were geared to bring about the complete destruction of the Negro's African cultural heritage. African American history was not taught in the public-school systems.

It is voiced in every quarter of this country, that immigrants from any nation can come to America and assimilate their religion, social culture and find the cohesion from their old country, so to speak – which gives them unity and a leg up? Along with all the many other things African Americans have had to endure in this country is the fact that for many years they were denied a past.

> Certainly, we can see and understand that the denial
> and destruction of these various basic elements of life so
> afflicted the Negro slaves; that the trauma continue to
> haunt Black America *in all of life* today [154 years later].

From all reports, the arriving new slaves with their African ways were subjected to the hostility of Negroes who had become accommodated to the plantation routine and had acquired the ways of their new environment.[23]

For more than 200 years, Africans were held in bondage in America. For two centuries, these people were systematically stripped of every right of personality. Racism was institutionalized, and the sacredness of the African American family was trampled in the dirt. Children were sold from their mothers, and fatherhood was made illegal. Many masters believed Africans were too "brutish" to comprehend the gospel: others doubted Africans had souls.

In his book, *Before the Mayflower,* Lenore Bennett, Jr. said, "The Mississippi court ruled that the rape of a slave woman was an offense unknown to common or civil law. A Kentucky court ruled that the father of a slave was unknown to the law.[24]

The lack of cohesion remains a major problem among African Americans today, even in many of our local Black churches. Can we expect 154 years of the spirit of racism, white privilege and perpetuated white supremacy in every institution in this country, stop-gap money thrown at suspected crucial problem areas, failed state and federal programs, atheistic clichés such as "pull yourself up by your own boot straps," "take responsibility for your own state," and many other derogatory sights and sounds to naturally try to squash the dilemma? One of the largest obstacles was and remains to this day is sheer racism – for white supremacy [a dream] that is very much alive and well in these United States today. In recent times we are seeing in some states the revival of redistricting-strategies and long-forgotten laws put in place as white politicians sought and continue to suppress black voting power that emerged during Reconstruction and propelled some black candidates to national and statewide office. African American candidates continue to face hurdles in some southern states. After Reconstruction, extremely few blacks were registered to vote until the mid-1960s because of poll taxes and deadly violence. Again, "ignore or forget the errors of the past and you are destined to repeat them!"

Though He is rejected by the world, Jesus Christ is still the answer!

A new basis for cohesion

Research shows that it was not the remembrance of African culture or African religious practices, but the Christian religious practices that provided the new basis for the slave's social cohesion and life. Amazingly from the beginning of the slave importations, Negros received Christian baptism by the Anglican church.[25]

Although slaves were regularly baptized and taken into the Anglican church during the seventeenth century; there was stiff opposition from the slave owners; however, their resistance against the practice began to wane when laws were established that made it clear that slaves did not become free through the acceptance of the Christian faith and baptism.

Though husbands and wives were sold apart, many honored their marriages as Christians, regardless of the lack of civil protection. In 1897, AME Bishop W.J. Gaines wrote this about his parents, who were former slaves:

> *"The negro had no civil rights under the codes of the Southern States. It was often the case, it is true, that the marriage ceremony was performed and thousands of couples regarded it and observed it as of binding force, and were as true to each other as if they had been lawfully married ... The colored people generally held their marriage (if such unauthorized union may be called marriage) sacred, even while they were yet slaves ....*
> *My own father and mother lived together for over sixty Years. I am the fourteenth child of that union, and I can truthfully affirm that no marriage, however made sacred by the sanction of law, was ever more congenial and beautiful. Thousands of like instances might be cited to the same effect."*[26]

Unfortunately, detailed records are not available on the religious behavior of the Negro converts to Christianity. It was noted that missionaries had encountered much difficulty in attempting to convert the adult Africans therefore; they turned their concentration to the children. A study of the situation has revealed that only a small portion of the adult slaves in the American colonies could be considered nominal Christians.[27]

According to Carter G. Woodson, the Negro historian, "The Dawn of the New Day" in the religious development of the Negroes came when the Methodists, Baptists, and Presbyterians began proselytizing the Negro slaves. When the Methodists and Baptists began their revivals, a phase of **"the Great Awakening"** in the South; large numbers of Negroes were attracted to that type of worship.[28]

The Baptist and Methodist preachers lacked the education of the Anglican Church and appealed to the poor and illiterate. The ministers placed emphasis on *feelings* as a sign of conversion. The "fiery" messages of salvation gave the slaves who were so repressed, hope of escape from their earthly woes and sorrows.[29]

- The slaves enjoyed some social solidarity in the emotionalism of the camp meetings and revivals; they were drawn into union with their fellow man.
- Later, common religious beliefs and practices provided a new basis of social cohesion in an alien environment.
- Moral barriers between the master and slaves began to breakdown.
- It became a part of the discipline on many plantations to provide religious instructions to the slaves. Home servants attended the family prayers.

Thus, the slaves, who had been torn from their homeland, kinsmen, friends and cultural heritage to include idolatry and pagan religions, were lost, isolated and broken – now responded to the religious overtures.[30]

Joining the state in its repression of slaves, white churches and denominations began to take theological steps to ensure that converted slaves did not interpret baptism or Christian freedom as grounds for temporal and physical freedom.

Moreover, the high literacy demands of most white denominations effectively barred illiterate Negro pastors from formal ministerial preparation. Coupled with slavery the mounting prejudice of white Christian churches presented nearly overwhelming circumstances for any aspiring Negro pastor.

As the enslavement of negroes developed in practice and confirmed by law, during the seventeenth century, Maryland and Virginia passed laws to the effect that Christian baptism did not confer freedom upon the slaves. Nevertheless, the free Negro population in the colonies and later in the United States continued to increase until the outbreak of the Civil War. The increase in the free Negro population came from five sources:

1. Children born of free colored persons
2. Mulatto children born of colored mothers
3. Mulatto children born of white servants or free women
4. Children born of free Negro and Indian parentage
5. Slaves who were set free

The Negroes who were free before the Civil War were concentrated in areas where the plantation system of agriculture either had not taken root or had died out. Most free Negroes were concentrated in the cities of both the North and the South. Among the free Negroes in both the North and the South there developed an organized community life. Most of these efforts were concerned with mutual aid societies and cooperations for economic welfare.[31] These organizations, included efforts to acquire an education, were generally tied up with their churches which comprised a large part of their wealth.

Preparation for effective ministry

Despite the odds, some Negros were able to prepare for and conduct effective ministry. In the late 1700's, some began to preach immediately after conversion. Through a kind on-the-job training they preached to anyone who would listen. Richard Allen (1760-1831) began to preach immediately following his conversion at age seventeen. For nearly ten years Allen preached to anyone who would listen – his family, his master, and blacks and whites throughout Delaware. He went to Philadelphia at age twenty-six, where he was ordained a deacon by Francis Asbury (1745-1816), the first bishop of the Methodist Church.

In 1816, Allen became the first black bishop of the African Methodist Episcopal Church, and the first bishop of the historically Black and independent African American denomination.[32]

Young Negro ministers also apprenticed with more seasoned African-American pastors. With the rise of independent Black churches, black pastors molded generations of black preachers. First African Baptist Church of Savannah, Georgia serves as an example, Andrew C. Marshall served this church from 1812 – 1856, having no academic training. He did serve however, what might be called an apprenticeship under his uncle.

Another example was Daniel Alexander Payne (1811 – 1893) a mainly self-educated pioneer in African American Christian ministry. He was born to free parents in Charleston, South Carolina, during the height of slavery. Between the ages of eight and fifteen, young Daniel received educational instruction from the Minor's Moralist Society and a popular Charleston schoolmaster named Thomas S. Bonneau. While employed as an apprentice to local shoe and carpentry merchants, Daniel taught himself and opened a school for both slave and free Negros in South Carolina until the South Carolina General Assembly forced its closure in 1835. He moved north and received further education and training at the Lutheran Theological Seminary in Gettysburg, Pennsylvania. Although he resisted full-time Christian ministry, the Lutheran Church licensed Payne to the ministry, and about two years later the Synod at Fordsboro, New York, finally ordained him. Later as a pastor and bishop, his significant contribution was raising the educational requirements for pastoral ministry in the AME Church.

The Negro Church

The Civil War and the Emancipation destroyed what stability and order that had been attained among Negroes under slavery. However, the fusion of the Negro church which had taken root among the slaves and the Institutional church which had grown up among the Negroes who were free from before the Civil War resulted in the *structuring* or *organization* of Negro life to an extent that had never been attained. This becomes evident when we recall that organized social life among the transplanted Negroes had been destroyed by slavery. Any efforts toward organization in their religious life was prevented because of the fear of the whites of slave rebellions.

This was all changed when the Negro became free. In his book, *The Negro Church in America,* E. Franklin Frazier sets out to show how *an organized religious life* – became the chief means for a structured, social life to come into existence among the Negro masses. He shows that the life of the Negro masses was centered on the merged "Invisible Institution" and the "Institutional Negro Church." Despite many difficulties mainly from the fact that:

- There were among the Negroes many mulattoes and unmixed free Negroes representing a higher degree of assimilation of white or European culture.
- This was often reflected in the differences of character in the religious services of the free Negroes and those just released from slavery.

- The social stratification of the Negro population after the Emancipation, a free and mulatto ancestry became the basis of important social distinctions.

However, through it all the church organizations established by the free Negroes persisted. The church provided leadership as an agency of:

- Social Control – The problem of monogamous and stable family life was one of the most difficult problems that confronted white missionaries from the north who came south bent on improving the morals of the newly liberated blacks through establishment of the family with the Word of God. However, with the removal of the authority of masters resulting from the Civil War and the Emancipation, promiscuous sexual relations became widespread along with the constant changing of spouses. Many ex-slaves resisted formalizing and legalizing their union because it was not in their mores. Some missionaries even tried to force the freedmen to legalize their sexual unions – marriage and the family life could not be imposed by the missionaries. Marriage and the family could acquire an institutional character only as the result of the operation of economic and social forces within the Negro communities.[33]
- Economic Corporation – economic forces within the Negro communities provided aid in housing. A great number of Negro families of freedmen continued to be dependent upon the Negro mother as they had been called during slavery. However, the new economic conditions which resulted from Emancipation placed the Negro man in a position of authority in family relations.[34] The local Negro church fortified the new economic position of the freed man by moral support. This topic will be further explored throughout the remaining chapters.
- Education – the initiative in setting up schools for the African American Negroes; and encouraging young people to pursue higher education was a high priority of the Negro church, Negros in the cities, and northern white missionaries. Before the Civil War one of the most important agencies in the education of Negroes were the Sunday schools mainly through the ministry of the church. Additionally, as the Union armies penetrated the South; the representatives of northern missionary societies and churches sent funds and teachers in the wake of the advancing armies. Working with the Freedmen's Bureau which was created by an act of Congress in 1865 to aid the freemen in assuming the responsibilities of citizens, they also laid the foundation for a public school system for the newly emancipated Negro. Negroes trained in these schools

supported by northern churches and philanthropy became the educated leaders among the Negroes. They laid the foundation for or established most of the Negro colleges in the South.[35]

- Political Life – In the fall of 1865, southern white voters made it clear that they did not plan to come to terms with freedom. Angered by southern whites' unwillingness to admit that they had lost the verdict of war, northern Republicans in congress, led by a faction called the "Radicals," took control of Reconstruction. They passed a series of bills that took the vote away from most ex-confederate officers, and they extended the power of the army and the "Freedman's Bureau" to impose new labor systems on the cotton south. The formerly enslaved Negroes wanted land to plow and raise food without someone riding behind them with a pistol. They wanted their children to go to school instead of field work all year. They wanted to grow crops. The freed people's dream of land for most was short-lived.

Yet the Radicals convinced Congress to pass the Fourteenth Amendment, which made former slaves equal citizens.[36] It wrote into the Constitution a nationwide standard of birthright citizenship that would eventually enable future generations of the slaves' descendents and immigrants alike – to undermine racial and cultural supremacy.

Reconstruction

During the period between 1866 and 1876 Reconstruction in the South seemed to be moving toward a transformed society. African American voting permitted former male slaves to make policy in state legislatures where deals were made to securitize their own blood and seed.[37] Preachers who took the lead in social control also took on political life. During the Reconstruction period, African Americans enjoyed civil rights. Though white resistance was fierce and brutal the national commitment to emancipation kept federal troops stationed in the South.

After 1873, the industrial economy fell into deep depression, white America's conscience wavered. Due to labor disputes in the north, Republican leaders lost interest in the plight of the ex-slaves in the south. Between 1868 and 1871, an estimated 400 African Americans were lynched across the South.

In 1876 to resolve the disputed presidential election, northern Republicans made an atrocious deal with the Southern Democrats to let them have "home rule." The "Redeemers," as the white southern Democrats called themselves, *changed the law to roll back as much of Reconstruction as they could*. A broad counterattack was mounted to undo the work of the 13th, 14th and 15th amendments.

This involved a campaign of murder and intimidation to disenfranchise black Republicans across the South as night riders went out hooded in white, burning, raping, beating and killing. They burned the homes owned by black folks. This also involved the imposition of economic systems (sharecropping and convict labor) that effectively recreated the conditions of slavery. After food and other living costs were deducted from their earnings, sharecroppers typically owed the landowners more than their wages due. There is little empirical data or evidence on which to establish the precise economic arrangements between most black families and the landlords who dominated their lives. Especially when it came to knowing how many black families lived in a form of uncompensated involuntary servitude.[38]

In many instances, African Americans were arrested for petty and false offenses, vagrancy and when they could not pay the fines and court costs, sometimes the warden sold the prisoners to plantations, mines, and factories. In his book *slavery by Another Name,* Douglas A. Blackmon estimates that from the end of Reconstruction until World War II, the number enslaved in this way exceeded 100,000. Mines operated by U.S. Steel alone used tens of thousands of imprisoned African Americans. The practice slowed during World War II, but it wasn't until 1951 that Congress fulfilled its Thirteenth Amendment to outlaw the practice. Across the nation under the first national New Deal program, the Federal Emergency Relief Administration, adopted in 1933, disproportionately spent its funds on unemployed whites, and frequently refused to hire African Americans in any but the least skilled jobs – and paid them less than the official stipulated wage. Increasing the minimum wages in the textile industry, resulted in price increases thoughout the entire production chain to include retail clothing. But the agreement bypassed jobs in which African Americans predominated: cleaners, outside jobs, and yardmen. Of the 14,000 African Americans in the industry 10,000 were classified into one of these jobs – which incidently were not included in the wage increases.[39] This was prevalent throughout te United States.

In his book, *"Stoney the Road,* Henry Louis Gates, Jr. recounts the massive coordinated betrayal of black citizens and denial of justice following Redemption by every white institution:

- The Supreme Court gutted civil rights protection.
- The scientific community justified white supremacy with bogus research.
- White churches ignored or blessed the oppression.[40]

Gates concludes Fredrick Douglass got closest to the truth – that there is no path to pride and equality that does not include *political power,* particularly the right to vote.[41]

Jim Crow – segregation

By 1900, they had taken away the vote from most black men, and many less fortunate white men as well. They dropped the bomb, segregation – "Jim Crow," as it came to be called. Actually it was an array of demoralizing and brutal rules, for instance:

- African Americans could not drink from the same water fountain as whites.
- African Americans could not eat in the same restaurants as whites.
- African Americans could not attend the same schools with whites.
- African Americans did not have equal rights to move in public spaces as equals with whites.
- African Americans could not ride in the front of the bus even if the back was packed [all seats occupied]; and there were empty seats in the front.
- African Americans had to give up their seat for any white person standing.
- African Americans had to give up space or make room for whites.
- African Americans did not have access to the same educational and economic opportunities as whites.
- Southern whites built monuments to their defeated generals who led their troops in the war for slavery.[42]

Only by knowing this period in our history can we understand how *white supremacy* became the broadly accepted, and current ideology and dream of many white Americans today. This was the main focus of the NAACP and eventually, of Dr. Martin Luther King Jr. The denial of justice recounted in "Stony the Road" was every bit as attrotious as apartheid. It is very important to note at this point, It was not just racism which is often viewed as an action performed by individuals. You may ask, why do Black families own less than white families? Why does school segregation persist? Why is it harder for Black adults to vote than for Whites? Would addressing economic inequality solve racial and gender inequality?

Many Americans are some-what familiar with the recorded histories of slavery and Jim Crow alike – yet we don't seem to grasp or maybe don't care to grasp an understanding of how the rules of those periods undergird today's economy, that produces the same racial inequalities 150 years after slavery and a half century after Jim Crow. Since the Civil Rights era racial practices that produce racial division in this country are:

- increasingly covert
- embedded in the normal operations of institutions
- avoid direct racial terminology
- invisible to most whites

The fight for racial equity has been a push and pull-back and forth [progress and retrenchment] for inclusion over exclusion in each generation. For example, today through a series of rules and customs, government employees and real estate agents have actively engineered neighborhoods and communities to maintain segregation.

Presently across this nation, rising polarization among the races is once again revealing *systemic racism*, which refers to how racial disparities operate within major parts of the United States society, that allocates:

- differential economic
- partisan politics
- education
- the racial wealth gap
- residential segregation [red lining]
- housing discrimination
- mass incarceration (which results in higher rates of unemployable African Americans
- dumping African American prisoners back in the ghettos upon their release
- targeted by the War on Drugs
- racial stigma of race is not limited to the individual; it extends to family members, friends and even to some whole communities
- police killings of unarmed blacks
- traffic stops
- higher infant morality rates
- unequal access to health care
- unequal job opportunities
- racially biased school discipline policies
- a subtle return to school segregation

Mass incarceration of African Americans

One of the hallmark rules of the War on Drugs was the sentencing disparity for using crack cocaine (whose users are more often poorer and black) compared to powder cocaine (whose users are often weathier and white). While the substances are virtually the same in composition, *sentences* for using crack cocaine are *one hundred times longer* than for powder cocaine. In 1994, President Bill Clinton oversaw the passage of the Violent Crime Control and Law Enforcement Act, which put more cops on the street, expanded the use of the death penalty, increased prison sentences, restricted education opportunities for prisoners, and significantly invested in the expansion of the U.S. prison system.

President Clinton's 1994 crime bill came under sharp scrutinty during the 2016 presidential campaign, some suggested that the bill was, in part response black concern of threats of violence in their communities. However, as Elizabeth Hinton, Julilly Kohler-Hausman, and VeslaWeaver explained, while Black America were concerned about crime, violence, and drugs in the neighborhoods – they were not simply asking for tough-on-crime measures to address them! They were not simply asking for tough-on-crime laws. Their calls for tough sentencing and police protection were paired with *calls* for:

- full employment
- quality education and drug treatment
- criticism of police brutality

Policy makers ignored these calls – but chose stricter surveillance and harsher punisherment.[43] In 2010, thirty thousand people were sentenced for crack cocaine offenses, under the harsher rules regime; 85% of them were African Americans.[44]

Throughout the criminal justice system, as well as in our schools and public spaces, young + black + male is equated with reasonable suspicion, justifying the arrest, interrogation, search, and detention of thousands of African Americans each year, as well as their exclusion from employment, housing and the denial of educational opportunities.

Structural racism in the U. S. housing system

Some critical for gaing wealth building and financial well-being in the United States and critical are homeownership and affordable housing. Therefore, American lawmakers have sought to secure land for, reduce barriers to, and expand the wealth-building capacity of property ownership and affordable rental housing. These efforts have almost exclusively benefited white households. For centuries, persistent racial disparities in wealth has haunted the financial well-being, especially between Black and White households. Federal, state, and local policies subsidized the development of prosperous white suburbs in the metro areas the country. Then they constructed new highway systems through Black communities to ensure access to jobs in urban centers mainly for white commuters. Many neglected Black communities are then displaced to make room.

Another nightmare for low income people happens during the process of repairing and rebuilding homes and businesses in a deteriorating area …. Which when completed will experience an influx of middle-class or affluent people resulting again in the displacement of earlier poorer residents. These government policies foster systemic removal of people of color from their homes and communities. Nowhere is this process more noticeable than Washington, D.C. Between 1970 and 2015, Black residents declined from 71 percent of the city's population to just 48 percent.[45] During the same period the city's white population increased by 25 percent.[46] From 2000 to 2013, the city went through the nation's highest rate of gentrification [Webster's Dictionary defines it: the process of repairing and rebuilding homes and businesses in a deteriorating area] resulting in more than 20,000 African American residents being displaced.[47] Today, almost 1 in 4 Black Washington residents live in poverty.[48]

Future outlook?

Future obstacles that threaten black Americans is the possibility of block grants by the State for Medicaid recipants, or public housing and the like. The fear is that the State could modify Medicaid and other social programs with an employment requirement; which would mean removal from the rolls if not employed for various reasons. This would certainly effect already overwhelmed low-income, and poverty-stricken African Americans; more than with the poor of others people groups.

Researchers at Mt. Sinai in New York in a recent study found that trauma suffered by Holocaust survivors was passed on to the *genes* of their offspring – is there a question as to whether the trauma of slavery, Jim Crow, *perpetuated* systemic racism, and white supremacy along with the many injustices continuously experienced to this present-day impact the *genes* of Black Americans as well? Research across this country reflects the wide-spread attempt to destroy through on-going systemic racism, violence, mass incarnation, threats to mockery – the dignity, political rights and social standing of all African Americans in this Country.

In the early days slaves and free-blacks sought refuge and relief from a hostile white world; they turned their hearts and minds from the suffering, many injustices and privations of this world to a world after death where the weary would find rest. Through it all they retained their faith in God and found refuge in their churches.[49] Like our parents, and foreparents of old we must repent and return to our Lord and Savior, Jesus Christ – and His church! He is our refuge and our strength.

Christ is all

Can we say with the song writer, "We've come this far by faith – leaning on the Lord? Trusting in His Holy Word – *He never failed me yet?*" In 1890, as white politicians across the South cracked down on the black population with Jim Crow laws, Mississippi inserted into its constitution an unusually high bar for getting elected governor or any other state office. The provision, which remains in force to this day; says that candidates must win not only a majority today of the popular vote – that is, more than 50% — but also a majority of the state's 122 House districts. On May 30, 2019 more than a century later, four Black Mississippians sued in federal court to put an end to what they say is a racially discriminatory system, unique in the United States and deliberately aimed at twarting the election of African Americans. No matter the argument, it was put in place as white politicians sought to suppress Black voting power that emerged during Reconstruction and propelled some Black candidates to statewide office.[50]

African Americans have faced many'other hurdles not only in Mississippi, but across the entire nation. How many other states still have such antiquated racist laws on the books? If they are there, Satan will make sure that one of his find them.

Present-day racial polarization across the country and partisan politics are at a very dangerously high level, even among some Christians. In many cases it's hard to get a Christian brother or sister to talk to their neighbor about Jesus and salvation; but if they find out that a brother or sister voted for a candidate from a different political party – Someone will be talking to them, sooner than later!

For some Christians it seems that an unsaved person belonging to the same political party is a more valued friend than a saved Christian brother or sister belonging to another party. Wouldn't you say that is putting partisan politics above the Word of God?

In the local church we promote the right to disagree, but still be agreeable in our business meetings – but not in our politics. As I stated in another section, partisan politics may be the new religion on the block in America! Lest we forget, after Reconstruction, many Blacks were not registered to vote until the mid – 1960s. Jesus made two very profound statements that we often preach to others, but can't seem to get our own knower [heart] wrapped around for our own spiritual growth and well-being:

1. *"Without Me you can do nothing"* (John 15:5).
2. *"With God all things are possible"* (Mark 14:36).

Systemic Racism

In America among the various elites there is a tendency of many to *still* believe that these disparities are the result of personal ambitions and individual choices, therefore, their solution to the problem of racial inequality is for individuals to take "presonal responsibility." Twenty years ago, two-thirds of America's general population including 71% of Whites and even 53% of Black Americans believed that Black Americans who *"have not* gotten ahead in life are mainly responsible for their own situation.[51] Certainly that was an incorrect conclusion, the proof is in the pudding: A progressive iniative to raise the minimum wage, for example, will benefit black Americans – *but it will not change the fact that every $100 dollars a white families earn in income; black families earn just $57.30.* You do the math – what an injustice! Couple that with the fact that Black Americans are paid less than their white counterparts, consider with these disparities the gender-gap. As epidemiologist Camara Phyllis Jones writes, "the association between socio-economic status and race in the United States has historical roots in unforgotten events and continue because of contemporary factors that has not or will not change them – thus, perpetuating these injustices. Therefore, the ways of wealth-building and income constraints of slavery and Jim Crow policies continue to reverberate in asset-poor Black communities.[52]

Systemic racism then, is where the government bases its policies and legal sanctions on the premise of racial stereotypes or when the government disciminates public privilleges and opportunities by race or color. This was a great concern and focus of Dr. Martin Luther King Jr. during the Civil Rights Era. Sadly, sixty years later we are in the same spot. Why? Mainly because we fail to understand the scope of the problem. The prince of this world (Satan) did a job on us as a people; but take heart, Jesus did a job on him on Calvary. Praise God!

There are acknowledged *perpetuated* disparities at every level of income, employment, education, lower rates of home ownership, unfair public housing practices, and criminal justice – just to name a few. The world has proven through deconstruction what they think of past heroes and heroines. Rather than duplication, our predicament needs enlightened young people to grasp the spirit of our past heroes and heroines be innovative and of great character, know themselves and the generation they are to serve. As in the other two calamities above only God can deliver us!

Many African Americans are doing their own thing without a true relationship with Jesus Christ – their attitude toward our problems as a people insist, "that's just the way it is." Yet, the records show that many slaves turned to God during that dark period of American history; likewise, the Black churches of the Jim Crow era looked to God – and here we are.

Today so few people in many of our local Black churches have been properly discipled that we now have a problem with the way they are living. Without a clear vision of discipleship, there is little or no spiritual depth in the lives of the people. Therefore, such churches have little or no impact in their society [world]. Many churches have taken secular humanistic view and prefer to look to science and reason, government and politician generated solutions for all of life. Again, review Jesus' sayings in the two passages above (John 15:5; Mark 14:36).

Even though they know that, "Christ is all!" It is high time we remember from where we've fallen, seek God's face, repent, return to Him, His church, and effective witness-evangelism and discipleship. That is His will for all of us. Church, "have faith in God!" His clear command two thousand years ago: "Go make disciples" (Matthew 28:19). The Word of God [the Bible] is still the will of God.

Discipleship is Spiritual Depth

We often hear the emphasis in Jesus' commission to His disciples placed on the verb, "Go" we think to the distant lands of the world" – but the main emphasis is really on the verb, "make disciples!" How? Three components:

1. Go – win them to Christ
2. Baptize – bring the into the church
3. Teach – teach them to obey the Bible [sanctification – deeper life]

As God allowed Magdalene and me to travel the world preaching and teaching the truth of God's Word for many years – I have noticed a common thread everywhere. That thread is [*voluntary* spiritual and biblical illiteracy] in many Christian families. Additionally, there is the de-emphasis of biblical education and through preparation for ministry. The major problem with this approach is the church's failure to fulfill Jesus' Great Commission instruction, *"teaching them to obey."* We must not relegate biblical teaching and training to a level of less importance when it is a primary and necessary means for fulfilling of the Great Commission. Right now, people all over the world are begging for help in this area. They want to be taught the truth of God's Word and be spiritually and biblically equipped for the mission.

Church, if we are not training believers to believe sound Christian doctrine and to interpret the Word of God correctly, the day will soon [and in some areas has already] come when those who represent Christ in this world will be preaching and teaching a gospel that Christ never gave. When people wonder what Christianity is all about, they will look to a "typical" Christian. The person they look at will *not* be preaching a gospel that biblical Christianity will recognize.

Doctrinally sound New Testament Christianity is shrinking in size and influence. Though this was denied our foreparents in slavery. Praise God, today a biblically sound theological education is possible. However, the day is rapidly approaching when many will be growing in such a way that truth will be considered, *"that which works for me;"* pragmatism rules in the absence of true truth. If this trend continues, we will one day shout truth in order to rebuke, reprove, exhort, instruct, and correct, only to be considered irrelevant and not to be heard.

Many people find it unbelievable when told that, the Southern Church, referring to [Christian churches] in Africa, Asia, and the nations of South America is growing exponentially. They not only outnumber those from the United States in Christians and churches; but they also send more missionaries than the U.S. and Europe combined.

This move of God is new, from the situation at the beginning of the twentieth century, when approximately 90% of all the worlds Christians lived in the United States and Europe, the beginning of the twenty-first century finds that 75% of the world's Christians are in the continents of the South and East [Latin America, Africa, and Asia].[53]

The movement's emphasis is on *experience* rather than *doctrine only.* While much may be said of the lack of their doctrinal preparation by those who offer scientific rationalism and traditional religion – the Holy Spirit makes the difference.

Magdalene and I were raised up in the Baptist Church, however, we found while serving with the Pentecostal churches in Panama and Seoul, Korea that in those settings Pentecostal persuasion is best suited, because a lot of the American institutional and traditional trappings are absent.

In fact, being led of the Spirit and the Word with much prayer; rather than science and rationalism with much intelect could be the key to revival of the American churches. Here in United States, the vibrant local Black churches that are led of the Spirit and the Word, no matter the denomination are growing. Are we walking by faith or by sight? Does your purpose statement reflect, "Our purpose to glorify God and enjoy Him forever?" Is your church hearing and acting upon what the Spirit is saying to the churches?

II Thessalonians 2:1-4, is warning people who live in the last days that a falling away will take place. A main cause for this tradgedy is, man has set *himself* up in the *temple* of God and serves himself as a god. In verse 4, Paul used the Greek word *naos,* not *hieron,* for temple. He is referring to the *human body* not the temple in Jerusalem. In Christianity mankind is the temple. In other countries many people served false gods. Satan's world [society] systems have made available many material goods and services – for the people to serve themselves.

The electronic media: TV, internet movies, and the press are very powerful tools in Satan's hands to influence the populance to accept worldly standards and decide right from wrong for our own personal taste. Biblical morals are no longer the norm. Satan has used these tactics to seduce and deceive Christians in America. Jesus warns us that the last days and the spiritual warfare we face is similar to the days of Noah. He said:

> *"And as it was in the days of Noah, so it will be also in the days of the Son of Man. They ate, they drank, they married wives, they were given in marriage, until the day Noah entered the ark, and the flood came and destroyed them all* (Luke 17:26-27).

Jesus' emphasis in the passage is not so much on the extreme wickedness of Noah's day. But it was on the people's preoccupation with the mundane matters of everyday life (eating, drinking, marrying, and giving in marriage"). When judgment fell *suddenly,* they had received warnings in the form of Noah's preaching (2 Peter 2:5) and the ark which was a testimony in itself to the judgment that was to come. Even so will it be when the Son of Man comes (Luke 17:30).

As the 2019 flu-season approaches, we are all encouraged to take the flu-shot; which has been reported to be only 30% effective. Faith in Jesus Christ is 100% effective – in all seasons of life. Try Jesus – He's alright!

As an African American, I pray that those who read this book will re-look the Big Picture salvation and the Great Commission. Our fore-parents looked to Jesus Christ and His Church for solace during slavery with a *hope* that He would deliver them from the bondage of slavery and give them hope of an eternal place of rest (John 14:1-9). They were willing to risk 200 lashes and possible death to come together for prayer and worship. What are we willing to risk for Christ?

Today many people believe that God is their just to supply their wants – right now! Much of the preaching today leads many to believe that to be true. I pray we'll all wakeup and get it right. Satan caused lawlessness and wickedness to become so vicious and terrible – God had no choice but to judge the Earth through a flood.

- People are falling back into the old thinking that to be poor, sick or hungry is the results of sin on the individual's part.
- In this thinking, God is there to not let the Christan suffer or lack anything their heart desires.
- Satan promotes this type of thinking. Buy into it and you are in for a great awakening. He is our enemy who in the past caused Adam and Eve to fall, don't be deceived by him.

Let's review a little history on the subject: In the first 300 years of the church, Satan attacked Christians through the Roman government. As a result, an estimated three million Christians were persecuted for their faith. They were hunted down and killed. Many were thrown to wild animals, beheaded, burned at the stake, crucified and buried alive. After Martin Luther and the Reformation in 1517, Satan stepped up his attacks against Christians:

- From country to country, Christians were brutally killed.
- In the Netherlands over 100,000 Christians were killed between the years 1566 and 1598.
- On August 24, 1572, in France, 70,000 Christians were massacred at one time.
- This should enlighten those who blame God for the slavery, and also the sad conditions of African Americans as a whole in America to this day.
- To take responsibility for the condition as many of the white race chides is totally impossible in our own strength – but with God all things are possible.
- Just as Satan deceived Adam and Eve, he has deceived this generation to turn from God to their own understanding. Daily more and more people are numbed to conviction and commitment to the gospel of Christ. What is at stake in all of this? Loss of the

gospel means the loss of the salvation and eternal life [again!]. Forget the errors of the past and you are destined to repeat them.

One thing that has hindered Satan in his attempt to bring down America has been the fact that God made this country, founded on biblical principles, the dispository of Christianity in these last days. However:

- the enemy is destroying the biblical standards in this country as we swiftly move [voluntarily] toward conditions similar to "as in the days of Noah."
- America no longer carries the big stick in the world; as is indicated by the enormous loss of respectability and influence around the world, even among our allies.
- As stated in a prior section, America has been labeled the most immoral nation on the planet. This is stated inspite of the past favor of God.

The Scripture says, "The wicked shall be turned into hell, and all the nations that forget God" (Psalm 9:17). America is no exception.

A Walk of Faith

We need renewal! Most people can understand how Jesus could heal the sick and raise the dead, after all He was God come in human form. Everywhere He went He preached the good news of the kingdom of God; and He demonstrated the kingdom by casting out demons and healing the sick. Here we see the pattern of proclamation accompanied with a demonstration of the kingdom of God.

What about His disciples you may ask? How were they able to demonstrate the kingdom? What about us? How can we add demonstration to our proclamation? By the Holy Spirit and His spiritual gifts and ministries operating in and faithfully through true believers in the body of Christ.

For three years, Jesus taught His disciples how to minister from:

- Hearts of love, compassion and mercy
- Hearing the Father
- Growing in dependence on the Holy Spirit
- Obedience to God's leading
- Our believing that God performs miracles through men and women

Christ taught them His *post resurrection commission* recorded in (Mark 16:9-20). At the present time, we still have a voice. God has revealed Himself in His Word, and as such:

The Bible is the only concrete absolute in the universe.

The teachings of the Bible will never fail, and they are sufficient for all faith and practice. Since expressions of Christianity are found throughout this nation, some bear little resemblance to what the Bible teaches. Pastors must bring their people to the teachings of God's Word – if they are to rightly know Christ.

God's revelation matters; the true knowledge of Him that comes through His Word is not some superfluous extra. In our evangelistic zeal, when we have brought the people to Christ – we must also teach them how to live. "Go and make disciples .... teaching them to obey everything I have commanded you" (Matthew 28:18-20). Remember, "if we forget or ignore the past, we are destined to repeat it." My prayer is that truth may ring out for the glory of God and the advancement of the gospel of Christ. Amen!

REFLECTIONS: "REPENT AND RETURN" CHAPTER 8

1. All sides in the slavery crisis in America turned to the Bible to interpret their experiences.

2. Slavery deprived the slaves of their African culture, broke up their social organization; all which in turn took away their sense of place in the world.

3. Christianity gave the slave a center for his or her life in their new environment.

4. Discuss the slave preacher and the "invisible church."

5. After reading Chapter 8; what are your thoughts? Jot some facts to pray and ponder about.

SECULARIZING THE
BLACK CHURCH

*"For the wrath of God is revealed from heaven against all
ungodliness and unrighteousness of men, who suppress the truth in
unrighteousness, because what may be known of God is manifest
in them, for God has shown it to them"* (Romans 1:18-19).

As African Americans, it is important to note, "Jesus Christ and His Church are the best legacy our parents and fore-parents could possibly have left us! Throughout the first half of the Twentieth Century, the church was the most important institution to the African Americans; and remained prominent in the lives of entire communities, especially in the South. At the same time, a much larger number of ministers were involved in the civil aspects of other institutions.

The great movement of blacks to the cities of the north and the south brought broad changes in the economic and social organization of American life; which have been responsible for increased integration of African Americans into the mainstream of American civilization. Sadly, the most significant change is that the church is no longer center of communal life or a refuge for African Americans that it was formerly.

This was brought about due to large-scale urbanization of African Americans after World Wars I and II; which was brought about, through secularization and transformation of the Black church – a change in their outlook upon the world and their place in the world. Soon the established Black churches placed *less emphasis on* **salvation** and *the life beyond* and increasingly directed their activities toward the *economic, social,* and *political problems* of African Americans in the world. As Christians we must always remember that our allegiance is *first* to God! When a nation *or a people* humble themselves before God, God blesses the nation whose people call on the name of the Lord (2 Chronicles 7:14).

The reorganization of the religious life of African Americans in the urban environment has been influenced mostly by the results of new class structures in the communities, due to increased occupational differences in the Black population. With an overwhelming urge to move up and away from the *spirituality* of the Negro church, many upper-and middle-class Black Americans joined the European model of church and institutionalized and traditionalized many of the local Black churches to *ineffectiveness!*

Remember, unless we've been born again from above through faith in Jesus Christ and Spirit led, our religion is "useless." Without overstating, the chief purpose of the church is to bring glory to God by accomplishing the Great Commission, commanded by Jesus Christ. Over a period of time, "Making disciples" and the responsibility to "teach them to *obey* all that Christ commanded" (Matthew 28:19-20); have been either lost, neglected, or simply disobeyed to a large number of local Black churches. For many others churches, it seems the Great Commission was never instituted.

Much of the church work today was at one point means to an end – however, over time the means have become the end. Herein then, is one of the *reasons* that the African American's problems are never solved – as a people, we blame our problems on everybody and everything but our own "disobedience," and inevitable *separation from God!* The Bible has recorded a number of people groups and nations who turned to God during a crisis and found grace in time of great need. God is full of grace and mercy; and it is not too late for America and the West to turn to Him. Lord have mercy on us!

The systemic racism and other problems we suffer as a people have proven over time to be beyond natural man's ability to fix. Especially when the people who caused the situation to exist in the first place refuse to take responsibility for it. In fact many white people have been led to believe that

African Americans should take responsibility for our own plight and pull ourselves up out of this mess. By the same token many blacks have been led to believe that "this is just our lot," "all there is." What would happen if the Black church would put the same amount of enthusiasm and emphasis on biblical teaching with practical application and evangelism – as it puts on partisan politics? I pray we become the Bible-believing church [spiritual organism], that Jesus Christ intended us to be. Some people think this thing has gone to the point that it is impossible. We tend to forget that all things are possible with God! He might ask us, "Where is your faith?"

Much Prayer – Much Power! & Little Prayer – Little Power!

As a concerned Christian, I am burdened by the plight of our people. Hurricanes over the past several years have presented problems that need to be addressed before the Father in heaven. Notice the number of storms coming off the coast of Africa today, September, 26, 2019 and turning north in the ocean away from our Eastern shores, this is indicative of what happens when the people of God pray! A few months ago, the evening news reported that a cloud of locusts 80 miles wide flew over a section of our western states. It was only news for a day because they didn't land on our crops out there. Are we really getting the message?

Scientists hurridly put a *natural spin* and label on every event that happens out of the ordinary. Why don't we believe that Creation is going through convultions as predicted in the Word of God over the sins of America; and other supposedly Christian nations that are turning their backs on God. In Deuteronomy 18:10-12; 7:1-5; Leviticus 20:6, God warned His people not to get involved in any way with those who did not serve Him. They were to tear down the enemy influences among them. We can see as we continue to read these Scriptures that the Israelites failed to obey Him. Read on and see what happened to them as a result. I would venture to say, "America is perhaps more vulnerable today than most nations, because through multiculturalism the assimilation of various gods, idols and supposedly harmless satanic influences are even found in our churches. As I mentioned earlier, secret lodges and fraternities, introduction of foreign religions, and other so-called harmless practices many; of which lead us away from God. Little by little we have incorporated or assimilated pagan practices until God has become just one god among many. Second Kings 17:33 says,

> *"They feared the Lord, yet served their own gods; according to the rituals of the nations from among whom they were carried away."*

Satan can stir up storms, but God can calm them – isn't our situation worth the revival of corporate prayer ministry in our churches? The point is we cannot afford *not* to revive our individual and corporate prayer life and true worship of the Living God. The world and even many in the church are asking, "What's going on?" Are we explaining to them that, "we do not wrestle against flesh and blood, but against principalities, against powers, against the rulers of the darkness of this *age*, against spiritual *hosts* of wickedness in the heavenly *places*" (Ephesians 6:14)? We need Jesus folks!

Jesus Christ is the only foundation on which to build any society. In the process of the slave masters dehumanizing the slaves, eventually the Muslim religion of their captors, animism, demonic spiritism and other paganistic beliefs were driven out of their belief system. However, like all people, God had given them a spiritual sensitivity toward Himself – and here in America, their adopted home, they became Christians characterized by a lifestyle of faith [praise God!] in Jesus Christ void of all idols and prior religious associations. Why as a people did we let that slip?

Enter Syncretism

The English word syncretism made its debut in the early 17th century. The word means the combining of different beliefs, while blending practices of various schools of thought.[54] The historian Phillip Schaff made the comment, "that going from the writings of the (Jewish) apostles to the (Gentile) fathers is like going from a city in a beautiful well-watered oasis, into a dry and barren wilderness!" This is a far cry from the level of spiritual insight expressed by the writers of the New Testament.[55]

Part of the big problem with many of these Gentile writers was that they wanted to embrace the message of Jesus without rejecting their pagan philosophy.[56]

Some of them had been students of Greek philosophy before their conversion and accepted the works of the Greek philosophers as wisdom given by God. Therefore, there was a deliberate attempt to blend the teachings of the New Covenant Scriptures with the teachings of secular philosophers. To accomplish this, required them to reinterpret Scripture to favor or include the secular worldview.

Syncretism is prevalent in many local churches where the ruling values of this present, passing world is *tolerance* and *inclusivity*; which is only acceptable as defined by the secular humanists' and atheists' agenda. Since society has <u>no moral authority that dictates the absolutes to which it should strive,</u> everything is legitimate if it [supposedly] doesn't harm or hinder another person? What is there, [especially sinful activity] that you can engage in that doesn't harm or hinder others in some manner?

Because earthly philosophers in their own so-called progressive liberal enlightenment have come to believe there is no real right and wrong – their thought is, to be truly modern <u>we must tolerate everything?</u> We are now a couple of generations deep into this diabolical belief system; which parallels a determined effort in the culture to distort and abolish Christianity. Their success is substantiated by the marked lack of spirituality and voluntary biblical illiteracy; which characterizes the secular worldview in this nation today.

Open rejection of Christ and His redemptive work on Calvary becomes more natural and the norm with every passing day. Lest we forget, the power of the gospel of Jesus Christ is still found in (Romans 1:16; 1 Corinthians 15:3-4), God's planned solution for a sinful world. Rejection of the blood of Jesus has caused some churches to abolish the Lord's supper.

During the mid-term elections of [2018], African Americans spoke as many local Black churches promoted candidates from a variety of worldviews, and secular immoral philosophies whose platforms hailed many items that were clearly biblically sinful and ungodly, yet, in the face of their known debilitating outcomes; many people in the Black churches continue to support such candidates out of loyalty and tradition. On both sides of the political aisle are those who would love to take away our religious freedom. As Christians we should realize that you can move too far in either direction [red or blue] and be so extreme that you lose purpose. If the Democrats have [demoralized] their party by accepting various fringe groups – the Rebublicans have moved so far to the right that they have [demoralized] their party through a conservatism that borders on self-righteousness, phariseeism and like it or not plain old racism.

I retired from the U.S. Army after having proudly served this country 26.5 years. Until recently, I flew the Stars and Stripes for the past 30 years out in the front of our home. I no longer fly my flag, even during holidays because to do so would offend many people – that same flag that we so proudly fought for in Vietnam and our Military representative of all races in America are still dying for, now symbolizes [spoken or unspoken], [perceived or unperseived] for many people – white supremacy. Much prayer must go into our decision-making in these matters. For many African Americans, if they vote, politics have become so partisan that to support the conservaties would further cut the throats of many poorer African Americans – for whom nothing is trickling down today. I spent five years in Europe three in Germany and two in France] arriving thirteen years after the end of WWII; while there were some scares of war – for the most part you would not know how quickly the United States through the Marshall Plan stepped in to rebuild Europe at war's end. We have spent trillions to liberate other people and nations – yet, the African Americans still don't deserve a hand up? Affirmative action was a start, but if fizzled out. Sadly, systemic racism, institutional injustice, stereotypes and pure segregation are very much alive in America today. Therefore, many poor of all races feel that the liberals will, see to it that they get food to eat, being driven to vote the liberal ticket or not vote period. For example: According to recent study released by the anti-hunger group, Feeding America nearly 8% of Americans 60 and older were "food insecure" in 2017, that equates to 5.5 million seniors who don't have consistent access to enough food for a healthy life.

We seem to be at a political stalemate: Perhaps it's time to create a third party? Remember, the Christian church in America is indeed communities of *believers* united by shared beliefs and missions.

Therefore, those practicing co-habitation, gay lifestyles, pro-abortion, sexual expression without limits, and other sinful lifestyles are slowly through assimilation are fully *tolerated* in society; but not in the local churches, they may be politically correct – but they are not biblically correct!

I read a comment coming one of the candidates for President of the United States on the early news, the other day concerning the two kissing in an ad on Hallmark channel. By the next hourly newscast his comments had been deleted. His comments left absolutely no doubt where he stood on the biblical view of homosexuality and same sex marriages. Love put above the truth of God's Word is the new normal for many. I'm sure that his lifestyle and platform would have to try to take away our religious freedom. Again, partisan politics may be the new religion on the block – but having been a pastor and Bible teacher for more than 30 years, to accept such a platform today would really be turning our backs on a Holy God. God is real, folks and one day we will stand before Him. Peter and the other apostles countered such thought with truth, *"We ought to obey God rather than man"* (Acts 5:29). The old adage says,"If you don't stand for something, you'll fall for anything."

When the church is properly aligned with Christ, they can enrich every dimension of our lives and provide great help and comfort to us, both in times of need and times of plenty.

My overarching objective in this book is to strengthen God's people in the Black Church to do God's work and to do it God's way; despite what the world is spewing out in the streets of this great nation, the Word of God [2000 years later] remains the standard for right living. African Americans cannot afford, "to not pray" and "to not trust God!" We are in the Christmas season (2019), I pray that the Church of the Living God doesn't get caught up in the party frenzy of the search for deals, sales and freebies – and forget the reason for the season: *Jesus Christ, the [incarnate]*

Son of God was born of the flesh through the virgin Mary to die, the perfect [sinless] sacrifice, for the sins of the whole world. He is the greatest gift ever! Though He died in our place, unless we recieve that truth in our heart by faith; there is no other way to heaven. All of the giving and gaiety of the season will cease in a few days, but what we do with the great gift, Jesus Christ, will establish our eternal destiny. The Scripture tells us that:

> **For God so loved the world that He gave His only begotten Son, that whoever <u>believes in Him</u> should not perish but have everlasting life** (John 3:16).

> **For God did not send His Son into the world to condemn the world, but that the world through Him might be saved** (John 3:17).

> **He who believes in Him is not condemned; but he who does not believe is condemned already, because he [or she] <u>has not believed in the name of the only begotten Son of God</u>** (John 3:18). Emphasis added.

Clearly, we see that "to believe in the name" means more than a mere intellect assent to the claims of the gospel of Christ, but it includes trust and commitment to Christ as our Lord and Savior <u>which results in receiving a new nature.</u> The new [divine] nature produces a change in heart and obedience to the Lord (see John 3:6-7).

Make no mistake, according to the Scripture [all must be born again] to be the people of God – who have been called to a task, and emphatically states that Christ has given us (His church) *a ministry of reconciliation* and has commissioned us as His *ambassadors.* That His appeal to the world is literally being made through us:

> *Therefore, if anyone is in Christ, he [or she] is a new creation; old things have passed away; behold, all things have become new. Now all things are of God, who has reconciled us to Himself through Jesus Christ, and has given us the ministry of reconciliation, that is, God was in Christ reconciling the world to Himself, not imputing their trespasses to them, and has committed to us the word of reconciliation. Now then, we are ambassadors for Christ, as though God were pleading through us: we implore you on Christ's behalf, be reconciled to God* (2 Corinthians 5:17-20). [Brackets are mine]

> Think about it – more than 59 million babies aborted in America since 1973; although African Americans account for only 12% of the population, African American women account for 36% per 1000 abortions (ages 15-44).[57]

When looking at such statistics as these; and to think, God decided to make His appeal to the world through you and me literally sends a chill down my spine. His *mission:* to reconcile the world unto Himself. His *strategy:* the church, His soldiers – you and me! Certainly, there can be no higher calling!

Therefore, as Christ's ambassadors we are admonished to *seek* and *speak* the truth in love, personally and corporately, knowing that often, we will be persecuted and rejected when we have found *the truth* and attempt to share it with others. Local churches are reminded that Christians find their lives formed by the *virtue of truth.* Many pastors of our Black churches are shying away from "the truth" because it inevitably puts them in conflict with the domain from which we have been delivered!

Due to a lack of biblical Spirituality and knowledge of the Truth – local churches everywhere are admitting to experiencing a higher interaction with the devil's disciples and their influence in all levels of church leadership.

This is the result of many churches no longer using the Spirit and the New Testament's truths, principles and practices as their genuine guide for all of church life. Many also have separated from repentance and a saving faith in Christ – this laxity should be laid right at the feet of pastors and teachers. Additionally, mesningful church discipline to include [Bible: applicable practical training] is almost unheard of in the Black churches today.

Truth by its very nature is *intolerant.* If there is truth, then there is error. If there is right, then there is wrong. A Christian who is committed to truth will always tolerate those persons who are in error – but will never tolerate the error itself. Many congregants are working to change that statement, beware of the counterfeits!

> We will not adjust the Bible to the age, but we will adjust the age to the Bible. Charles Spurgeon

Sin is still sin according to the Scripture and we are not to buy into ignoring it or watering it down to say that it is some incurable disease as the social scientists and some other cultural elites insists. We have to explain to this generation that love and truth are not in conflict with each other, that a conscience informed by truth can be very loving even though it draws a line and says, "I refuse to do this." Thus, no matter what my personal conviction is, love should always be true, even when I refuse to compromise my convictions. The Scripture reminds us, "For whatever is not of faith is sin" (Romans 14:23). Having said that, "personal holiness" in many local churches seems to have been ruled optional; as is clearly reflected in the voluntary lack of corporate prayer and choice of spiritual and biblical illiteracy within the local churches' membership. Certainly, these are eternal matters.

Like the culture, many people in our congregations operate on feelings today, demanding compromise on secular issues, with the anger and fervency of their cultural counterparts outside. For the good of all, we must overcome our failure to counter sin in our midst; not only sexual immorality, but the sins of cold love, disobedience; and the open rejection of the true interpretation of God's eternal Word.

We counter through prayerfully engaging in accountability, Spirit-led biblical mentoring, teaching and practice, modeling righteous living, and speaking the truth in love, even toward our enemies. Many of our people through voluntary ignorance of the truth – remain under the judgment of God.

We are reminded of the many local churches who no longer pray together regularly as a corporate act, not realizing they are courting distinction. When church leadership gets entirely to busy; prayer ministry is often what is neglected. We are so busy in the work of the Lord – that we have little time for the Lord of the work!

Oswald Chamber's observation of the matter says, "Remember no one has time to pray; we have to take time from other things that are valuable in order to understand how necessary prayer really is."

Much Prayer – Much Power! [or] Little Prayer – Little Power!

The things that act like thorns and stings in our personal lives will go away instantly when we pray; we won't feel the smart anymore, because we have God's point of view about them. Prayer means we get into union with God's view of other people.[58] Certainly, seeking God for information, answers, strength and wisdom is a must. However, we must be reminded that the necessary changes sought cannot be accomplished without people whose lives have been transformed. In fact, God told us what to do.

"If My people which are called by My name,
Shall humble themselves,
And pray, and seek My face, and turn from
Their wicked ways;
Then will I hear from heaven,
and will forgive their sins,
And will heal their land."

– 2 Chronicles 7:14

Unless we obey the Word of God, we are simply kicking the ball [error] down the road to the next generation. A truly transformed life is God's deterrent against sin and evil! As a people, African Americans are losing much of the religious ethos that was our cultural norm until secularization which was only a mumbling before; but has now become mainstream – We are growing up a generation, who accept the secular humanistic worldviews over the Biblical Christian worldview [of which most in this generation were never exposed] at the same time, carnal-living is increasingly being paraded as right living in many churches. Something to ponder:

R. T. Kendall says, "If the Holy Spirit was completely withdrawn from the church today, speaking generally, 90% of the work of the church would continue as if nothing happened. This can apply to an individual as well."[59]

Isn't it sad that the truth of God's Word is being ignored or redefined and rejected by our newly-allowed selfish *progressivism, secular humanism, consumerism, and materialism;* which deem doctrinal purity as too narrow for many of the members in our local Black churches today? By rationalizing and compromising the truth of God's Word concerning our *repentance* and *acknowledgment* of sins; we have brought much of the grief and poverty upon our families and communities ourselves. "Ethical respectability" cannot substitute for the required salvation experience, of being "born again from above" and living a righteous life by the Word and Spirit of God.

The culture with its rejection of godly lifestyles and obedience to God's biblical standards, cannot over-shadow the great deliverance a person experiences who *returns to Jesus Christ as their Lord and Savior.* Praise God, some people in the culture still have a conscience convicting them of the wrath of God – then there are some people beyond conviction, their conscious has been seared through their ignoring it. Our conscience, like the "engine warning light" on the dash of our cars. It does not correct, but if we keep ignoring it, the thing comes to past and oh how we wish that we had heeded our conscience's warning. Sadly, we are living in a time when people seem to no longer fear God or His Word. They speak of His love, but want to think that His love for us pre-empts His wrath. All of this is deception from Satan – don't fall for it. Obeying the Word of God yields eternal rewards; so disobedience can yield God's wrath! We should confess it, seek His forgiveness and move on in our life of faith.

Even with ample knowledge of this fact, many Christians will not interact with an unsaved person at work, school, recreation or other opportunities – thus, failing to share the gospel of Jesus Christ with them. At the same time, many backsliders with their names on the church rolls need to be reminded of the truth of Christ's forgiveness, if they will repent and confess their sins to Him and enter a personal relationship acknowledging Him as Savior and Lord – He promises forgiveness (see 1 John 1:9).

Yet, of all the principles of *righteousness – truth must reign supreme*. It is not that we proudly claim to know truth; it is rather that we are the people of our Lord and King, Jesus Christ, who by His very nature is Truth. In fact, the impression Jesus made on earth was that *He was full of truth* (see John 1:14) and that His truth reflected the glory of His Father. Likewise, the believer's truth reflects the glory of Christ.

True Black New Testament churches both embrace and express truth, however, we don't pursue it the way our foreparents did [in the slaves' invisible church] and **the fervent prayers of the saints** during the [50's, and 60's] Civil Rights Movement. The source of truth is the authoritative Word of God – which gives us solid life-related conclusions that are true no matter the *circumstances, conditions,* or the *state of denial* in our present culture, therefore:

- We must be people who speak the truth in love.
- We must be true to our word and commitments.
- We must be true to who we say we are – and claim to be.
- We must not erode what is true by either action or attitude.

Christ is truth. All that He says and does is true. You can bank on that! He is true to His Word, His promises, and to His people. In His rule there is no error, no hypocrisy, no unselfishness, and no deceit or injustice. Truth is a virtue toward which each Christian must strive! As stated earlier, Christ's biblical mandate to "make disciples and teach them to obey all that I have commanded," has become lost or overshadowed by secular-driven curriculums at all levels of so-called Christian education, false teaching, philosophies, agendas, fund-raising programs and other priorities – such as secret lodges, fraternities and of late partisan politics (probably the new religion on the block in this country); which have become hinderances and ends in themselves rather than means to ends – and having absolutely no eternal value. Even knowing the truth; these activities are not designed to give God any glory whatsoever – and even knowing this to be true, the church is getting in step with the times.

Renewing the Black churches depend upon re-aligning our whole lives on living in God's calling and purpose. Upon His departure, Jesus gave the disciples in several key passages; what is generally referred to as the Great Commission.

The Great Commission was a clarion call to follow Him by joining Him in His mission to reconcile humankind to His purposes. This is His biblical *will* for every true believer. The very Son of God became flesh and lived among us. He died and arose the third day so that we could find forgiveness and reconciliation with God. He has commissioned every true born again believer to bring the same good news to the nations of the world – sadly we have failed to do so! The will of God for His church should be common knowledge of every Christian. Yet, everyday people are asking, "What is God's will for my life?"

It seems God's people have lost their sense of purpose in the world. Corporately and individually, if we are not personally engaged in God's great mission to the world, then we have missed the very thing He created us to do. "How else can He receive glory?" In the service of the Lord, we need more than ability and skill, we need the manifest presence of:

- the Holy Spirit
- the Word of God
- the righteous life and practical living of the local Black Christian community
- along with some new wineskins

No healthy Christian or church can live that does not nourish itself on the indwelling fullness of the Holy Spirit and the life-giving Word of God. Many traditional institutional Black churches in America should conduct a stand-down [stop all operations] for as long as it takes to conduct a spiritual and present-truth examination, to see if they are still in "the faith" of Jude 3 and obedience to Christ's Great Commandment and Great Commission for building His kingdom.

Nor can any Christian be continously and completely satisfied in his or her calling without the powerful anointing of the Holy Spirit. Additionally, in order to provide the necessary spiritual soul-food, the pastors in our local churches must revive their preaching so that the main point of any biblical text be the main point of their sermons.

Sadly, today expository preaching and teaching are cast aside by many preachers and churches as not relevant, and too narrow; although we know that biblical exposition does the best job of honoring the Word of God, exposing its meaning, and providing the people with the true Word of life.

When the Bible's content truly occupies the central position in the life of the church and the preachers commit to preaching the message of the Bible, then the message heard will really be the truely anointed message Christ has sent through His messenger!

There exists in the Black Church as in other quarters, various theologies which include: a prosperity gospel, a liberation gospel, a social gospel, and New Age religion, [these few in no way exhaust the list]. In this book we will be concerned with a fifth, the recovery and restoration of the "evangelical gospel" which is precisely what the Bible teaches the gospel to be.

The Evangelical Gospel in the Black Church

The oldest and dearest explanation to that question adopted by the Black Church is called the "evangelical gospel." This is the gospel message encountered and embraced as the slaves listened to the preaching of many white evangelists, itinerants, and preachers in the 1700's. According to Henry Mitchell it was particularly the preaching of Evangelist George Whitfield. He writes:

It would be an over-estimate the influence of George Whitfield for it was he more than any other who not only revived a dying Protestantism but also built the bridge over which it could travel to a spiritually hungry and brutally oppressed people from Africa.[60]

In addition to the popular and influential preaching of Whitfield, as stated in an earlier section, many African-American preachers, and pastors received their training through apprenticeships with white clergymen. Naturally their training would have included immersion into the evangelical assumptions of the broader white church. However, this does not mean African Americans adopted verbatim whatever was being taught by the white preachers.

Yet, the historical record clearly establishes that from the earliest generations until the present day an evangelical gospel tradition has existed in the Black Church. The gospel according to Black evangelicals is summed up in four points beginning with the truth about God:

1. Black evangelicals believe that God created the universe and that as Creator He owns it. God is righteous and holy, and He is sovereign and He rules the universe with justice for His own glory and the highest happiness for His creatures.
2. Black evangelicals believe the gospel tells us the truth about the nature and the future of humanity. God made humankind in His own image and likeness for an eternal fellowship with Himself (Genesis 1:26-27). However, our first parents, Adam and Eve, rebelled against God by breaking His commandment not to eat of the tree of the knowledge of good and evil. When they disobeyed God, sin entered and corrupted and distorted the world and everyone who would be born in it. Sin has alienated humanity from God. Because of sin every person faces a coming judgment (Romans 1:18-32; Revelation 20:11-15).
3. Black evangelicals believe God has made a way of escape from His wrath. Man is unable to save Himself. But God in His love (John 3:16), sent His Son, Jesus, into the world, born of a virgin, fully God and fully man, sinless and perfect to be righteousness for us (Romans 5:8; 1 Corinthians 1:30) and to become a curse for us so that sinners through faith in Him, could become the righteousness of God (Galatians 3:13-14). Jesus' death [crucifixion], burial, and resurrection accomplished the reconciliation of sinners with a holy God. And He has made us His ministers of reconciliation.
4. Black evangelicals believe that the "good news" centers on the reconciliation of fallen humanity with a perfectly holy God. And the righteous life, atoning death, and justifying resurrection of Jesus Christ; which demands a response from those who hear and receive it (1 Corinthians 5:1-4; Romans 10:9-10; Acts 2:38). Those who turn from sin and follow Jesus, trusting His promise of righteousness and eternal life, are forever joined to Him and His life now becomes theirs (Galatians 2:20).

The gospel of liberation

Another view of the gospel in the Black churches is the "gospel of liberation." The main champion of the liberation gospel or black theology as it is called is Dr. James H. Cone, professor of systematic theology at Union Theological Seminary in New York. Cone's view is centered on the person of Jesus Christ, but his definition of Jesus and His work is different from the evangelical view. Cone wrote, Jesus is God Himself entering humanity for the sole purpose of setting free blacks whose existence is threatened daily by white power.[61]

One of the foundational texts Cone used for Black Theology is Luke 4:18-19 where Jesus cited Isaiah's prophecy of His work concerning human liberation:

- Preaching the good news to the poor,
- Release of the captives,
- Recovering of sight to the blind,
- Set at liberty those who are oppressed.

Many in the Black Church heard of Black Theology or liberation gospel for the first time, when on national and international media Rev. Jeremiah A. Wright Jr. called on God to "damn America" for her many historical and contemporary acts of oppression.

The prosperity gospel

Then, there is a view of the gospel growing in many local Black churches, the prosperity gospel. The definition of this gospel is expanded to include physical, emotional, material, social, and prosperity *in this life*. Through their dominance of television and other media; promoters of the prosperity gospel have tremendous influence on many members in Black congregations.

The world has its lottery and the American church has her prosperity gospel!

Sadly, in many cases the people mostly attracted to these prosperity philosophies, are the poor and others who can least afford to participate financially. At every flip of the TV channels these days we find so-called "evangelists" who tell us to send them "seed money" and by obediently doing so:

- the very act will break curses
- we can watch for our inheritance because it's on the way
- we will be healed from all physical ailments

- God will open the windows of heaven and send financial and physical blessings

Like Israel of old, today people love what they are hearing. Jeremiah wept over the people, but the false prophets did not. They were prophets of a false hope – but a hope indeed. Jeremiah rejected the false prophets' lop-sided emphasis that God had chosen the nation and therefore they could presume on His unending favor – despite their lifestyle. Look again at the promises above (see Jeremiah 5:30-31). Too many are preaching a gospel as a means of self-exaltation that humbles no one.

Prosperity knits a man to the world. He feels that he is "finding his place in it," while really it is finding its place in him.[62] C. S. Lewis

---

We can obviously see from the Scriptures, the fact that Jesus values the soul of a person well above all the riches and benefits this world has to offer. Nothing of any earthly value comes near the worth of the eternal human soul. Therefore, the salvation of souls carries the highest priority of importance for the church and the individual Christians as well – over liberation and prosperity in this life. In his evangelical critique of both the prosperity and the liberation gospels Anthony Carter writes:

"What was once the treasure chest of the church namely, [the person of Christ and the message of the gospel has during the last half of the twentieth century been exchanged for social expedience and financial gain]."

What has been lost, indeed forfeited, is an uncompromised, orthodox, biblical view of Jesus and the message of the gospel that saves sinners from the death that is due all of us because of our sin. What has been lost is the unique message and calling of the church."[63]

New Age spirituality

Many of our children do not feel at home in most local churches today; they prefer to be involved in groups where they are personally involved in sharing, caring for the poor and continuous relationships. Neither do they like normal worship services that follow a printed script or for that matter to follow the dictates of organized religion.

They are not moved by the standards of decorum of formal worship, to them there is no vitality to be found there. This generation is uncomfortable with being told what to believe – but are committed to finding a faith that fits them:

- They are more comfortable with marginalized people who don't meet the formal demands of the church.
- Despite great qualities, they are prone to seek spiritual experiences outside of Bible doctrines.

New Age, a widely accepted spirituality in our culture, and sadly in some cases taught right alongside biblical teaching in our churches – some say in order to be more relevant? They believe that through "contemplation" they can connect with God in the soul of their being. About 28% of practicing Christians strongly agree that "all people pray to the same god or spirit, no matter what they use for that spiritual being. The same percentage believe that "meaning and purpose come from becoming one with all that is." There is no need for a specific doctrine or biblical teaching; what matters is a technique to access the "god within.[64]

New Age spirituality is attractive to many who are disappointed with traditional church for a number of reasons. People want spirituality, but not religion:

- Listen to Professor of religion Jerome P. Blaggett, people are saying, "Yes, I want to have a connection to the sacred, but I want to do it on my own terms, terms that honour who I am as a discerning, thoughtful agent and that affirms my day-to-day life.[65]
- Thomas Merton a Catholic who was greatly influenced by Eastern religion writes that "at the center of our being is a point of nothingness which is untouched by sin and illusion, a point of pure truth….. This little point of nothingness ….. is the pure glory of God in us… It is in everybody."[66] Merton also wrote that "it is a glorious destiny to be a member of the human race … Now I realize what we all are …. If only people could really see themselves as the really are … I suppose the big problem would be that we would fall down and worship each other."[67]
- The bottom line is, as you find God in the depths of your soul, your consciousness ends up being "god." Everyone has "god" already within them. These people want a theology that waters down the horrors of sin and elevates the goodness of humanbeings.
- They want a god who thinks like they think – who is broadminded as they are. A god who winks at all the moral depravity, and human secularism that's bringing God's judgment upon America. Certainly, as the American church stands by silently, their agenda is being fulfilled! The apostle Paul has some input, listen:

"For the time is coming when people will not endure sound teaching, but having itching ears they will accumulate for themselves teachers that suit their own passions, and will turn away from listening to the truth and wander off into myths" (2 Timothy 4:3-4). We are living in that day, folks.

Sadly, it seems we find people in every generation who willingly follow these false prophets from pillar to post waiting for the bonus they promise – namely a special revelation from God just for you (see Jeremiah 14:14). Not only was their apostleship false, so also was their doctrine, as Satan's emissaries of false teaching, they were under the curse of (Galatians 1:8,9).

Paul knew that we would encounter the same deceivers in our day:

"For such men are false apostles, deceitful workmen, disguising themselves as apostles of Christ. And no wonder! For even Satan himself transforms himself into an angel of light. Therefore, it is no great thing if his ministers also transform themselves into ministers of righteousness, whose end will be according to their works" (2 Corinthians 11:13-5).

Where is the Black Church Today?

More and more African American churches are facing a crisis in today's culture. They are out of touch with the shifting culture and going through many questionable activities just to keep their doors open. These churches are living in the past as the world moves away at a high-rate of speed. This condition has led many churches to the inability to reach the post-civil rights generations.

I believe the Black church reached her peak [spiritually and influence wise] during the 50's, and 60's, a period known by some historians as the Civil Rights era. During that period the church was considered the bedrock of the community impacting and often transforming the lives of people inside and outside of the church [do you remember the chairs in the aisles] during preaching services and community meetings?

However, this is no longer true, particularly among the post-Civil Rights generations. Why? Because many African American churches are still working with [now more than 60 years old] evangelistic and discipleship programs and practices from the Civil Rights era.

What seems impossible with men is possible with God.

Insistance and reliance upon those assumptions have put many churches *out of touch* with people not in the church. Noticably, much of the Black Church is losing her spirituality [voluntarily]. There is a struggle for such churches to embody the gospel of Jesus Christ in a manner that speaks to the people in post-Civil Rights generations. This is especially true for many of the Black traditional institutional churches; that follow a set format introduced many years ago by their founders. Many have a form of godliness that denies the Holy Spirit and His gifts and ministries.

Haste makes waste

Through frustrations many local churches are frantically "brain storming" and making various attempts with new assumptions to maintain their status quo. However, such surface changes prevent them from growing and reaching new people for Christ. Failure is inevitable when churches attempt to introduce new wineskins of evangelistic methodolgy and discipleship practices into old wineskins from past generations, because the old wineskins will "burst." Jesus continues, "No one pours new wine into old wineskins ….. instead, people pour new wine into new wineskins for the safety of all [paraphrased]. Even though some old assumptions and practices from prior generations are slowly disintegrating all around them, many Black churches continue to believe the problem is not them and have begun finger pointing:

1.   The old unanointed wineskin claims that the church was founded on the old practices; and new practices are not needed.
2.   New people come in here with the intention of "upsetting the apple cart." It was good enough for my mother – it's good enough for me.
3.   The unanointed wineskin mentally begins to blame the struggle on limited resources in comparison to other churches.

Lest we forget, the Civil Rights Movement's successes were built on much corporate prayer and faith in Almighty God to lead and guide them:

Much Prayer – Much Power! & Little Prayer – Little Power!

As mentioned in another section, our light is borrowed, as is the light of the moon. Only Jesus Christ, the Light of the World, is able to keep us.

It was recorded that when Augustine was told about the fall of Rome to the Vandals, he felt deep sadness because he loved that city. He also believed its demise was a judgment for its sins, lamenting, "Whatever men build, men will destroy." Let's go on with Christ building His Church.

Love your Church

It is part of Christ's eternal plan that He have a beloved body of people called out of the world, redeemed by His blood, and truly committed in love to Him. Jesus said, "I will build my church" (Matthew 16:18). As stated throughout:

- "He is the Head over everything for the church" (Ephesians 1:22).
- "He is the Head of the body, the church" (Colossians 1:18).
- "He wants God's wisdom to be proved to the angels and the world by the church" (Ephesians 3:10).
- "Christ loves the church; and He chose the church to be His eternal bride (Revelation" 21:1-3).
- "Christ wants the church to be spiritually well-fed, spiritually secure, spiritually radiant, and spiritually adorned as His beloved bride."

If we are to share in the blessings of the Lord, the Black church individually and corporately must come into the knowledge that there is a price to be paid for the church. When asked why people line up for blocks around the Brooklyn Tabernacle before the doors are opened for their Tuesday night prayer meetings, the pastor Jim Cymbala said, "Your people would pray too if they actually believed that God answered prayer!"

"Your people would pray too If they actually believed that God answers prayer!"

We are to love the church and give ourselves away in service and even suffer for her. Christ was willing to give Himself even to die for it. As ministers of reconciliation, we may not be called upon to make that extreme a sacrifice, but as every-member ministers, we are committed to time, love, effort, and life-blood; which will make us the servants of the church.

Paul called himself a servant of Jesus Christ (Romans 1:1) and a servant of the gospel (Colossians 1:23), but Paul went on to rejoice in being a servant of the church (v. 25). Yes, for Jesus' sake we become in many respects servants of the church. Amen! Let's us remember, repent, and return to our first Love!

REFLECTIONS: CHAPTER 9

1. Discuss the new class structure in communities resulting from the great urban movement of African Americans to the larger cities.

2. How did placing more emphasis on economic, social and political problems; and less emphasis salvation and the life beyond, affect the African American Churchrs and communities?

3. Discuss the effects of syncretism in the local Black churches.

4. Compare prosperity and liberation gospel with evangelical gospel.

5. What was George Whitfield's contribution to African Americans during the "Great Awakening?"

Chapter 10

THE CHURCH A
LIVING ORGANISM

*"But you are a chosen generation, a royal priesthood,
a holy nation, His own special people, that you may
proclaim the praises of Him who called you out of darkness
into His marvelous light; who once were not a people but
are now the people of God, who had not obtained mercy
but now have obtained mercy"*(I Peter 2:9-10).

We need to recover and restore the true meaning of the gospel of Jesus Christ and the body of Christ that gives light and life to every person who believes and recieves it. Sadly, much of the African American church missed the great Spiritual move of God in the great Azusa Street revival – wherein an African American preacher named William Seymour was invited to preach in an integrated revival at a Black Holiness Church in Los Angeles in April 1906. The revival set for a week or so, lasted three years.[68]

Born out of that great move of God were: The Church of God in Christ, the Assemblies of God, the Church of the Nazarene; and other churches of the Pentecostal persuasion were formed later.[69] With that revival, the Holy Spirit and His gifts and ministries returned to the local church. The Pentecostal flame began to move after more than eleven hundred years of Roman Catholicism as the dispository of Christianity. Later, that flame became the Pentecostal/ Charismatic Movement that is still sweeping across many traditional and institutional denominational lines throughout the world today.[70] We witness this move of the Spirit especially in what was called third world countries in South America, Africa, and parts of the Middle East. Praise God!

Many Black institutional churches are in decline or no longer active due to the church no longer being the center for the African American community. Additionally, numerous losses in attendance and membership – are the results of the churches [resistance to change] having settled for a modified European model that relies mainly on science and reason; and views the church as an organization rather than a living spiritual organism.

The spiritual organism is totally dependent on the Holy Spirit and the Word of God for life and guidance. The context of the letter to the Laodiceans (Revelation 3:20), demands that Christ was seeking to enter the church that bore His name but it lacked a single true believer. If one member would recognize his spiritual bankruptcy and respond in saving faith, He would enter the church. Many churches and individual Christians find themselves in this same predicament today. Though this letter was written to the church of the Laodiceans, [the people's church] note the concluding verse [pertains to today's churches also]: *"He who has an ear, hear what the Spirit says to the churches."*

I read an article concerning a person who took specific action when the plane that hit the Pentagon on 9/11, no doubt saving lives. One of the large rooms was so filled with smoke and fast approaching fire that people were blinded, disoriented, unable to find their way out. But one person who did find the exit door, kept shouting, "Follow my voice!" So even though the people were blinded by the thick soot and smoke, they followed the voice that led them to safety. Blessed are those who hear what the Spirit is saying to the churches – today! "Follow My voice!"

More than maintainers?

Sadly, many of our pastors are mere "maintainers." They are striving to preach to please and maintain the status quo, (hierarchy), formed when their denomination was first established. Their attitude is, "that which works for me." Additionally, many are busy maintaining the organization and the physical facilities; while their congregations slowly fade away.

It is Christ's desire to use *all* of His church members for greater demonstrations of His glory and kingdom power in the manifestation and growth of His body, a living spiritual organism. At the same time, those Bible-believing Black Pentecostal/ Charismatic churches in spiritual organism, [no matter the denomination] are continuing to be among the fastest growing churches around the world.

We will see in a later chapter how God is doing this through the Holy Spirit's gifts and ministries in spiritual organism[71] through the five-fold ministers ministering all present truth to the church worldwide until it becomes sanctified in humility, purity, maturity, ministry and unity (Ephesians 4:11-15; I Cor. 12-14; Romans 12).

We were made for more

I believe God will deploy a generation of Spirit-filled and Word-empowered [ordinary people] to come forth with courage and extraordinary ministry – to restore witness-evangelism, discipleship, and the other tenets of the Great Commission. If we do our part, God will do His. Embeded in the larger story of redemption we find a principle: <u>God uses ordinary people to do extraordinary things in the lives of others.</u> They will bring compassion and salvation to the greatest ever harvest of souls on a global level. What synod, convention, conference or church today would use:

- Moses – an exiled murderer?
- David – a shepherd boy with no military training?
- Peter – who publicly denied Christ?
- Paul – persecuted the Church of Jesus Christ?
- Jesus – had no place to lay His head?

God wants to use the "all My people" – "all the time" New Testament model. Many would be pleased if God used only trained pofessionals; but it's not so with God. However, with God we need the ministry of the whole body of Christ until sanctification is complete in glory. The whole body [a living organism] will grow to perfection [completion]. We are sanctified through the Word; so that we are not tossed about with every wind and doctrine.

We were made for more – in fact, today we can't effectively witness until we are maturing in Spirit and in Truth – note the goals:

- Unity (oneness)
- Faith (Jude 3)
- Knowledge of Christ (Doctrine)
- Speaking the truth in love (every member)

Evangelism, discipleship and all other Christian service means, God is invading a battlefield and you and I are the weapons He uses to attack and defeat the enemy. When God builds a ministry, He needs somebody's *surrendered* body to get the job done. It was reported that at Evangelist Billy Graham's funeral a news reporter asked, "Who will replace Billy Graham?" A lady standing near by, heard the question and boldly replied, "We will!"

Praise God! Remember, "God shed His love abroad in the hearts and gave us the Holy Spirit," who came into each true believer at conversion and took up residence [Romans 5:5]. We see reflected in the lady's answer to the question – Christ's goal for evangelism is [all believers to be committed and deployed in His kingdom work equipped with the gospel of Christ].

We are to interact with the world in our places of employment, neighborhoods, schools, recreation, family, and public service areas, however, we are to represent Christ at all times and do all things "for the glory of God." All true believers are clothed in Christ's righteousness (2 Corinthians 5:21) which sets a righteous atmosphere in and around us satuated with His Presence. Remember, we are not to allow the world's polution to contaminate us. We are in the world, but not of the world. Spiritual ministry demands spiritual power (see Acts 1:8; John 7:38-39; 16:13).

If our loved ones, friends and contacts go to hell because they were not properly loved, blessed, prayed for, witnessed to and warned, who will be held accountable? In Ezekiel 318-19, we [the members] will be accountable. But if pastors fail to teach their people, they will be held responsible. At any rate the pastor will be held accountable. Ezekiel says, "this will mean blood on their hands."

Today, a chief responsibility of all pastors and other church and ministry leaders is to prepare every member to participate in an all-out harvest of intercession and witness-evangelism to complete Christ's unfinished task, His great eternal plan. For all we do to that end, He will eternally reward us. Although we know this is God's priority for the church in this age, many local churches for some generations have so neglected this task that they are like dead men walking.

Restoring Church membership

Today it is not uncommon to see a number of local Black churches operate without concern for visible church membership; with the main interests on building size and numbers, the Old Testament approach, while others just think it is unbiblical and emphasize the importance of spiritual membership in the body of Christ. However, in the Old Testament (see Isaiah 52:11) and New Testament (see II Corinthians 5:17), God called His people to come out from among the other nations:

Old Testament

In the Old Testament there was to be a clear line between being *in covenant* with God and being *outside the covenant* of God's people. They were treasured by God because He loved them, He chose them, and He fought for them. Israel was to be a visible, distinct, holy community in which He lived with His people.

Their future was guaranteed because God was sure to keep His promises. Moses reminds Israel that "as for you, the Lord took you and brought you out of the iron furnace, out of *Egypt, to be His people of His inheritance, as you are this day*" (Deuteronomy 4:20).

> *"For you are a holy people in the Lord your God;*
> *the Lord your God has chosen to be*
> *a people for Himself, a special treasure above*
> *all the peoples on the face of the earth.*
> *The Lord did not set His love on you nor choose you*
> *because you were more in number*
> *than any other people, for you were the*
> *least of all peoples; but because the Lord loves you,*
> *and because He would keep the oath which*
> *He swore to your fathers; the Lord has brought you*
> *out with a mighty hand, and redeemed you*
> *from the house of bondage, from the hand*
> *of Pharaoh of Egypt.*
> *Therefore, know that the Lord your God, He is God,*
> *the faithful God who keeps covenant*
> *and mercy for a thousand generations.*
> *with those who love Him and keeps*
> *His commandments."*
> Deuteronomy 7:6-9

An Israelite's entire identity and purpose depended on their membership in the community. As God's people, Israel needed to be *separated* from the moral pollution of the Canaanites all around them. The choosing of Israel as a holy nation set apart for God was grounded in God's love and His faithfulness to the promises He made to the patriarchs – not through any merit or intrinsic goodness in Israel.

New Testament

Many people personally and corporately fail to understand that the same pattern of *separation* for the Old Testament follows in the New Testament pattern. However, they do understand that the coming of Jesus Christ opened the way for a new covenant not with Israel only, but all the nations of the earth.

> *But you are a chosen generation, a royal priesthood, a holy nation. His own special people, that you may proclaim the praises of Him who called you out of darkness into His marvelous light* (1 Peter 1:9).

The New Testament takes the foundation laid out to Israel in the Old Testament and extends it to all those brought into new covenant relationship with God through faith in the redemptive work of Jesus Christ. The New Testament's view of church membership also includes and "in" and "out," but not dependent upon sociology nor ethnicity. The New Testament church membership relies upon union with Christ through faith. The word "member" or "part" comes from the *"body of Christ"* metaphor used by Paul to describe the Christian church. He wrote, *"You are the body* [a living spiritual organism[72]] *of Christ, and each one of you is a part [member] of it"* (I Corinthians 1:27). Emphasis added throughout. It is very important that we keep in mind, Paul wrote this letter to a visible local church not to the invisible, universal church.

I believe the Lord is producing a people who stand in their identity, fully realizing who they are *"in Christ"* and who Christ is *in them*. A new breed of evangelism and discipleship is not impossible. So, the "in" and "out" means that people are either "in Christ" or they are "out" and "separated from Christ, alienated from the commonwealth of Spiritual Israel and strangers to the covenants of promise, having no hope and without God in the world" (see Ephesians 2:12).

God took great care in designing the body of Christ. Each Person in the Trinity plays a part in assembling the members of the local church. The body is a unit [spiritual organism] though it is made up of many members; and though all its members are many, they form one body. So, it is *in* Christ.

> *"For as the body is one and has many members, but all the members of that one body being many are one body, so also is Christ. For by one Spirit we were all baptized into one body — whether Jews or Greeks, whether slaves or free — and have all been made to drink into one Spirit. For in fact the body is not one member but many"* (I Corinthians 12:12-14).

While stressing the gifts in (vv. 4-11); Paul also emphasized the single Source, the Holy Spirit, (vv. 4-6, 8-9). We are united to Christ through faith, and our status is reflected in our membership in visible local churches. In conjunction with membership there is the foundational requirement of a two-fold separation from whatever is contrary to the mind of God, and unto God Himself. Clearly, the member is not to compromise with evil:

1. Separation from anything which unites a child of God and an unbeliever in a common purpose is "unequally yoked."
2. Separation from evil desires, motives, habits, acts; and they are to disengage themselves from all forms of false teaching and idolatrous patterns of religion (II Corinthians 6:17; Ephesians 5:6-12; 2 Timothy 2:20-23).

Be separate is a command not a suggestion nor recommendation, but all believers to be as Christ was. As a result of their separation from false doctrine and practices, believers will know the full riches of what it means to be children of God. In the next chapter, we'll see that the Source of spiritual gifts is the Holy Spirit who gives the gifts as He wills – but they are to be received with love, humility and in the unity with other believers (see Hebrews 10:25).

The special covenant relationship is transferred to the church, which Jesus purchased with His own blood. Peter said, *"You are a people of God's own possession"* (I Peter 2:9). Out of all the peoples [ethnos] of the earth, there is *a special people* [Laos] who are God's "called-out people." It is key that we understand that the people of God [Laos] is a new creation of humanity, a token of the kingdom of God [a work He has begun and will complete], **a people of the future living in the present!**

It is very instructive to note the apostle Paul's salutations in the letters he wrote to the churches always addressed the *whole* church never in terms of a select leadership [top down, hierarchy]. The church is *all* the people of God, not a representative group such as pastors, elders, deacons or stewards as is seen in much of the American church.

In six of the nine epistles addressed to the churches, Paul's salutation is to the "saints" (Roman 1:7; 1 Corinthians 1:2; 2 Corinthians 1:1; Ephesians 1:1; Philippians 1:1; Colossians 1:2).

The term "saints" is used fifty-six times in the New Testament – but never in the singular. "Saints" is a noun, but as a verb it means "sanctified, holy and godly." It always refers to the entire body of believers, not to an a individual.

I believe this is a very important point today as individualism is promoted as a godly trait even over humility in many local churches. Again, notice Paul's usage in his greeting to the Corinthians,

"To the church of God which is at Corinth, to those sanctified in Christ Jesus, called to be saints, with all those who in every place call on the name of Jesus Christ, our Lord, both theirs and ours" (I Corinthians 1:2).

The phrase that precedes "called to be saints" is the key to the meaning of the word. We are saints because of what has been done for us – *"sanctified in Jesus Christ."* "Sanctified" means we are made holy by Christ, and not through our own efforts.

Remembering what was said about the Corinthian Church in other chapters; does it surprise you that the Corinthians would be the church to receive such distinction? Saints refer to keeping one's ways pure.

The Corinthian church was:

- Marked by a party and proud spirit (1 Corinthians 1:12).
- Carnal and on the milk of the Word (1 Corinthians 3:2-3).
- Immorality was allowed in the church (1 Corinthians 5:1).
- Profaned the Lord's Supper (1 Corinthians 11:27).

Paul demonstrates the all-around scope of sainthood by calling the Corinthians "saints together with *all* those *everywhere* who call on the name of our Lord and Savior, Jesus Christ (I Corinthians 1:2). We have wandered so far from *biblical inclusivity* by narrowing saints to a restrictive few whom the people in many cases are led to believe excel them in godliness.

The best witness for Christ is a changed life!

We need to return to the Reformation doctrine of the communion of the saints, which views all of God's people – past, present, and future as a part of an eternal fellowship linked by our common life *in* Jesus Christ. The theme of this chapter is an explanation why the church did not make a totally clean break from the traditional Roman Catholic institutional concept of ministry.

If the church is going to be recovered, restored and returned to the people of God, we must experience the church as a living spiritual organism rather than the non-spiritual organization found within many Black *traditional institutional* churches that practice the top down concept of leadership.

The Body of Christ, an Organism

In the introduction I stated that we live in perilous times, but at the same time we live in a moment when the ministry is rightly being returned to the people of God. Therefore, to receive the fruit that the Holy Spirit is producing, we must recapture the biblical vision of the fundamental nature of the church. For those who are hearing what the Spirit is saying to the churches and *are* obediently *"teaching them [their people] to observe [obey]* **all things** *that I have commanded you"* realize (see Matthew 28:18-20), that many of the local Black churches are experiencing a radical shift from the church as a traditional institution to spiritual organism, body life, through the power of the Holy Spirit and His gifts and ministries resident in the believers or they join the list of dying churches. The church was never intended to become a *cultural* social club [emphasis added throughout].

The theological position of each church will serve as the basis for our discernment of truth concerning God's will for His people. Organism means the church in its essence is quickened to life in Christ, *".... ... because the love of God has been poured out in our hearts by the Holy Spirit who was given unto us"* (Romans 5:5). **1)** Now justified by His blood – these are [*seeds of righteousness to be developed*] to maturity through **2)** sanctification through the Word of God. It's high time for evangelism to move from getting someone to simply decide. Christ's command was and remains to "make disciples!" Believing right things is imperative; however, like Jesus' disciples, we must also seek to do the right things:

- Disciples *[learners]* are dedicated to learning their master's truths, so they can imitate His life and grow in Christlikeness.
- Disciples embrace His mission and serve His purposes.
- Disciples plan their lives around His teachings and commands.

Those who believe without practical application make their own plans for their lives – then expect the Lord to bless them. Listen to Jesus' rebuke to them:

> *"But why do you call Me Lord, Lord,*
> *and not do*
> *the things which I say?"*
> (Luke 6:46).

It is not healthy to give lip service to the service of the Lord! Genuine faith produces genuine obedience to all He commands. "A good man out of the good treasure of his heart brings forth good; and out of the heart of an evil man comes evil. For out of the abundance of the heart his mouth speaks" (Luke 6:45). Many Christians today are like the people in Jesus' parable of the sower who "hear the word; but the worries of this life, the deceitfulness of riches, and the desires for other things come in and choke the word, and it becomes unfruitful (see Luke 4:18-19).

There is a shallow gospel [tickle the ear type] making the rounds that is void of such terminology as: "repentance," "sin," "forgiveness," "blood," "righteousness," "sacrifice," "commitment," "dedication, faithfulness, and truthfulness." As stated earlier, concerning such a gospel:

- It is not the gospel the apostles preached?
- It lacks power to change people and win them for Christ.
- It is comfortable with the status quo.
- It does not make any demands on our lifestyle or behavior.
- It let's us do what we want with our money.
- It does not require you to feed the hungry, clothe the naked, or heal and care for the sick.
- It does not require taking a stand against injustice in our world.

Certainly, there is nothing mentioned about such a gospel to require the radicalism of Christ's disciples. What happened to Jesus' great mission to transform humanity, model the values of the kingdom, and make disciples of all nations? He said the church would storm the gates of hell! Sometimes I think we forget that this is an eternal matter. We are in a revolution! That is why it is imperative to get the *gospel* right, the *whole* gospel, because without *real* disciples the revolution will die!

Embracing the call to decide for Christ – is not the same as embracing the call to become a *disciple* of Christ!

I shudder when I think of the many years, I had little understanding of the Kingdom of God and the Church's mission therein. Yes, becoming a disciple of Christ does begin with a decision – but that decision must be followed by a *radically* new way of living:

1. Under God's authority
2. Under God's truth
3. Under God's virtues and values

Think about it, I am not concerned with entering God's kingdom when I die; through Christ's death and resurrection – I am in His kingdom now! Praise God! The gospel is all about Jesus, His story, in that God's kingdom has come and Jesus is the King (see Colossians 1:13-14). Oh! How much more serious is our commitment to follow our King, Jesus Christ, and to embrace His mission in the world.

Jesus' death on the cross to atone for our sins made it possible for us to get citizenship in His kingdom. I will illustrate what this means by example: I enlisted into the U.S. Army and upon doing so I turned my life over to a higher authority. From the first day everything about my life became governed by the U. S. Army. For the next 26 ½ years until retirement: where I would live, and how I would spend the day were subject to the will of the Army.

I was trained according to the Army's purposes and I embraced the Army's goals and mission. I went where the army sent me, to include combat in Vietnam. In battle our mission was to win; and to die for this nation while engaged if necessary. We can expect no less as we are involved in kingdom building with our King!

It begins with our personal transformation. Like the military, Jesus taught us a very different way of living based on:

- His truth
- His virtues
- His values
- His priorities

We submit our will for God's will for *our lives*. We commit to the lifelong process of becoming like His Son. We make that commitment to be His disciple the number one priority in our lives, organizing every other aspect of our lives to support that goal – to the glory of God! He has invited each of us [who are His], to partner with Him in offering *life* in the kingdom *to others*. How? We do this by manifesting the glory of God.

To Paul this power was so essential in his ministry, that he was willing to pay any price so that Christ's glory could rest on him. It was Paul's heart cry to God for more of Your power upon me: Oh! For more of Your power manifest through me!" More of the abiding power of Christ communicated through the Spirit (see 2 Corinthians 12:9). Christ had promised power when the Holy Spirit came upon His disciples (Acts 1:8). Paul had experienced that power over and over again. He wanted that power to *"rest"* on him. The Greek word means *"to tabernacle."* Just as Christ came and *tabernacled* among us during His incarnation (see John 1:14, where the same Greek word is used), so Paul counts his highest ambition in ministry to have Christ's power day by day *tabernacle* over him.

Most commentators recognize in this heart cry a reference to the *Shekinah glory of God:*

- It was over the tabernacle in the wilderness, and entered the tent and covered the ark of the covenant.
- Later it entered the temple and "tabernacle" over the ark in the holy of holies.

As the Shekinah glory covered the ark, Paul wanted Christ's power to cover him, overshadow him, and continually rest upon him. Jesus had told him that such power *"is made perfect in weakness"* (2 Corinthians 12:9). Weakness does not create power. But weakness drives us *all* the more to God, the source of our hearts. When through revelation Paul recognized his *thorn in the flesh* (v. 7), all the other opposition, dangers, and sufferings during all the years of service to Christ (see 2 Corinthians 11:23-30) served to drive him closer to God and to constant dependence upon God, the apostle responded, "That is why hardships, in persecutions, in difficulties, for which I am weak, then I am strong" (2 Corinthians 12:10).

How important is having the power of Christ tabernacling, resting, remaining upon you? Filled with that power, clothed with that power, energized by that power, endued for your ministry by that power! That power is the Spirit, that power is Christ Himself (1 Corinthians 1:24) manifest and available through the Spirit today (see 1 Peter 1:11).

The anointing for liberty and skill

The Scripture declares, "We all have sinned and come short of the glory of God" (Romans 3:23). It is a reality, man is incapable of satisfying God's justice apart from Christ, except by spending eternity in hell (see 1 John 2:2).

Every kingdom is organized into communities as states, cities, or villages. The local church is the organizing factor of God's kingdom, because those who chose to live under God's rule and according to His truth, must be shining examples of a radically different way for people to live [personally and corporately].

These local Christian communities come together around worship, discipleship, and mission *all for the glory of God* – described in the New Testament as the household of God, the people of God, the Bride of Christ, and a fellowship of the Holy Spirit. But the flag-ship image that dominates the New Testament and serves as a hold for all of them is the body of Christ – which is the proper metaphor to paint a picture of the church as a spiritual and living organism. Imbedded in the phrase "the body of Christ" we find *three essentials* which provide the essence for understanding who we are *in* Christ:

1. Christ's relationship to His church

The apostle Paul selected the image of the human body to illustrate the spiritual truth of Christ's relationship to His church. Note: 1 Corinthians 12:12:

> *"For just as the body is one and have many members, and all the members of the body, though many are one, so it is with Christ."*

For Paul the body of Christ is more than a metaphor, as it points to the reality of the truth that Jesus dwells in His people and gives His life to them. In his book *Body Life,* Ray Stedman writes, "The life of Jesus is still being manifest among people, but no longer through an individual physical body, limited to one place on earth, but through a complex, corporate body called "the church."[73]

Jesus dwells in His people, His corporate body, to whom He has given His life. When you touch Christians, you have touched Christ. Christians are a sacramental people. A sacrament is a means of grace – it is a symbol that mysteriously bears the presence [shekinah glory] of Christ and through which believers encounter Him (Hebrews 10:25). The church then is a conduit of Christ.

In John 12:20-22, several men from Greece had heard about Jesus, His teachings, and His miracles, and they wanted to meet with Him. Phillip serves as a conduit and leads these foreigners to Jesus. Once again, those who want to see Jesus can do so through Phillip. How nice it would be if we could all do witness-evangelism that way, taking people to meet Jesus face-to-face? We don't have the same tangible access to Jesus that Phillip had. However, in John 14, Phillip also wants to see someone who is unseen and invisible. He wants to see God the Father? Later when Jesus declares to His disciples, "I am the way, the truth and the life. No one comes to the Father except through Me" (John 14:6). Phillip, don't you know me, even after I have been so long with you? Anyone who has seen Me has seen the Father ... Don't you believe that I am in the Father, and that the Father is in Me?" (14:9-10). Jesus is making clear to Phillip that He is the One who makes the invisible God visible.

In the beginning of his gospel, John says of Jesus, that "the Word was made flesh and dwelt among us. We have seen His glory, the glory of the

One and Only, who came from the Father, full of *grace* and *truth*" (John 1:14). John concludes with these words:

"No one has ever seen God, but God the One and Only Jesus, who is at the Father's side – has made Him known" (1:18). Jesus came to make the invisible God visible to us, full of grace and truth; and from that fullness "we have all received one blessing after another" (1:16).

In othe words, Jesus was so full of grace that when people interacted with Him, they were amazed by something very different. "He must have come from God," people exclaimed, no other explanation was sensible after meeting Jesus.

Jesus, by His very nature, made the invisible God visible to sinful human beings. "He is the image of the invisible God ... For God was pleased to have all His *fullness* dwell in Him." Jesus was so full of God's grace that when you interacted with Him you knew, that you were dealing with the invisible God.

The church of God as the living spiritual organism, Christ's body is further upheld in Paul's conclusion:

> *"..... And He [God] put all things under His feet and has made Him the Head over all things for the church, which is His body, the fullness of Him who fills all in all"* (Ephesians 1:22-23). Emphasis added.

We do not understand what the church is and its nature until we grasp the unspeakable truth that Jesus extends His life on earth through a corporate people that can literally be called, "the body of Christ."

2. The church's relationship to Christ

Just as we can all testify that the parts of the human body cannot function without the head; neither can the church which is totally dependent upon its Head, Jesus Christ. The church's relationship to Christ is cemented in Paul's expression that Jesus is, *"Head over all things for the church"* (Ephesians 1:22). Biblically the word *Head* in reference to Christ has two meanings:

(1) source of life
(2) supreme authority

By their actions, too many pastors seem to believe that the church has two heads. It has been said, anything with two-heads belongs in a circus. The church has only one Head, Jesus Christ. The pastors like the rest of the body of Christ take their commands from the Head.

Source of life

We are totally dependent on Jesus Christ our Lord and Savior, our Source of life for everything. Head is commonly used almost exclusively to refer to the one in charge. However, biblically it can also mean "origin." Paul uses this imagery of head as the source of nourishment in the church:

> *Rather, speaking the truth in love, we are to grow up in Him who is the Head, into Christ, from whom the whole body, joined and knit together by every joint with which it is supplied, when each part is working properly, it makes bodily growth and upbuilds itself in love* (Ephesians 4:15-16). Paul reminds the Ephesians that:

- The only way Christians become spiritual adults is to recognize their absolute reliance on Jesus Christ to supply their life.
- Christlikeness through sanctification is the goal to which they are growing to mature discipleship.

The church is dependent on Jesus Christ for its life. It is on life support! The church dies when the lifeline is cut. This is the point Jesus was making when he says, "He is the true vine and we are the branches" (study carefully John 15:1-11).

> *Abide in me, and I in you. As the branch cannot bear fruit by itself, unless it abides in the vine, neither can you, unless you abide in Me. I am the vine, you are the branches. He who abides in Me, and I in him, he it is that bears much fruit, apart from Me you can do nothing* (John 15:4-5).

Jesus did not say, "Apart from me you can do a little, or do the best you can." This is a lesson we all have to learn over and over again. Pray and seek God until He gives you His instructions, His word for the person or people. Then pray and ask God's presence for the mission. Also pray, hunger, and trust for God's special anointing on you as you lead or minister in any way:

- Don't plan and then ask God to bless your plan – Get your plans from God.
- Don't prepare and ask God – to bless your preparation.

First, get your plans from God. Ask God to guide – not in a second of prayer, but take time to seek His face. Then ask God to anoint and empower you as you minister in His name. Those who receive fresh blessings upon there own hearts before they lead, speak, or sing in the service of God on any particular occasion will see the Spirit descend in blessing upon those present as they minister.

Those who move forward in their own *self-sufficiency,* without fresh anointing from on High, may give a beautiful speech, song, or other ministry, but spiritually speaking it will be barren. Barrenness is a continuing tragedy in too much of the Black church. It may be intellectually stimulating, emotionally moving, and may receive a standing ovation from people – but the long-term spiritual results will be minimal.

The fact that the special touch of God is upon you as you witness or counsel today is no guarantee that the same touch will be upon you tomorrow. Even though you may have been powerfully anointed in one service, you may not necessarily experience the same anointing the next time. You are not so much the apple of God's eye that He will bless you whatever you do regardless of how constantly you hunger for and seek His help. Don't take God's empowerment for granted.

The Christian life is a life of faith and our calling and ministry is an activity for which we constantly appropriate by prayer and faith the ministry of the Holy Spirit.

We experience little of God's touch upon us because our asking for it is so casual and superficial.

Remember, the branch *has no life* of its own. Life flows from the vine (source) to the branches. Branches live and die by their connection to the vine. So, our responsibility as the church individually and corporately is to stay connected to our Source, Jesus Christ; and be "ready" to meet the Living God in public, private worship and service. We do that by "living to the praise of His glory." Emphasis added throughout.

Supreme Authority

Christ is the Head [Supreme authority]; and the church is under His *direct* authority. The church [His body] in relationship with Him is to faithfully and obediently fulfill the role that God has assigned to each *through the Holy Spirit.* "Jesus is Lord" means that He arranges life in the body:

- Each member is directly connected to the Head.
- Each member can receive signals from the Head.

- Each member as a part of the body in the role consummates with spiritual gifts assigned to him or her by Christ through the immediacy of the Holy Spirit who determines each person's function (1 Corinthians 12:18).
- God, the Holy Spirit arranges the spiritual gifts in the body, each one as He wills" (1 Corinthians 12:11).
- The church functions as a *spiritual organism* when those who make up the body of Christ seek to obediently fulfill their, role [spiritual gifts] that God has given them.

When coordinated according to design, the human body properly functions in a beautiful manner. The head sends the signals through the nervous system, which activates the body parts. Notice, these important facts concerning body parts:

- They have no will of their own.
- They operate or function in response to the head.
- If the hand, ear, or any other body part could operate independently of the head – there would be utter chaos in the body.

The Church is alive when it remains connected to its Source of life and is *directly* under His [Christ's] authority.

So, the body of Christ is harmonious in perfect coordination with the Head when *each* person [who makes up the body] seeks to faithfully and obediently exercise his or her *assigned* gifts. The church *is alive* when it remains connected to its life Source and is directly under His authority. The Body of Christ is gifted by the Holy Spirit in 1 Corinthians 12, and the operation of their spiritual gifts are recorded in chapter 14 – but to get there you must go in the unconditional *love* of chapter 13; trying to operate your gift without love – would be like pulling an empty wagon – just making a lot of noise.

A Word of warning

Why do so many Christians have a restless awareness that something is lacking in their Christian life and ministry? They have had adequate training; they use time wisely in preparation; they work faithfully and hard. But it all remains largely on the "fleshly" or human level:

- If you rely on training, you accomplish what training can do.
- If you rely on skills and hard work, you get what skills and hard work can obtain.
- If you rely on committee meetings, you get what committees can do.
- But when you rely on God – you get what God can do!

We are in danger of being better trained and equipped on the human level than we are empowered by the Spirit; of being more skilled and more experienced than Spirit-anointed. We can be schooled and trained to be adequate in our various skills, and administration. But we cannot be trained to be anointed and empowered – these are divinely added! Sadly, it seems that most of the church is attempting to do God's work depending only nomininally upon God – but in reality depending primarily upon ourselves, our training, our personalities, our past experience, and our knowledge.

The most important change that could happen to your Christian life and service would be for you to receive and continually experience the divine empowerment and anointing through the Holy Spirit. The difference it makes – you will never want to live or attempt anything for God individually or corporately without it (see Luke 24:49), but we must receive renewal. Once begun with the Spirit it would be foolish – trying to attain your goal by human effort (see Galatians 3:3). God has made every provision for you to have as much of the Holy Spirit's presence and power as you need to live and serve effectively for Him (see Luke 10:17-21).

3.Our relationship to others

The reality that characterizes the essence of the church is realized in spiritual organism. Being the church means sharing in divine life. Jesus lives in us. We are drawn into a new life from above. It has been said, the ground is level at the cross.

Therefore, in spiritual organism we have no choice about who our brothers and sisters are [all of us are adopted into the family of God]. The only thing we may have in common with the person in the pew next to us *in worship* service is that we are there through the mercies of God, totally undeserving.

Human organizations can set standards for membership which eliminate those they don't want or don't like for various reasons. Paul declared that racial, ethnic, socio-economic status, nor religious heritage in life has no meaning or distinction in the church. Through [one] baptism by [one] Spirit we enter this [one] divine body of Christ, and therefore find ourselves with others who have been chosen of [one] God.

According to Paul's body image, all the parts or members are interdependent and necessary for the health of the body. No individual part can function without a connection to the other parts:

- Many try to function independently inspite of the Word of God.
- "The body does not consist of one member but many" (1 Cor. 12:14).
- The church of Jesus Christ is meant to reflect the corporate restoration of the broken and marred image (Colossians 1:27).

Into our Ministry

The Scriptures say we all have ministries: "To each is given the manifestation of the Spirit for the common good" (1 Corinthians 12:7). Our ministries are defined by our spiritual gifts, through which we contribute to the good of the whole:

> "There are diversities of gifts, but the same Spirit. There are differences of ministries, but the same Lord. And there are diversities of activities, but it is the same God who works all in all. But the manifestation of the Spirit is given to each one" (I Corinthians 12:4-7).

These categories of giftedness are not natural talents, skills, or abilities such as are possessed by believers and unbelievers alike. No matter what the gift ministry is – all spiritual gifts are from the Holy Spirit. The gifts make the Holy Spirit known, understood, and His presence evident in the church and in the world, by spiritually empowering all who *receive* their ministry.

Now to conclude this section on the biblical vision of the church as spiritual organism means we are a spiritual people through whom Christ transmits His divine life to one another. We must remain connected and receive direct signals from the Head of the body, Jesus Christ. The apostle Paul exhorts, "Now you are the body of Christ and members individually" (1Corinthians 12:27).

Organization within the Organism

When the church is receiving life from the Head, the body grow organically. The congregation multiplies and ministry within the body arises spontaneously, and things begin to happen that would be impossible without the presence of God. Many in the local churches and ministries throughout this nation and the world are being led to *understand* that the church *is a* spiritual organism rather than just another organization however, that does not mean that the church is without order.

There must be some organization within the organism, the body of Christ. When Paul speaks of the church as a body, he makes it clear that no one joins that body *except by the new birth from above* through faith in the finished work of Jesus Christ. Imagine what the human body would be like without necessary order. Authority among Christians is not derived from the same source as worldly authority, nor is it to be exercised in the same manner.

As stated earlier, the world's view of authority places people over one another, as a business [hierarchy] or the military [organizational structure]. For the world system this is as it should be – the Adamic sin nature [the old man, the flesh] would have it no other way. If the church is to function properly, we must heed:

> Jesus' saying, *"It shall not be so among you"* (Mark 10:42–43). He made it clear, *"You have one teacher, and you are all brethren"* (Matthew 23:8). We can easily see that spiritual organism without Jesus Christ, the Head – the body is out of control.

Thus, Paul's analogy of the human body shows us a harmonious *relationship* between spiritual organism and order [spiritual gifts]; which allow the unity in organic life. He defines the nature of the church as organism, but at the same time he is persistent about spiritual gifts for the necessity of institutional order. Paul uses the gifts of tongues and prophecy to illustrate the confusion and chaos that could arise within the worship service if allowed to be operated in isolation:

1. Tongues without interpretation (see 1 Cor. 14:27).
2. Uncontrolled prophecy (see 1 Cor. 14:29-33).

Paul ends this portion with a statement summarizing his overall concern. "All things should be done decently and in order" (1 Cor. 14:40). Despite the absolute priority of the church as spiritual organism, there is a dire need for the spiritual components of leadership, policy, and structure – servant leadership.

During the second and third centuries a ridgid hierarchy of the Roman Catholic Church developed the threefold offices of bishop, presbyter, and deacon, positions of status and honor. For three hundred years the church followed the apostles' established doctrine and pattern experiencing a life and a power that the world could not comprehend. Then in the fourth century, through a compromise instigated by the pagan Roman Emperor, the church allowed the early church of Pentecost to die having been cut-off from its life-giving Source (Jesus Christ).

By the year 500 A.D. almost nothing of the early apostolic church remained. Notice what was lost:

- the entire ministry team of Ephesians 4:11)
- the gospel of Jesus Christ (Romans 1:16)
- eternal life (John 3:3, 16)
- the Holy Spirit with His gifts and ministries (1Corinthians 12-14) were *lost* to church.

Praise God! The Word of God was preserved during this period through monastic life. Throughout these Dark Ages, the church headed by a hierarchy of priests became a corrupt political organization with vast wealth, land holdings, and military power but little to no spiritual reality.

These stratified [top down] positions gave the hierarchy power equal to and in many cases above the state. Additionally, they did all biblical interpretation for the people.

Institutional [ism]

The Church's dominance over the people sharply changed to a false theology that said, Christ delegated to the *church* the right to dispense grace [God's favor] or withhold it; meaning for all practical purposes through institutionalism the church controlled the physical and spiritual life of the people in time and eternity, by taking authority for:

- Controlling the people through creating two categories: clergy and laity
- Controlling biblical interpretation
- Controlling forgiveness of sin
- Controlling who received eternal life

This clerical order was in place at the time Luther rediscovered the doctrine of *justification by faith,* [righteousness]; which after some eleven hundred years of the Roman Catholic Church's dominance and damaging influence had a profound impact on ministry. Martin Luther's rediscovery of the gospel of Jesus Christ, the doctrine of justification by faith, and the priesthood of all believers was a great move of God, in deed.

Justification by faith

- Puts all the people on equal footing.
- An individual is made right with God through a personal response to the saving grace of Christ.
- Priesthood of all believers in Christ.
- Come boldly to the throne of grace through our High Priest, Jesus Christ.
- We can pray to God without a human priest.

Defining the church as a spiritual organism begins with God's Spirit-filled people. However, all aspects of leadership, policy, and structure are needed and must be maintained in spiritual organism, for order (1 Cor. 4:40; 14:29-33). As I pointed out in an earlier section, Paul makes it clear that there must be order. For example, I Corinthians 13 and 14 provide guidance governing the chaos and confusion created by the abuse of freedom and mismanagement of spiritual gifts. The church at Corinth became self-focused and performance oriented. Paul assured the church that unless the gifts are motivated by love – there is no value (see 1 Cor.13:2-3).

Elimination of clergy and laity arrangement

The elimination of the clergy-laity arrangement has great potential to change the view of ministry. The rediscovery of the priesthood of all believers meant the end of the distinction within the church between clergy and laity. Martin Luther's conviction was that every Christian should by nature be a priest, a mediator, and intercessor between God and man. Additionally, he attacked the hierarchy of callings. His stance was that because of the gospel, the call of God comes to *all* of us with much potential in our ordinary status of life as ministers of the Word of reconciliation.

Rather than the reverse of the Roman Catholic concept of ministry, the rediscovery of the gospel which included preaching, was not realized. The facts show that as a sign of the change from a priestly concept of ministry; the clerical vestments were replaced by the academic robe. In 2017, we celebrated the 500th anniversary of the Reformation. And yet in review, we find that there are promises of the Reformation that have yet to be realized:

- Why didn't the recovery of the gospel produce the new wineskin of spiritual organism, body life ministry?
- Why, to this day is the gospel ministry and the church sill in the hands of top down hierarchy?

To answer those questions would settle the problem for the bulk of local churches today in this country. The church was empowered by its top-down leadership, a priesthood within a priesthood. If leadership is made up in representative terms – one group doing for another – then the doctrine of the priesthood of all believers is undermined. In the institutional form the priesthood of all believers along with the Holy Spirit His gifts and ministries were affirmed in theory, but denied in practice. As the old saying goes, "action speaks louder than words."

Bottom up

If the ministry is to be returned to the people of God, we must have a bottom up view of the church. A spiritual organismic view of ministry begins with *all* the people as the place where ministry resides in each person every day, and it receives servant leadership from the Holy Spirit *within the body*. In contrast, an institutional view operates around its ordained leadership and then tacks on a role for lay ministry. Thus, operating from an institutional mindset that tried to mesh a traditional institutional concept of ministry with the spiritual organism doctrine of the priesthood of all believers. As you can see today – it did not work!

The local churches in this country presently enjoy freedom of religion from the coercive power of the state; however, we are not to take our religious freedom for granted as it is tested daily.

Many may think that this means the end of the ordained minister [pastor]; not so, the pastor as under shepherd is key to spiritual organism. The idea being the illumination of the spectators, thus, freeing *all members* to do the work of ministry as a body under the authority of Christ by the Holy Spirit. By comparison the relationship between the church and society is like that of the first century.

The church's authority is derived from its Lord, who indwells *all* of His true people through the indwelling Spirit. Thus, starting with the Protestant Reformation, God has set periods of restoration within the church lost during the eleven hundred years of Roman Catholic authority – beginning with salvation and eternal life to the people. Give Him praise and glory.

The Spirit's return

Stated in an earlier section an African American preacher named William Seymour, leading the Azusa Street Phenomenon launched Pentecostalism. In it God restored the Holy Spirit with His gifts and spiritual empowerment of the people to minister to people everywhere (see Acts 1:8). In more recent times during the 20th Century the Holy Spirit has restored the ministers of Ephesians 4:11; I believe all is a vital part of the restoration of spiritual organism, His body, the Church. The church is fundamentally *organism* and secondarily *organization*.

Organization puts innovation on wheels, translates faith into action, and enables our ministry to become a viable reality. If organism is the heart of the church, a solid organizational structure is the muscle and skeletal systems for planning and implementing for getting things done. All the people power [unconditional love, time, and Spirit-filled, Spiritual-giftedness] is the muscle implementing and bringing to fruition the mission and ministry of the church. Both spiritual organism and limited-organization are essential if the church is to fulfill its high calling.

The implication here is profound – the chief purpose of the church is to bring glory to God by obediently accomplishing the Great Commission commanded by Jesus Christ, the Head of the Church. Three warning shots indicate a need for restoration:

★A lack of spiritual organization – there is a saying, "If you think education is expensive, try ignorance." By the same token, while organization takes time and energy – the cost of disorganization is even more staggering! The goal of spiritual organization in spiritual organism is for the right people to be assigned according to their proper spiritual-giftedness, instead of constantly having to do emergency repair work in a broken operation. In many local churches, unspiritual disorganization substitutes for Spirit-led spontaneity. Local churches offer excuses for tolerating disorganization. Here are a few common excuses offered:

- "We have to tolerate it; in order to keep the peace."
- God said, we are to let the wheat and the tares grow together."
- "We just go with the flow and let the Spirit have His way."
- "We really don't have time to get organized."
- "We can't afford to be organized."
- "We have to be right, our heads remain above water year after year."
- "That's just the way it is."
- "That's all there is."

God desires order in the church (see 1 Corinthians 14:40).

★The means become the end or goal – when a church does not keep the higher purpose for its existence clearly in view; they may fall for the delusion that doing church work is the equivalent of doing the work of the church. In a church where the highest order is keeping the customs, traditions, and programs – resistance to change is likely to be the order of the day. Such structures leave little or no room for spiritual relationships nor is there room for the Holy Spirit to deploy His gifts and ministries.

★The church is well organized and functions on purpose, but the wrong purpose. Sadly, many churches are disobedient toward what God has called them to do – and are doing their own thing, for example the church may be organized to meet the needs of its own membership or simple to enhance its status in the community through facility size and numbers.

The structures in the church's organization must be determined by its mission [often, the opposite is true]. It is essentially appropriate to create organizational structures to carry out the church's mission; however, the church itself must be biblically sound.

Remember, a local church is an assembly of professed believers in the Lord Jesus Christ, living for the most part in community, who assemble themselves together in His name for the breaking of bread, praise and worship, prayer, testimony, the ministry of the Word, and discipline – all for the glory of God; and the furtherance of the kingdom of heaven (see Hebrews 10:25; Acts 20:7; I Corinthians 14:26; 4:26; Philippians 4:14-18; I Thessalonians 1:8; Acts 13:1-4). Such a local church exists where two or three are gathered in His name (Matthew 18:20). According to the Word of God every such church that has Christ in their midst, is a temple of God, and indwelt by the Holy Spirit (see I Corinthians 3:16, 17).

In a nut shell

It has been noted that many families are withdrawing from many local Black churches, because in their own words, they think their church is doing more harm than good for the families. Although, many pastors and other church leaders have come to the realization that many of the old traditional structures and methods are not working – they are afraid to trust God for new wineskins.

Research reflects that continuing on its present course that the American church is traveling, within the next seven years 55,000 churches will be closed for good. That would put the United States on par with Europe; where there are many beautiful churches, but they are open to tours, not for worship. In fact, a couple of years ago, the evening news anchor spoke of two very prominent churches in London beinging rented to Muslims to hold their services during Ramadam – even promising to cover all crosses during their presence.

Restructuring the church is not a substitute for Spiritual renewal. The same gospel that worked on the Day of Pentecost is the same gospel that worked for our great grand parents' generation; grand parents, and our parents is the same gospel working in the world today (Romans1:16; 1Corinthians 15:1-4). There is no restructuring without repentance when we know that we are on the wrong track will not make the people more loving toward God, Christ nor their neighbors – but it can define and clarify the direction in which you are asking the congregation to go. There was an old saying in the military, that said, "loose lips – sink ships!" Well in reference to the church, we can say, "closed lips closes churches!" Certainly, there will be many questions and choices, for example:

- Should we revise our mission statement?
- Should we start some new ministries?
- What qualifications should be required of prospective leaders?
- Is it time for your church to create some new wineskins?

Today the church is undergoing a greater transformation perhaps than it did in the days of the Protestant Reformation. Christians are calling out to God to restore all that was lost. We are seeing spiritual growth through persecution, tragic events, and conditions. Make no mistake; God's people have been called to a task, and the church's responsibility is to equip them to do it. In many cases the Black church suffered even after slavery because of the denials during slavery by the slavemasters' preachers and the white churches in general:

- Many families never heard the true gospel of Jesus Christ.
- They were never taught "the faith."
- They were not taught to obey "all that Jesus commanded" in the Great Commandment.
- How far have we come in the past 174 years since the Civil War – especially, after having been blocked from the true Christian faith once delivered to the saints.
- How do you pack all that was lost or never offered in 174 years?
- Though many of our African American churches began as Evangelical, sadly, the many black congregation has never fully embraced and involed themselves with the Great Commission.
- The widely acclaimed homogeneity principle used for many years in church growth and development, while practically guaranteed success is not consistent with Scripture.
- Clearly, as the late Dr. C. Peter Wagner questioned, homogeneity [birds of a feather flock together] does produce rapid growth and stability within church structures – the question must be asked is it

at the heart of God for the physical manifestation of His body and bride?

- I first heard of this *principle* in Bible school – where I was also told that methods change, but principles stay the same.

The power (and the problems) of homogeneity lie in the fact that it creates an artificial "safe" environment in the church. Could this "great divide" could well be a subtle form of racism? Certainly, God loves diversity, notice:

> *You are worthy to take the scroll, and to open its seals; for You were slain, and have redeemed us to God through your blood. Out of every tribe and tongue and people and nation, and have made us kings and priests to our God; and we shall reign on the earth* (Revelation 5:9).

Jesus was slain to purchase for God with His very blood people from every tribe and tongue, and people and nation. The Cross was designed to redeem a kingdom of people that would be incomplete if it did not include an appropriate, representative group of people consistent with His creation. This group of people would be a thoroughly *diverse* representation of humankind. However, when it comes to the church – we chose?

I'm sure that some will object that churches should reflect the diversity of the body of Christ reflected in Revelation 5, but it is the calling of the church to go and "make disciples of all nations." Paul powerfully states that Christ has given us [His church] a ministry of reconciliation and has now commissioned us as His *ambassadors;* that His appeal to the world is literally being made through *all* of us:

> *Therefore, if anyone is in Christ, he is a new creation; old things have passed away; behold, **all things have become new.** Now all things are of God, who has reconciled to Himself through Jesus Christ, and has given us the ministry of reconciliation, that is, that God was in Christ reconciling the world to Himself, not imputing their trespasses to them, and has committed to us the word of reconciliation* (2 Corinthians 5:17-20).

Some pastors seem afraid to confront or offend their congregations by challenging them with the considerable demands the Lord makes upon those who choose to follow Him. They rarely if ever talk about cultural issues, sexual distinctions, the suffering and needy around the world, or the demands of holiness that Scripture makes on behavior and lifestyles for *all* believers. We could label such claims, "the silent issues in the church."

The Great Commandment and Great Commission have for many churches become simple oppositional suggestions.

If churches are going to be a counter cultural to change the world, pastors must abondon their caretaker roles and become like battle-tested platoon sergeants always ready to carry the battle to the world which involves:

1. Preaching the true gospel [the Good News]
2. Inviting people to enter the kingdom of God
3. Discipling and teaching those who believe and receive
4. Baptizing them
5. Establishing outposts of the kingdom

They must provide direction and bases for the members to launch into the world on mission. Battles are fought outside the walls of our local churches – its better to have no walls at all than to stay hidden within them! Any true Christian in any local church can begin to see what God is doing and join Him. We are witnessing things for which men and women of God have prayed for hundreds of years.

Most Christians waste many opportunities which could increase their usefulness to Christ and increase their reward. This is why pastors must plead with their people, carry a tremendous burden for them in prayer, weep for them, and like Paul warn them with tears.

Woe to the shepherd-leader who fails to prepare his or her people for Christ's judgment of rewards (see 1 Corinthians 3:1-15).

Christ is no respector of persons, but He is a respector of our response to His love, His commands, and the work He has assigned us. Folks, it is not enough to flee from sin, attend church, do a little Bible reading, and spend a few minutes a day in prayer. Christ will reward the time we spend in prayer blessing others, and extending His kingdom. It is our responsibility as their shepherd-leader [pastors, Sunday school teachers, small group leaders – to teach and warn them concerning the questions Christ will ask them when they stand before the judgement seat of Christ.

Time is for sowing – eternity is for eternal reaping!

This adds to the seriousness of our life-living as Christians, to our priestly intercession for others, and to our witness-evangelism and discipleship. Christians who live and think primarily of only today and [more stuff] are fools – eternal fools. They will be ever-mindful throughout eternity and regret that they made such little use of their time sowing for Christ and His body, the church. Be ever mindful – any Christian may be the only one who will ever pray for some people or ever witness to them. We may be their only hope for heaven.

Commitment

Diverse and truly reconciled churches are built upon the foundation of committed relationships. Speaking of racial alienation in this country goes back centuries and affects everyone. Effort is needed to bridge the pain of past experiences. Those of us who are true Christians need a *deep commitment* to cross the chasm and build significant relationships across racial lines. Racial understanding and acceptance are the essential catalysts for setting the *miracle* into motion.

No matter what our effort to win the world for Christ, the Spirit must guide us as we reach out. The wonder and beauty of pursuing diversity in our churches is that there is a miracle in it that reflects the heart of Christ. There is no human way that such churches could grow or even exist without Christ's hand on them.

Reflections: Chapter 10

1. Explain why Paul always addressed the whole church, but never in terms of a select leadership [top down hierarchy].

2. Contrast sanctification with justification

3. Discuss experiencing the church as spiritual organism rather than organizational institution.

4. Explain what is meant by the statement that Christians are a sacramental people.

5. Explain Ephesians 4:15-16 regarding Paul's imagery of "head" as the source of nourishment for the church.

SECTION IV

IT'S NOW OR NEVER

Chapter 11

EVANGELIZE OR FOSSILIZE

"Be transformed by the renewing of your mind" (Romans 12:2)

"Service," "worship" or "ministry" captures the spirit in which spiritual organism is to be rendered on behalf of the whole body. Jesus captured the essence of the model servant when He said, "For even the Son of Man did not come to be served, but to serve, and to give His life a ransom for many" (Mark 10:45).

Under institutionalism the terms "ministry" or "minister" refer to a certain class of people set apart from the rest of the church. The Gk. noun *diakonia* is translated "service," "ministry," or "mission." The personal form of the "diakonic" is translated "servant," "minister," or "deacon," depending on the context. In Paul's description of spiritual organism, spiritual gifts and other grace abilities are distributed throughout the entire body of Christ by the Holy Spirit as He pleases (1 Cor. 12:18):

- A synonym for "spiritual gift" is "service" or "ministry." "And there are varieties of gifts [ministries], but the same Lord" (1 Cor. 12:5).
- Ministry is to be done "for the common good" (1 Cor. 12:7).
- Ministry is to be done by the *entire* body (1 Cor. 12:27-30).

It is sad that in the *institutional mindset:* "the apostles are the only ones set apart as a class by themselves to do ministry" (see Acts 6:4). A crisis arose among the Greek-speaking and Hebrew-speaking widows. The apostles were being distracted from their call which was to "devote themselves to prayer and the ministry of the Word" (Acts 6:1, 4). In these two verses the word translated "ministry" in (Acts 6:4) is translated "distribution" in (Acts 6:1). The term *"ministry"* is used in *two* different senses in these two verses.

The apostles were called to a function of prayer and proclamation, while the seven were appointed to oversee the ministry to the widows. Again, the institutional model of the church leads us to two peoples – two ministries. Changing this concept of ministry was the intent of the Protestant Reformation; which requires *a renewed mind*. However, what happened – instead of the adoption of spiritual organism, or whole body ministry, the denominations coming out of the Reformation settled for different variations of the institutional model over the New Testament model of spiritual organism ministry and attempted to address it, by word of mouth only. The bottom line is the institution model of ministry with its top-down hierarchy has *quenched* the Holy Spirit and *denied* His gifts and body ministries for hundreds of years in those churches that *refuse to change*.

The battle for the mind

In the mindset of most clergy and so-called laity; it is the responsibility of the dominant pastor to handle the spiritual concerns of the Christian church; while the laity are mere spectators, critics, and recipients of pastoral care. This model frees the laity to go about their *own* personal business and do their own thing; because the pastor is taking care of the church's business personally! At the same time such churches are [voluntarily] producing a *biblical* and *spiritual drought* of tremendous proportion among the people. People are wandering from church to church [they say they are seeking a place "to be fed?"]. No wonder a growing number of families feel that the church does them more harm than good. That is dangerous in these days of consumerism rule.

In a nutshell this is probably the greatest single hindrance to spiritual restoration, witness evangelism and discipleship in the Black community. The hierarchal top-down "ordained" structure is denying and destroying the New Testament doctrine in the local churches. It seems the thinking of many pastors is that the Bible consists of only five books: the four gospels, and the Book of Revelation. Others rely solely on their denominational discipline/ manuals for guidance; along with an annual program calendar established by the founders many years ago; therefore, most of those local churches simply [appoint a new chairperson and change the date on the [traditional] bulletin.

Sadly, many men lack theological training, and there seems to be an anti-intellectual, anti-training attitude in many denominational circles. In the meantime, the number of women seeking theological education and training is consistently rising.

However, regarding pastoral ministry, a great number of men and women are called to the churches, but they are totally unprepared for a life of equipping ministry:

- Biblical preaching
- teaching
- shepherding
- counseling
- mentoring
- witness-evangelism
- servant leadership

In many traditional institutional Black churches, the means to an end have become the end. Therefore, nothing ever happens there that requires the supernatural.

When we speak as a member of the spiritual organism – we have a role to play according to our spiritual giftedness within the body of Christ.

Many pastors recognize the shortcomings of the institutional model of top down hierarchy – but chose to sit *silently by* rather than *repent* and *change it!* Today is not a time to be silent, it's time to repent and do the right thing. True biblical repentance requires a change of heart – transformed by the renewing of our minds, that we may know what the will of God is (Romans 12:2). So, the emphasis in our churches must be on the Spiritually-gifted organism model of ministry. This renewal allows us to experientially discover what the Bible teaches and demonstrates.

Again, unlike the institutional church wherein [the laity] are mostly spectators – in the spiritual organism/ body community we are *all* conduits through whom the Holy Spirit works, bringing grace-giftedness to [win] the lost and [build-up] others in the body of Christ so that we grow together in Christlikeness through sanctification.

As Christians, we are all called by Christ to serve. Whether it be to preach, teach, sing, console and; certainly, all are called to witness-evangelize wherever we are – no Christian is exempt from this calling! Our greatest glory is to serve God.

As individual Christians our deepest purpose in life is to find our specific calling in building God's church. Jesus said, "If anyone desires to come after Me, let him deny himself and take up his cross daily, and follow Me" (Luke 9:23).

- Does answering God's call and serving Him carry its proper weight in your life?
- What motivates you to serve Christ?

"Once you have decided you are willing to lose your life for Christ, the rest – money, pleasure, possessions, comfort – is easy to give up." __ Benny Prasad

---

For years now, the Holy Spirit has been moving across denominational lines establishing spiritual organism, body ministry. Unless we shift the priestly ministry from the institutional model of [*top down*] ministry to the body model of [*bottom-up*] ministry – the return of the ministry to the people of God cannot take place. It bears repeating again and again, traditional institutionalism has wreaked havoc on many of the local Black Churches in America.

The idea of the Reformation was to rid the church of the top-down [few ordained and non-ordained spectator] ministry and bring it back to every member ministry. However, as with the early Roman Catholic church that has gone before, the heretics are alive and active in too much of the American church. Emphasis added.

"How can one ever become a Christian in an atmosphere in which the pure Gospel of Christ is rarely if ever preached?" R. T. Kendall

---

Since Christ has come, we have no excuse for being separated from the ordained in the winning of souls to Christ. Witness-evangelism is the responsibility of every believer. What a national tragedy and waste; when God has already provided the means for all to be rescued! We should heed the example of the early Christians who focused their teachings upon the Person and work of Jesus Christ. They declared that He was the sinless Servant and Son of God:

1. Who gave His life to atone for the sins of all people, who put their trust in Him (Romans 5:8-10).
2. He was the One whom God raised from the dead to defeat the powers of sin (Romans 4:24, 25; 1 Corinthians 15:17).

The work of God's mercy has one great purpose – to show believers the riches of His grace throughout all the ages to come. God has done so much for us, His Church, through Jesus Christ that it will take an eternity to show it all off!

A growing spiritual organism

The apostles and prophets were the foundation of the church because they pointed and witnessed to Jesus Christ. The early church was established on their teaching and preaching (see Acts 2). Yet Christ Himself is the rock foundation on which the whole church rests (see 1 Corinthians 3:11).

> "Having been built upon the foundation of the apostles and prophets, Jesus Christ Himself being the chief corner stone; in which the whole building, being fitted together, grows into a holy temple in the Lord, in whom you also are being built together for a dwelling place of God in the Spirit" (Ephesians 2:20-22).

The cornerstone can be called the instructional stone – upon it all the lines and instructions of the building are based. So, it is with Christ. He is the Person who gives the directions and instructions to God's people. We – the local churches – are to obediently build our lives upon His instructions and His directions only. If we follow any other's instructions and directions, we will be out of line; and when we are noticed, we will have to be removed, cast aside, and replaced with a stone that can be set in line.

God used Jesus Christ to give directions to all the other stones. Jesus Christ is the Chief Cornerstone. If He is removed, the church will collapse; no Christ, no church. Christ holds it all together within the church. Therefore, it is an absolute necessity that He alone be preached, taught, and lived! The word "grows" is a biological term, conveying the idea of a living organism. The church then, is pictured as a living organism – the *union* of various parts of a living and growing being. This may seem impracticable to speak of a building that grows. The point is that more and more parts [more believers] are brought and fitted into the building. The building grows and grows and shall continue to grow until the Lord Jesus Christ returns.

Another fact, the apostle Peter calls Jesus Christ the *living stone*. Christ is the living stone upon whom all others are built. To live and have their spiritual sacrifice accepted by God all others must be built upon Christ.

> *"To whom coming, as to a living stone, rejected indeed of men, but chosen by God, and precious, you also, as living stones, are being built up a spiritual house, a holy priesthood, to offer up spiritual sacrifices acceptable to God through Jesus Christ"* (1 Peter 2:4-5).

It's important to notice that it is all due to God's work. He is the One who raised up Christ. The church and its believers face two challenges:

1. The church must be bringing in new believers [stones] and fitting them into the building of God. God expects the church to grow.
2. Every believer within the building is a part of the building and expected to fulfill his or her function within the building; the ministry of every believer to bring in new stones (see 2 Timothy 2:2); which is God's multiplication plan for church growth.

Expected [local] church growth

Each local church is pictured as a building structured for God's presence; and each member is seen as an integral, necessary stone being and fitted into the building (Ephesians 4:16; 1 Peter 2:5). The stability of the church lies in:

- *Each stone's* being placed, fitted, and cemented by the same Lord.
- *Each stone's* holding up its load, fulfilling its purpose in the structure.

Throughout the ages, Satan has opposed the growth and destiny of the church. History shows that he will stop at nothing to achieve that goal. We can picture the church's miraculous growth through a very proficient technology called, "Ultrasound" for observing [the similarity] the growth of new birth, *a growing organism*, a child with little hands, feet and other body parts developing in the womb. No matter the opposition, the church will be triumphant – Jesus promised, *"...... upon this rock I will build My church; and the gates of hell shall not prevail against it"* (Matthew 16:18). He said it – that settles it!

The *gospel* of Jesus Christ is open to all people everywhere. There is no place for division, prejudice, privileged, partiality, class or caste systems, and definitely no systemic racism in the Church of the Living God. The Spirit of God dwells within the church to conform the church to the image of God's Son. Christians who are not filling their hearts and minds with the Word of God are like soldiers going out to battle without a helmet.

A raging battlefield is a frightening place to be when your head is exposed. As a Vietnam war veteran myself, I can witness that the head is the most guarded part of a soldier's body. Likewise, when the helmet of salvation is smugly wrapped around your mind, the devil has to flee for his strategies are negated. That's why salvation is listed as a defensive weapon in Ephesians 6. Note: The effectiveness of *any* local church depends upon how much [individually and corporately] it allows the Holy Spirit and the Word working in tandem to dwell within and control the entire body (see Romans 12:2).

Here again, the mind is in focus, Paul instructs his readers, "do not [allow yourself] to be conformed to this world, but [allow yourself] to be transformed by the renewing of your mind. We allow the process and participate in it, but God actively does it in us with our cooperation. It's His work. You may ask, why is God so concerned about our minds?

If the enemy can get a foothold in your mind – then he gets a foothold in your body.

According to Scripture the mind is where the battle takes place. If Satan has no say-so in your mind, then he has no say-so in your body. Many Christians believe the war is primarily about their circumstances, their behavior, their work, or their relationships. Even though all those things are relevant, they are not the top priority. The major part of the battle is in our thought life – that is where Satan is most effective in manipulating people towards his goals subtly and invisibly.

If Satan can distort our thoughts, our emotions, and *our knowledge,* then our behaviors and relationships will fall in line for him. He doesn't have to succeed in turning us to overt evil, just a little *distorted thinking* can neutralize and make us practically ineffective for the master's work. Human thinking is the battlefield in this war, and if we have not diligently filled our minds with God's *truth* and operate out of His teaching – we lose! God wants us to have a sound mind. In his Book, *Dressed to Kill,* Rick Renner offers concerning the question, "What is a sound mind?" Quoting one translation which says it means "sensible thinking" taken from the Greek word *sophroneo.* It is a compound of the word *sodzo,* which means *saved or delivered,* and the word *phroneo,* which refers to *intelligent thinking.*[74]

That is why God is so concerned about our minds, and likewise with Satan and his concern. Our minds are a threat to him. Many passages of Scripture emphasize just how critical protection of the mind is in this area.

II Corinthians 10:3-5 describes the weapons of our warfare as spiritual, not physical, and then applies them directly to "speculations and every lofty thing raised up against the knowledge of God." The goal is to take "every *thought* captive to the obedience of Christ." When Jesus prayed what some call the real Lord's prayer in John 17:17 before the Father, He asked that His disciples would be *prepared* and *protected* – primarily in their knowledge of the truth. *"Sanctify them by the truth,"* He prayed, and notice, the next line made it indelibly clear what He was talking about: ***"Your word is truth."***

Romans 8:6-7 also gives us a clear picture of the critical role of the mind: "The mind set on the flesh is death, but the mind set on the Spirit is life and peace, because the mind set on the flesh is hostile toward God." Then remember, the "god of this world" can thwart unbelievers from accepting the truth. How? He has blinded their *minds* (2 Corinthians 4:4). The believer's mind must be saturated [like a sponge submerged in water] with the real knowledge and truth of God's Word and transformed [sanctified] by the Spirit – there remains no room for counterfeits!

Reaching the world

Certainly, we hear much today on the gifts of the Spirit and the power in which they operate [Praise God!] in many local churches, but, many with limited results, because they have lost sight of the biblical twofold reason for the manifestation of these gifts. The Scripture clearly states them:

1. unto the work of the ministry (outside the church)
2. unto the building up of the body of Christ (within the church body)

Notice, in these two realms: in the world, and the church these spiritual gifts are useful. Lest we forget, the work of the ministry is to the world. The church exists by God's design as His instrument for reaching the world for His glory (see John 3:16).

It is clearly God's intention that, through the true church the world *might see Jesus* working through us. The body of Christ was created by God to be incarnate in the world, visible in the marketplace, other public squares, and institutions of the world who need the ministry so desperately through her influence and testimony – but He never intended for the world to actually have to come to the church building to find Jesus.

A three-fold mystery

Before Jesus came, if a person wanted to be saved, he had to approach God through the Jewish religion. Scripture declares that "salvation is of the Jews" (John 4:22). However, since Christ came, no people of the earth can approach God except through Him. No matter who we are, we are not able to approach God through any other people or religion. We can now approach God face to face through His Son, the Lord Jesus Christ. When the world can see the body of Christ among them:

- Ministering to them
- Challenging them
- Loving them
- Reaching them

They will understand that Jesus Christ is not gone, but He is right here among them, in the form of ordinary believers. He is alive and has been involved in human society for two thousand years, just as He said He would be: *"Lo, I am with you always even to the end of the age"* (Matthew 28:20) KJV.

No longer does man have to approach God through one body or nation of people. God's love is universal, and He is now creating a *new body* of people, the body of Christ (1 Cor. 12:27). Jesus Christ is present as Head of the local church (Eph. 4:15). Every member is placed in the body as it pleases God (I Cor. 12:18). The Holy Spirit manifests Himself through each believer for the good of all (I Cor. 12:7).

The whole body is fitted together by the Father. Members are enabled and equipped by the Holy Spirit to function in the body wherever He sees fit. What one-member lacks, other members in the body supplies. God made the church up of people of all races, nations mutually interdependent – and all are [*one*] centered "in" His Son, our Lord and Savior, Jesus Christ:

- We the Gentile believers – are fellow heirs of God with the Jews.
- We the Gentile believers – are of the same body with the Jews.
- We the Gentile believers – receive the same promises of Christ as the Jews did. God had promised Abraham that he would inherit the promised land and a great nation would proceed from his loins.

The Body of Christ in Motion

You may ask, "What specifically, is the ministry of the body of Christ? Jesus answered that question in Luke 4 – stating what He came to accomplish on earth, whether in His physical body of flesh or in His corporate body, the church:

> *"The Spirit of the Lord is upon Me, because He has anointed Me to preach the gospel to the poor; He has sent Me to heal the brokenhearted, to proclaim liberty to the captives and recovery of sight to the blind, to set at liberty those who are oppressed, to proclaim the acceptable year of the Lord"* (Luke 4:18-21).

Therefore, knowing what God is doing in and through His body is essential to my knowing how to respond to Him. Where I see Him working in the body, I adjust and put my life there. In the church, I let God use me in any way He chooses to complete His work in each member. This was Paul's goal when he said, *"Him we preach, warning every man and teaching every man in all wisdom, that we may present every man perfect in Christ Jesus"* (Col. 1:28).

Reflection: Chapter 11

1. In Paul's description of spiritual organism, spiritual gifts, and other grace abilities are distributed to the entire body of Christ (the church) by the Holy Spirit as it pleases Him.

2. Explain the difference between the apostles' calling and that of the 7.

3. In what manner is the ordained structure of the church destroying the New Testament doctrine?

4. Explain the purpose or intent of the Reformation?

5. The stability of the church is dependent upon:
    a.
    b.

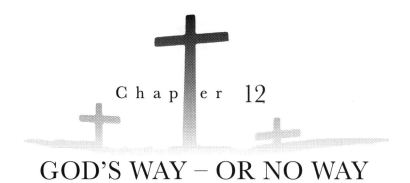

Chapter 12

GOD'S WAY – OR NO WAY

"A new commandment I give unto you, that you love one another, as I have loved you, that you also love one another. By this all will know that you are My disciples, if you have love for one another" (John 13:34-35).

Here the Lord was speaking to His disciples for the last time before He walked the last step to Calvary. He was giving them His last message, and that message was "love one another" – and He set a new standard, they were to love one another "as I have loved you." Unbelievers recognize Jesus' disciples:

- Not by their doctrinal distinctives.
- Not by dramatic miracles.
- Not even by the Christian's love for the lost.
- But by their love *agapa* [unconditional] for one another.

That is a command not a suggestion. We are to love fellow believers as God has loved us. If we do this, if we love one another as Jesus loved us, what would be our action toward other Christians? Paul answers that question in his letter to the Roman believers: "Love worketh no ill to his neighbor; therefore, love is the fulfilling of the law" (Romans 13:10).

In God's love letter to His "little children" we find the kind of love that we are to show toward fellow believers:

"For this is the message that you have heard from the beginning, that we should love one another, not as Cain, who was of the wicked one, and slew his brother. And why did he murder him? Because his works were evil, and his brother's righteous. Do not

marvel, my brethren, if the world hates you. We know that we passed from death unto life, because we love the brethren. He who does not love his brother abides in death. Whosoever hates his brother is a murderer, and you know that no murderer has eternal life abiding in him. By this we know love, because He laid down His life for us. And we ought to lay down our lives for the brethren.

"But whoever has the world's goods, and sees his brother in need, and shuts up his heart from him, how does the love of God abide in him? My little children let us not love in word, or in tongue, but in deed and in truth.

For if our heart condemns us, God is greater than our heart, and knows all things. Beloved, if our heart does not, condemn us, have we confidence toward God. And whatsoever we ask, we receive of Him, because we keep His commandments, and do those things that are pleasing in His sight. And this is His commandment, that we should believe on the name of His Son Jesus Christ, and love one another, as He gave us the commandment. "Now he who keeps His commandments abides in Him, and He in him. And by this we know that He abides in us, by the Spirit whom He has given us" (I John 3:11-24).

What is the message of love?

The message is that we love one another, and we know we are believers because we love one another. If we have the goods of this world and our fellow believer is in need – and we refuse to help him [or her], how can we say the love of God dwells in us? Additionally, we are to love unbelievers, that is love them in Christ, witness to them, and do all in our power to win them to Christ, but we are to love [unconditionally] our fellow believers as God has loved us. And this love should be evident before the world – in our attitude toward other Christians.

Jesus reinforced this command by His own example [*we are to love as He loved*]! The frequency of the command to love one another proves that. Sadly, there is so little of it displayed today! Many Black church leaders are held in high esteem in the hearts of church people: pastors who preach great sermons; teachers who teach great lessons; and others in all areas of church who all too often in their private life do not demonstrate the love of God.

One of the most noted theologians of the twentieth century, Dr. Francis Schaeffer put forth the following thought: The way Christians interact with one another is the final apologetic for whether non-Christians believe the gospel of Christ message. He furthered expanded on this idea in his book:

"The Marks of a Christian."

> *"Yet without true Christians loving one another, Christ says the world cannot be expected to listen, even when we give the right answers." Let us be careful, indeed, to spend a lifetime studying to give honest answers. For years the orthodox, evangelical church has done this very poorly. So, it is well to spend time learning to answer the questions of men around us. But after we have done our best to communicate to a lost world, still we must never forget that the final apologetic which Jesus gives is the observable love of true Christians for true Christians."*[75]

What is the measure of love?

> **"Greater love has no one than this, than to lay down one's life for his friend"** (John 15:13).

Here, Jesus teaches the measure of love believers should have for one another. As born-again children of God, our love should be self-sacrificing – even to death if need be. Christ died for us because He loved us! He proved His love by His death on the cross – but that's not the end of the story: He died not only for His friends, but He also died for His enemies!

> **"For when we were still without strength, in due time Christ died for the ungodly .... God demonstrates His own love toward us, in that while we were still sinners, Christ died for us"** (Romans 5:6,8).

That is the full-measure of love. Dying for one whom we love is the greatest possible demonstration of love!

> **"By this we know that we abide in Him and He in us, because He has given us of His Spirit. And we have seen and testify that the Father sent the Son as Savior of the world. Whosoever confesses that Jesus is the Son of God, God abides in him [or her], and he or she in God. And we have known and believed the love that God has for us. God**

is love, and he that abides in love abides in God, and God in him [or her]."

"Love has been perfected among us in this that we may have boldness in the day of judgment; because as He is, so are we in this world. There is no fear in love; but perfect love casts out fear, because fear involves torment. But he who fears has not been made perfect in love. We love Him because He first loved us" (I John 4:13-19). Brackets are mine.

Unity is the Goal

True Christians are indwelt by the Holy Spirit, who energizes and empowers them. He creates a spiritual union by melting and molding the heart of the Christian believer to the hearts of other believers. Therefore, through the Spirit of God, believers become one in life and purpose.

> *"For you did not receive the spirit of bondage again to fear, but you have received the Spirit of adoption by whom we cry out, "Abba Father." The Spirit Himself bears witness with our spirit that we are the children of God, and if children then heirs of God and joint heirs with Christ. If indeed we suffer with Him, that we may also be glorified together"* (Romans 8:15-17).

> *"I do not pray for these alone, but also for those who will believe in Me through their word: that they all may be one as You, Father are in Me, and I in You, that they may be one in Us, that the world may believe that You sent Me. And the glory which You gave Me I have given them, that they may be one just as We are one: I in them, and you in Me; that they may be made perfect in one, and the world may know that You have sent Me, and have loved them as You have loved Me"* (John 17:20-23).

In His prayer, Jesus not only prayed for those the Father had given Him (v. 9), but for all future believers – for their unity and their future glory (vv. 20-26). If you are a believer – Jesus was praying for you also!

We can't have unity without love! Jesus was praying for the unity that takes place through the sanctification of believers. This is what Jesus was commanding. His followers had to love each other so that the world may believe in the reality of Jesus' love.

Gospel unity

The loving relationship of believers to each other is the greatest witness to Jesus Christ. The revelation of Jesus Christ through the disciples, is the means of unity. The only thing strong enough to build and sustain such a Christian community is the gospel and the refuge found therein.

- When a gospel community begins to operate like a unified body, spiritual organism, with a common objective – it unlocks the power of transformation for those involved.
- This gospel unity begins with correct belief and correct thinking about Jesus and God the Father will bear fruit (a life that demonstrates God's love and produces the unity between all the believers).

The gospel element is last here because all the other elements work together to build toward this one. The more the others are practiced, the more there will be unity among believers. However, the Holy Spirit brings unity to a body of believers. Notice the way Paul explains it:

> *I, therefore, a prisoner for the Lord, urge you to walk in a manner worthy of the calling to which you have been called, with all humility and gentleness, with patience, bearing with one another in love, eager to maintain the unity of the Spirit in the bond of peace. There is one body and one Spirit – just as you were called to the one hope that belongs to your call – one Lord, one faith, one baptism, one God and Father of all, who is over all and through all and in all. But grace was given to each one of us according to the measure of Christ's gift (Ephesians 4:1-7).*

There is one body and one Spirit that unites that body. As He had promised, Christ gave the Holy Spirit to the believers as a guide after His ascension. The Holy Spirit empowers, enables, and unifies life in a Spirit-guided Bible-believing church.

That means:

- We must be energetic to entrust the gospel body [spiritual organism] to God Himself through regular prayer.
- We must be energetic to maintain unity, and beyond to defend it.

- We must be ready to counter sins like gossip, slander, and deceit; which are like setting fires in the church.
- We must quell fires quickly or they will consume or contaminate everything around them.

The gospel is our only weapon against the destructive fires of sin; therefore, we must be vigilant in attacking sin with the overwhelming power of the gospel. The devil knows there is nothing less effective for advancing God's kingdom agenda on the earth than a disunified local church. So as leaders and Christ followers all of us should be eager to maintain the unity we have in Christ.

The gospel must be at the center of any group of believers. When it is, we open ourselves to a power experience of the church that we were created for and for God to begin to do powerful works in and through us (see Ephesians 4:11; 1 Corinthians 12; Romans 12).

There is no church that has ever or will ever perfectly live out its calling to portray the image of God Himself. We must remember, churches are filled with sinners, us included. Yet God created this people, the church, to declare something about Himself – even in our imperfection! Today, it is quite evident that God uses different methods and models to reach different kinds of people. Experiencing the Spirit and the Word give credence to the image of Christ that the watching world sees when it looks at the church.

Don't count the Traditional Church – out!

If God is effectively using your church to reach the community, drive on! Traditional like all the other models listed in this work is just a model. Any model discussed above is a tool – and useful, as long as it doesn't become the rule. Churches on mission look different from place to place. The objective is not to make all churches look alike and use the same techniques – but seeking to glorify God by being the visible expression of the gospel: A place of radical hospitality, inexhaustible hope, and transformational healing. A place where we recover what was lost in the fall. A place where God is at work, changing lives, everyday!

REFLECTION: CHAPTER 12

1. What was Jesus' last message or command to His disciples?

2. What was Jesus' stated standard for the disciples' love?

3. What is the measure of love?

4. Through the Spirit of God believers become one in _____.

5. In John 17, Jesus was praying for the unity that takes place through the _____ of believers.

Chapter 13

THE DEADLY COST OF SILENCE

"I fear, lest somehow, as the serpent deceived Eve by his craftiness,
so your minds may be corrupted from the simplicity that is in
Christ. For if he who comes preaches another Jesus whom we have
not preached, or if you receive a different spirit which you have
not received, or a different gospel which you have not accepted —
you may well put up with it" (2 Corinthians 11:3-4).

Deception and idolatry are still very much alive today. And there is no argument that deception has corrupted the pure devotion to Jesus Christ in many preachers and local churches today. Paul made it clear that this deception comes through preaching a counterfeit Jesus and a counterfeit gospel, which many believers and churches have accepted or just tolerate.

If we remain silent and continue to leave this problem unaddressed, it will only further weaken Christians and keep them from experiencing God's presence and resurrection power. The truth of the matter is, when a lie is tolerated for too long, it will eventually become truth. That's why *silence* is not the answer!

You may be asking, "How have we preached a different Jesus? Simply by what we've failed to communicate — the true Jesus Christ wherein His power and presence manifest through the pure gospel of the cross. This is especially crucial today, when the progressive religious culture creates their own "Jesus:"

- Who will give us whatever our hearts desire — much like Aaron did for Israel at Mount Sinai (see Exodus 34:2).
- Who is depicted as just a Savior and not Lord.
- Who offers [a bloodless] salvation on our terms.

- Who we believe will give us the benefits of His salvation, without relinquishing our lives to Him.
- Who overlooks willful sin.
- Who believe God and Satan, light and darkness, sin and righteousness can cohabit the same vessel.

The Jesus of the Bible commands that we deny ourselves, take up our cross [daily] and follow Him. When we make Jesus our Savior – He becomes our Lord as well. A counterfeit gospel twists the *truth* concerning Jesus Christ. This false gospel puts forth a salvation without repentance. However, we cannot experience the life that God has for us without repentance. Repentance is a foundational part of life in Christ. It is the decision to receive Jesus as Lord, turning away from living life our way. Repentance means changing our minds and attitudes – deeply as we partake of the God's divine nature; which changes us from the inside out and gives us the ability to see Jesus as He truly is!

No time for playing

In 2006 the widely-known atheist Richard Dawkins created heat waves with his bestseller, *The God Delusion*. It galvanized the intensity with which the secular agenda is striving to aggressively destroy theistic creation at any level possible. He emphatically argues,

The god of the Old Testament is arguably the most unpleasant character in all fiction: jealous and proud of it; a petty, unjust, unforgiving control-freak; a vindictive, bloodthirsty ethnic cleanser; a misogynistic, homophobic, racist, infanticidal, genocidal, filicidal, pestilential, megalomaniacal, sadomasochistic, capriciously malevolent bully.[76]

Most people simply dismiss Dawkins, and his cohorts as angry, uninformed, unregenerate people of intellect. I think those making such a declaration about him give the [atheism, secular humanism, progressivism] and people of other such groups who agree with him a boost; simply because [our silence] advances their personal agenda. After all, the only thing the average person has to offer about him is mostly their undivided *silence*. Of course, we can see the fruit that such silence produces in all areas of society. Even many local churches across this nation are falling silent in answer as the people cry, "What is going on?" How can we remain silent while the secular agenda continues to promote any religious claims foreign or domestic with their gods, and at the same time dispel true Christianity as invalid? Are we going to remain silent as these religions including the New Age philosophical religions are openly taught and spread in our public schools and embraced by our secular non-Bible reading society?

Sometime back, I read an article concerning the Treasury Department and their handling of counterfeit money. The question arose of their use of counterfeit money in the basic training of new agents. The answer came back, "The only thing we do with counterfeit money is burn it!" Choosing not to study fake money – they study real money to the degree that the false would be detected instantly.

God intended that His children be able to do the same with sin and evil. He has provided the resources, [the Spirit and the Word of God] needed to ensure that the believer with proper study, practical training and life application be able to instantly discern and counter the false – and at the same time display the true through their life and testimony. A truly transformed [sanctified] believer is God's best display to a cynical and unbelieving world.

There are many Christians caught up in the false "works righteousness" and "super grace" [God owes it to me] beliefs and forget all about "God's "mercy" and His "sovereignty." This has been a strategy of Satan from the early days of the church – we witness the increasing secular-influened fall-out in our pulpits, boards, music, and other church auxiliaries as more and more people silently harbor these foreign beliefs. Rather than a biblical spiritual conversion today, some local Black churches chose to by-pass conversion and accept people into membership based solely on their resources, talents and other abilities. In many cases it seems that this voluntary silence by the church is communicating that a life of righteousness is optional. As the Spirit and the *truth* of God's Word are continuously being rejected within many Black churches as not relevant and too narrow – we can be silent no more!

Silence on the part of Christians is really the results of voluntary spiritual and biblical ignorance. Many in the church today are falling for the same old deception that Satan is feeding the culture outside, that the church should retreat to their own premises keeping their faith to themselves [a private matter]. Sadly, many churches have turned to promoting prosperity and personal empowerment at the loss of evangelism and discipleship. However, the Spirit is telling us personally and corporately to repent, stand on His revealed truth of God's Word and return to our first work [the Great Commandment and the Great Commission]. Be silent no more!

Back to Bible-Centeredness

What does a truly Bible-centered church look like? Certainly, from the number of Bibles sold each year it seems that the Bible should be center to the life and practice of all local churches. However, the problem arises in striving to get Bible-centeredness to become the experiential norm rather than other sought-after goals. Jonathan Leeman illustrates a Bible-centered church this way:

"Electricity leaves the power plant and buzzes through power lines. Then it makes its way into street lights, grocery store freezers, office computers, and rows and rows of neighborhood homes. Lamps glow and refrigerators hum. In the same way, I'm contending that God's Word buzzes and hums through people and the local church, giving light to their eyes and hope to their hearts."[77]

The Word of God must become as central to the Christ-honoring life and body ministry of the church as a power plant is to the life and activity of our cities and homes. The Word wielded by the Spirit must course through every aspect of our faith and practice, giving energy and life to everything it touches.

Local Black church renewal in general depends on deep and wide [all members deployed], to effective witness-evangelism, discipleship training, and intersessory prayer, all guided by the Spirit and the Word of God everywhere. The norm today tends to limit this ministry of the Word only to that part of the worship service dedicated to the "invitation to discipleship" after the sermon. As a PK, [preacher's kid], I noticed during my childhood that the local Black churches were pretty well packed with chairs in the aisles during "preaching." Of course, the church was the center for almost everything in those days. The members were missional and even the sinners showed up on Sundays if for no other reason to get the latest interpretation of the news within and outside of the community.

Christian preaching and teaching make the gospel *audible* – but Christians living lovingly together [in unity] in Bible-centered churches [spiritual organism] make the gospel [Christ] *visible* (John 13:34-35). Emphasis mine.

The enduring authority of Christ's commands should compel Christians to study the Bible's teaching on the church. Where there is wrong ecclesial teaching and practices – clarify it, through a deeper and wider Word:

- It is imperative that pastors and other leaders prayerfully lead the church in teaching the Bible in various settings throughout the week.
- The Bible must be taught, read, and studied in midweek Bible studies, and small groups.

- Individuals meet one-on-one to search the Scriptures and encourage one another.
- Biblical counseling is another way to apply the truth of God's Word to individual lives – yes, and renewal of marriages and families.
- And the members of the church *must* take the Word of God into the marketplace and community in their roles as committed stewards of the Lord's Word of reconciliation (see II Corinthians 5:19).

Wait on the Lord

In his book *The Pursuit of God*, A. W. Tozier describes how the Holy Spirit germinates the Word of God in our hearts, then grows it, first the blade, then the ear, and finally the full ear. It is important that we get still to wait on God, preferably with our Bible before us. In the Scripture God makes clear promises to those who wait on Him:

> *"But they that wait upon the LORD shall renew their strength; they shall mount up with wings as eagles: they shall run and not be weary; and they shall walk, and not faint"* (Isaiah 40:31).

Hearing the wonderful promises of this text, we must confess these blessings are not usually found in the lives of Christians. In fact, we do run and be weary, we walk and do faint, and the wings of our souls do not habitually beat the upper air. Why is that? It's very simple, the blessings are dependent upon our meeting one condition. The Scripture says, *"Wait on the LORD."*

That is the one condition and it is in the reach of every Christian for our role in witness-evangelism and discipleship. Therefore, it's obvious if the blessings do not manifest in us and our churches, then we didn't meet the requirement. Often, we talk about the beauty and strength of a passage of Scripture – perhaps we have never stopped to read it and consider what it means. These blessings are made sure by the **"shall"** of Almighty God:

1. They **shall** renew their strength – "renew" means "change" denotes a change of garments. I lay aside my strength and take on a garment of His strength. Isaiah 40 contrasts our weak, frail, strength with God's greatness.

2. They **shall** mount up with wings as eagles – Why an eagle? Why not a dove? The eagle is the only bird that flies so high that he is lost to sight. The eagle is a peculiar bird; you've never heard of a flock of eagles. He has to do with great things [mountain peaks]; and sits

very still. There is no restlessness in him. At first light he gets up, stretches his wings and launches out over the abyss. He begins his ascent higher, higher, and higher, all day he is up there mounting up. Before God uses a man or a woman greatly – He spends time alone with them. For example: Moses attained the highest level of education in Egypt – but he spent forty years alone with God. Paul spoke five different languages, held Roman citizenship, and studied at the feet of Gamaliel, – but he spent three years alone with God in the Arabian desert. Though you may consider yourself to be an ordinary person, God will prepare you [wait on Him!] and then He will do His work through you, revealing Himself to a watching world.

3. They **shall** run, and not be weary – we run in service – but only to the degree that we know the upper air [separated unto God] can we run without weariness.

4. They **shall** walk and not faint – we walk in everyday life with our relationship with God, family, church, and occupation living the Word of God in daily tests and trials – representing Christ well in the world.

When we draw near to God, we begin to hear Him speak to us in our hearts. I think for the average person progression will be something like this: First a sound as of a Presence walking in the garden. Then a voice, more intelligible, but still far from clear. Then the happy moment when the Spirit begins to illuminate the Scripture, and that which had been only a sound, or at best a voice, now becomes an intelligible word, warm and intimate and clear as the word of a dear friend.[78] As the Bible is unleashed in the lives of saints and sinners, it will fall like a hammer and break up stony hearts (Jeremiah 23:29).

The Doctrine of the Church

Over the years many Black churches have asked and answered the hard questions simply by reason and prudence. Others have relied on their experiences to determine their answers. Still other local churches answer the debatable questions by looking to what the people want, or what the pastor says. For most churches the answers are found through some form of decision-making according to what works.

The goal for many churches is to be sensitive to the culture that God has placed them in. How do we contextualize our message in such a multicultural setting as we are in today? Do we observe the business world and try to learn and adapt their best practices? What about letting their standards, creativity, innovation, and efficiency be our guides – to help us reach the most people and extend our influence?

Everything we know about God and His will for the church comes from His own revelation. That includes such important issues as doctrine, worship, polity, and certainly the church's life to include:

- Its nature and purpose
- What the church is
- What it is for
- What it does

We only know "the Good News" of Jesus Christ because God has revealed the truth about Himself to us – and He has done that in His Word, the Bible. The truth of Christ is the means God uses to reconcile us to Himself. New life in Christ comes through the Spirit and the Word. Jesus prayed: "I do not pray for these alone, but also for those who will believe in Me through their *word*" (John 17:20). Emphasis added throughout. That is what happens throughout the remainder of the New Testament. For example, Peter preached to Cornelius and his household; and "while he was speaking, the Holy Spirit came on all who heard the word" (Acts 10:44). Of course, God had told Cornelius to expect this: "Peter will tell you words by which you and all your household will be saved" (Acts 11:14).

Unfortunately, when it comes to witness-evangelism and discipleship training in the Black church; the scarcity in the pews of the average congregation clearly shows that the place for these ministries individually and corporately are fading-away fast. Many pastors are no longer preaching and teaching the great biblical doctrines of the faith.

Much of the Black church in America has virtually the same morals as the world, so, where does that leave the majority of the "church" members today? Sadly, Christians in America are losing a desire to share their faith. When we have enjoyed a good meal at a restaurant, the first thing you want to do is share it with somebody – you want them to know every aspect of such a wonderful experience! This seems to be true for everything except witness-evangelism, making disciples, and particularly learning the doctrines of the faith, systematic theology: God, Christ, the atonement, angels, sin, regeneration, justification, adoption, sanctification, glorification, etc. (see 1 Peter 2:2; John 5:3; 17:17; Psalm 119:11). Even realizing to not win and train souls today, puts the next generation in jeopardy of not hearing the gospel. Have you considered the fact that salvation is just one generation from extinction? Its just natural to want others to experience what we love.

Why this selfish attitude toward the Lord's mandate? As a pastor for many years, I have seen the causes of declining effectiveness in witness evangelism over and over again. It seems that the glory days of evangelism ended with the methodology mentioned above after the civil rights era. Today, many churches are still using the traditional methodology of the 50's and 60's with very little success.

Several generations of pastors has grown up and are in the churches with little or no plans for carrying out the Great Commission nor preaching and teaching the great foundational doctrines of the faith. Therefore, many are preaching and promoting a false substitute fitted to their own local church's four walls [a what works for us gospel]. In fact many of them:

- Are preaching some truth, but it's the truth many are *not* preaching that brings concern [they are preaching another kind of gospel].
- Have rejected God's Word as old Israel did (see Malachi 2:12, 13).
- Seldom if ever preach the faith once delivered to the saints [the great doctrines of the Bible].
- Think evangelism is obsolete.
- Fail to preach the true full gospel of Christ (Romans 1:16).
- Think the Holy Spirit and His minisries ended at Pentecost.
- Priority is numbers in attendance and entertainment, rather than saved souls.
- Prosperity and enablement preaching and teaching draws the crowd.
- Ignore multiculturalism and the post-Christian culture and worldview.
- When empowerment left the church and moved downtown; it seems the pursuit of faith left also.
- In a post-Christian society, trust in the church and the Bible has slipped away.
- Each generation of Christians share the gospel and their faith less and less.
- People are not trained to cope with the cultural ills today.

However, Paul's warning *"do not be deceived,"* to the church at Corinth is just as appropriate for the local churches in America today:

> *Or do you not know that the unrighteous will not inherit the kingdom of God? Do not be deceived; neither fornicators, nor idolaters, nor adulterers, nor effeminate, nor homosexuals, nor thieves, nor the covetous, nor drunkards, nor revelers, nor swindlers, will inherit the kingdom of God* (1 Corinthians 6:9-10 NASB).

In Galatians Paul *again warns* the church (children of God) that if they practice the works of the flesh, that they would not inherit the Kingdom of

God. What does that say to the old once saved, always saved – you can live and do as you please false doctrine? (see Galatians 5:19-21).

Remember, repent, and return

Praise God for Jesus! No matter the strategy, we must keep in mind that Romans 10:13-14 remains true as it was the day the Lord revealed it to Paul:

> *For whoever calls upon the name of the Lord shall be saved. How then shall they call on Him in whom they have not believed? And how shall they believe in Him of whom they have not heard? And how shall they hear without a preacher? And how shall they preach unless they are sent?*

Remember, when we have confessed and repented, the Spirit and the Word of God working in tandem brings about the new birth from above. God's relationship to us is loving and redemptive and He wants our relationships to be the context for the change, growth to maturity/discipleship He works in and through us. Scripture describes the work He does in us with four words: justification, adoption, sanctification, and finally glorification.

Justification and adoption

In justification God declares me to be righteous based soley on Christ's perfect life, death, and resurrection. Christ righteousness is legally credited to my account; taking away my sin and and giving me His righteousness and adopted me into His family with all the rights and privileges of a son and through adoption full and complete *standing* and relationship with God, a gift of His grace (see 2 Corinthians 5:21). If we stop here feeling that we don't need anything else as so many false preachers and teachers are leading people to believe today, when considering our *condition* as a person, we can't stop here. We still struggle with sin daily; unless a radical change takes place in my soul I won't be fit for God's service. While justification and adoption are *events*, this work of personal transformation is a *process* called sanctification.

Sanctification

Sanctification is the process by which God actually makes me what He legally declared me to be in justification – holy. God did not justify and adopt me because I am okay – but because I am not okay. God knows that a lasting change will take place in me only when I am living and loving in a personal relationship with Him. The relationship God establishes with us through Christ is the context for His continuing work of transformation [sanctification] in us. We are to be ever mindful that our relationships do not belong to us; but they belong to the Lord and they are holy.

God uses relationships to prepare a people for Himself. Our everyday relationships are essential to the process of sanctification ordained before the world began. Everyday God gives us opportunities to serve those who are afraid, troubled, angry, discouraged, defeated, blind and confused. Contrary to what we see in our churches today; this is the way God works, and He calls each of His children to join Him and be a part of it.

Paul explained, "the gospel is the power of God unto salvation" (Romans 1:16). Again, He said that, "faith come from hearing the *message"* (Romans 10:17). The Bible is our lifeline – to our end result, Christlikeness. Toward the end of his life, Paul wrote to his son in the ministry, Timothy:

> All Scripture is God-breathed and is useful for teaching,
> rebuking, correcting, and training in righteousness, so that
> the man of God may be thoroughly equipped
> for every good work.
> In the presence of God and of Christ Jesus, who will judge
> the living and the dead, and in view of his
> appearing and his kingdom, I give this charge:
> Preach the Word: be prepared in season and out of season;
> correct, rebuke and encourage – with great patience and
> careful instruction.
> (2 Timothy 3:16-42)

The Scriptures teach us about all of life and doctrine, including how we should assemble for corporate worship and how we are to organize our corporate life together (Hebrews 10:25).

Glorification

Though believers endure suffering now, they will enjoy glory when Christ returns. It is the will of God that believers be conformed to the image of Christ (glorified). Note that all the verbs in Romans 8:30 are *past tense:* The believer has been *called, justified,* and *glorified.* We have been justified, and that standing never changes. "There is therefore *now* no condemnation for those who are in Christ Jesus" (Romans 8:1, emphasis added).

Oh, there is so much more to salvation than the decision at the door, a grand finale to this process of sanctification and the gospel of Jesus Christ. Paul said, "If in this life only, we have hope ...." For in this hope we are saved (v. 24). I'm pushing my 80th birthday in April. Here is the blessing. We've been climbing the heights of justification and sanctification and we are glorifed already in Christ Jesus. The Spirit's indwelling presence (Romans 5:5) is the down payment on our final stage of glory.

We wait with patience as we hope for what we don't see (v.25). For the meeting of our human spirit witnesses with our inner witness [the Holy Spirit] that we are saved. We are the children of God. Yet believers like unbelievers still suffer common ills as well as blessings. They eventually die, but believers die with the hope of the resurrection in a renewed heaven and earth. Eventually, the sunset of life's deterioring effects begin to appear in our bodies.

O yes, I say with Paul, "I press toward the mark for the prize of the high calling of God in Christ Jesus" (Philippians 3:4). "Henceforth there is laid up for me a crown of righteousness, which the Lord, the righteous judge shall give me at that day; and not to me only, but unto all them also that love His appearing" (1 Timothy 4:8). By His Spirit, Christ is now gathering a people for Himself.

Corporate Worship

Worship wars are destroying the essence of many of our local churches today. We have conflicts over the use of instruments, contemporary songs or traditional hymns. However, the problem lies much deeper than the singing. If the church life is going to be Bible-centered then the music, singing, and worship of the church must be Bible-centered also.

Most local churches spend a great deal of time together praising God in song. But fewer give attention to the place of the Word of God in determining what we sing. Additionally there is little emphasis on understanding what we are singing. Therefore, many in the churches think of Christian singing in terms of emotions or entertainment; which over time will begin to erode Christian worship and eventually the people. So, over a period of time the word "worship," consists only of respectful and formal recognition of God, on certain occasions, in buildings specifically designed for that purpose and marked on the outside with the sign saying, "Welcome."

Upon entering the building one would hear a preaching service with a sermon and singing which may or may not lead the hearer ultimately to worship. Listening to a sermon is not worship. Worship is the upspring of a heart that knows the Father as a Giver, the Son as Savior, and the Holy Spirit as the indwelling Guest. It is apparent from this definition that only the regenerated believer can spiritually and intelligently worship the Father and the Son, through the power of the indwelling Holy Spirit.

Therefore, an unsaved person may be able to recognize God as supreme and Creator of all – but he or she has not been brought into a living relationship with Him as Father, and consequently is unable to really appreciate what only the Holy Spirit can reveal. The Scripture says, "the natural man receives not the things of the Spirit of God: for they are foolishness and undiscoverable to him: neither can he know them, because they are spiritually discerned" (1 Corinthians 2:14-15).

Christ used the analogy of "living water" to provide a pictorial image to describe the spiritual life which He came to make possible for all who believe in Him (John 4:13-14). This "living water" enters the believer at the new birth from above (John 3:3, 5). It springs up within the believer in worship (John 4:14). Then, it flows out, from him or her in service (John 7:37-39).

Thus, worship really consists of this "living water" returning to its source. King Solomon adds, "Unto the place from whence the rivers comes, to there they return" (Eccles. 1:7). So, we see, the spiritual life which flows from God to us, returns to Him in worship from us – and thus the Divine cycle is complete.

It was never God's intent for us to try to sustain our souls through experiences and entertainment. That is the place of the Spirit and the Word of God. That is why His Word must hold center stage in our singing as well as in our preaching and worship.

It's important to note that we are not truly worshipping, if we are not engaged upon the redemption we have through the Person and work of Jesus Christ. Sadly, we have the Spirit and the Word desiring to work in and through us – but in many local churches the pastors and worship leaders are bowing to pressure to entertain congregations in order to attract larger crowds and money.

We should desire and search out everything that God has revealed about Himself and then to:

- joyfully accept it,

- adopt it,
- submit ourselves to it, and
- enjoy God's blessings in it.

In everything and every topic, our practice as Christians should spiritually seek God's will and the truth of His Word. The Bible says, if we want to find life, we must give our lives away:

> For who desires to save his life will lose it, but whoever loses his life for My sake will find it" (Matthew 16:25).

This can be like the difference between the Dead Sea and the Sea of Galilee. The Jordan River flows into the Dead Sea, but there is no outlet. That great sea gives out absolutely nothing of itself – as a result nothing in it can survive. The Jordan River also flows into the Sea of Galilee – but it also flows out. The Sea of Galilee by contrast has an abundance of life.

The Church at Work

This same principle above applies to the Christian individually and the local church corporately. When believers are at work evangelizing the lost and pursuing the prodigals – *giving themselves* away carrying out their ministry of reconciliation, the Lord will bless that church and give back to her many increases.

The story is told of a young laborer who was given an address and told by his boss to draw necessary paint and supplies from the warehouse; and go paint the house, white. Give me a call when the job is finished, added the boss. The young man finished the job and called the boss. While awaiting his arrival and inspection; he stood there admiring his work. When the boss arrived and surveyed his work he told the young man that his work was outstanding – but the house he was supposed to paint was next door. He painted the wrong house! The Lord Jesus commissioned the Church to proclaim the gospel message of salvation, sacrificial love, and ultimate hope – the "good news" to all the world. Are we painting the right house?

We must understand it's not about facility size and numerical growth; which are by-products. As I stated in an earlier section, it's about the possibility of *losing the gospel* and without the gospel there would be no *eternal life!* We are always only one generation away from extinction! Are we faithfully sharing the good news? Cultural concerns such as decline and fragmentation will not destroy the integrity of the Church, but failure to share the gospel of Christ and pursue the prodigal certainly will!

Historically, the local Black church has been the source of stability, hope and encouragement in the face of uncertainty and social ills. But the difficulties we face today are compounded by the fact that many Christians themselves, are affected by the destabilization of the present season of unprecedented challenges. For example, recent research reports that a majority of practicing Christians do not consistently support evangelism and 47% of Millennial Christians *believe it is flat-out wrong to evangelize.*[79]

More and more of our youth and young adults feel little cultural pressure to maintain a Christian faith identity or any other for that matter. Barna research shows that practicing Christians agree strongly that faith is very important in their lives and have attended church within the past month. All others fall in one of two main groups:

1. Lapsed Christians identify as Christians but have not attended church within the past month. Only 4% consider their faith very important.[80]
2. Non-Christians identify with a faith other than Christianlty ("religious non-Christians") or with no faith at all ("atheists/agnostics/nones").[81]

The cultural view coupled with Christianity's poor reputation are actively *de-converting* those people who were raised in church; while non-Christians are hardening as they openly oppose all attempts of evangelistic efforts.

Looking at Christian history, the good news has been preached and spread in every century [even monastically during the dark ages], and though there have been failures as well as successes of mission the original commission from Jesus has been carried forward by every generation across the centuries. This generation is faced with an unprecedented number of obstacles; which counters *effective* evangelism. A few are listed below:

- The overall number of practicing Christians is falling against a cultural backdrop that is increasingly difficult to define.
- Societal discoveries such as the internet and social media.
- Generational shifts [i.e. millennials].
- The breakdown and redefinition of institutions such as the traditional marriage and the family.
- The racial and ethnic makeup of this country.
- Rising social tensions.
- Sexual aggression and abuse at all echelons of public service and life.

- The Christian faith is seen by non-Christians as irrelevant, and morally hypocritical.
- Christians are often too poorly equipped in their relational skills to navigate in a new era of witness-evangelism.
- Christians must realize that we cannot do evangelism with the same playbook used by Christians 40 or 60 years ago. It's a totally new ball game!

Finally, as Christians mature they confess their faith vocally, in song, and prayer, showing personal affection, and can share this faith in natural and persuasive conversation with others, being ready to explain and defend the faith (1 Peter 3:15). In this way, they build up other saints with their spiritual gifts and introduce unbelievers to Christ. Along this whole process, there really is no clear division between knowing, feeling, and doing. Especially as we mature in Christ doctrine and life become intwined.

When churches see souls saved on a regular basis; they enjoy a unique happiness and spiritual life that is contagious. I'm sure you'll agree, there is nothing more fulfilling or life-infusing than leading a person to Christ. With this perspective it is hard to see how anyone can grow and become Christlike without consistently sharing and defending his or her faith. BE SILENT NO MORE!

Discussion and Reflections: Chapter 13

1. Discuss how the Bible-centered church makes the gospel visible.

2. Everything we know about God and His will for the church comes from His own revelation.

3. What is the impact on the church as Bible reading in or out of church seems no longer important?

4. As Christ's ambassadors of reconciliation, we are not to draw back in silence, but declaring the whole truth in love and compassion.

5. Sadly, it has become the norm in many local churches that people hold on to the sins that Christ died to deliver us from thinking that He covers our ungodliness and lifestyles.

"GO
TELL IT ON THE MOUNTAIN
OVER
THE HILLS AND EVERYWHERE!"

"For I delivered to you first of all that which I also received: **that Christ died for our sins according to the Scriptures, and that He was buried, and that He rose again the third day according to the Scriptures,** *and that He was seen by Cephas, then by the twelve. That He was seen by over five hundred brethren at once"* (I Corinthians 15:1-6a).

HE IS RISEN!

We preach: *"That if you confess with your mouth the Lord Jesus and believe in your heart that God has raised Him from the dead, you will be saved' for with the heart one believes unto righteousness, and with the mouth confession is made unto salvation"* (Romans 10:9-10). Amen.

NOTES

INTRODUCTION

[1] Andrew Cohen, "The Speech That Shocked Birmingham the Day after the Church Bombing," *The Atlantic,* September 13, 2013, https://www. theatlantic.com/national/archive/2013/09/the-speech-that-shocked-birmingham-the-day-after-the-church-bombing/279565/.

[2] *Wayne A. Meeks, The First Urban Christians: The Social World of the Apostle Paul (New Haven, Conn, Yale University Press, 1983), p. 75*

[3] John L. Locke, *The De-Voicing of Society: Why We Don't Talk to Each Other Anymore* (New York: Simon & Schuster, 1998), p. 131

CHAPTER TWO: A NEW CREATION

[4] Though Nichodemus was a ruler of the Jews, Jesus informed him that he had to be born again to see the Kingdom of heaven (see John 3:3). Further the Scriptures says, "You must present your body a living sacrifice to God and be *transformed* and *enabled* by the renewing of your mind through the Word of God (study carefully Romans 12:1-5; also, chapters 1-8; II Corinthians 5:11-21).

[5] Webster's Dictionary (G. & C. Merriam Co. 1964) 482

[6] D. Michael Henderson, *A Model for Making Disciples* (Evangel Publishing House 1997) 131. As taken from Alfred North Whitehead's, *The Aims of Education,* p. 10.

CHAPTER FOUR: A BURDEN FOR THE LOST

[7] C. Sumner Wemp, *Teaching from The Tabernacle* (Moody Bible Institute of Chicago 1978 Third Edition) pages 77-86

[8] W.E. Vine's Greek Grammar Dictionary (Thomas Nelson Pub. 2012) 443 Note: The Greek terms [*agape* and *agapao*] are used in the N.T. Love can known only from the actions it prompts. God's love is seen in the gift of His Son, 1 John 4:9, 10. Love was an exercise of the divine will in deliberate choice, made without assignable cause save that which lies in the nature of God Himself, CF Deuteronomy 7:7,8. Love has God as its primary object, and expresses itself first of all in implicit obedience to His commandments, John 14:15, 21, 23; 15:10; 1 John 2:5; 5:3; 2 John 6. Self-will that is self-*pleasing, is the negation of the love of God.*

CHAPTER FIVE: TRUE CHRISTIAN FELOWSHIP

[9] Ibid. Vine's Dictionary 311

[10] Watchman Nee, *The Normal Christian Life* (Tyndale House Publishers, Inc.) 15

CHAPTER EIGHT: LEST WE FORGET

[11] E. Franklin Frazier, *The Negro Church in America* (Schocken Books Inc., New York 1974) p. 26

[12] Ibid.

[13] Ibid.

[14] Database of Transatlantic Slave Trade online at http://www.slavevoyages/ estimates at least 1,464,200 slave deaths at sea.

[15] Frazier, *The Negro Church in America* p. 10

[16] Ibid, p. 20

[17] Walter Johnson, *Soul by Soul: Life Inside the Antebellum Slave Market* (Cambridge, MA: Harvard University Press, 1999), 60

[18] Harriet Ann Jacobs, *Incidents in the Life of a Slave Girl,* ed. L. Maria Child (Boston, 1861), 83

[19] Lerone Bennett Jr., *Before the Mayflower: A History of Negro in America* (Chicago: Johnson Publishing Company, Inc, 1966), 70-71.

[20] Frazier, *The Negro Church in America* Page 23

[21] Ibid, p. 24

[22] From article located at: https://www.christianitytoday.com/ct/2014/ february-web-only/inconceivable-start-of-african-american-christianity. html.

[23] Frazier, *The Negro Church* p. 13

[24] Bennett, *Before the Mayflower* 7

[25] Frazier, *The Negro church* 14

[26] Gaines, Wesley John (1840-1912), *The Negro and the White Man* (Philadelphia: AME Publishing House, 1897), pp. 143-144

[27] Frazier, *The Negro church* p. 15

[28] Ibid.

[29] Ibid.

[30] Ibid. pp. 16-23

[31] Ibid. pp. 28-29

[32] Ibid. pp. 32-33

[33] Ibid. pp. 38-39

[34] Ibid. p. 39

[35] Ibid. p. 43-47

[36] Baptist, Edward E, *The Half Has Never Been Told* (New York, NY: Basic Books, 2016) 400-408

[37] Ibid. 408

[38] Ibid.

[39] Rothstein, Richard *The Color Of Law* (Liveright Pulishing Corp. 2017) 146-156

[40] Gates, Henry Louis Jr. *Stoney the Road* (New York, Penguin Press, 2019)

[41] Ibid.

[42] Baptist, *The Half Never Been Told* pp. 409-410

[43] Hinton, Elizabeth, Julilly Kohler-Hausman, and Vesla Weaver. 2016. Did Blacks Really Endorse the 1994 Crime Bill? *New York Times.* April 13. Retrieved. April 28, 2016

[44] Ibid.

[45] David Rusk, "Goodbye to Chocolate City," D.C. Policy Center, July 20, 2017, available at https://www.dcpolicycenter.org/publications/goodbye-t-chocalate-city/.

[46] Ibid.

[47] Jason Richardson, Bruce Mitchell, and Jaun Franco, *"Shifting Neighborhoods:Gentrification and cultural displacement in American cities"* (Washington: National Community Reinvestment colition, 2019).

[48] Henry J. Kaiser Family Foundation, *"Poverty Rate by Race/Ethnicity,"* Timeframe: 2017. Available at https/www.kff.org/other/state-indicator/poverty-rate-by-raseethnicity (assessed December 2019).

[49] Frazier, *The Negro Church* pp. 37-51

[50] Accessed May 31, 2019 from the Fayetteville Observer, page A5.

[51] Andrea Flynn, Susan R, Holmberg, Dorian T. Warren, and Felcia J. Wong, *The Hidden Rules of Race* (Cambridge University Press, New York, NY, Reprinted 2018) 2

[52] Ibid.

[53] M. David Sills, *Reaching and Teaching* (Moody Publishers, Chicago, IL, 2010) 28

CHAPTER NINE: THE SECULARIZATION OF THE BLACK CHURCH

[54] Syncretism involves the merging or assimilation of several originally discrete traditions, especially in the theology and mythology of religion, thus asserting an underlying unity and allowing for an inclusive approach to other faiths. Assessed on life from Wikipedia (November 10, 2018).

[55] Phillip Schaff, *History of the Christian Church, Volume II: Ante-Nicene Christianity.*

[56] Ibid.

[57] Accessed December 13, 2018 at https/abort73.com/abortion and race.

[58] Oswald Chambers, *Prayer – A Holy Occupation* (Grand Rapids: Discovery House, 1992). 97

[59] Extracted from the article "Spoiled Fruit" by R.T. Kendall, (Charisma Magazjne, February 2019) 36

[60] Henry H. Mitchell, *Black Preaching: The Recovery of a Powerful Art* (Nashville, TN: Abingdon Press, 1990) 66

[61] Ibid., 121

[62] C.S. Lewis, *The Screwtape Letters* (New York: Harper Collins, 2001) 155

[63] Thabiti Anyabwile, *Reviving the Black Church* (B&H Publishing Group, Nashville, TN 2015) 77

[64] "Competing Worldviews Influence Today's Christians," Barna, May 9, 2017, https://www.barna.com/research/competing worldviews-influence-todays-christians/.

[65] Anthony Bright Arwarm, *Building Your Life on the Principles of God: The Solid Foundation* (Bloomington, IN: Author House, 204), 86

[66] Thomas Merton, *Conjecture of a Guilty Bystander* (New York: Doubleday, 1989), 157-58

[67] Ibid.

CHAPTER TEN: THE CHURCH IN ORGANISM

[68] Jay R.Leach, *A Light unto My Path* (Trafford Publishing 2013) 86–87

[69] Jay R. Leach, *Grace That Saves* (Trafford Publishing 2014) 115–116

[70] *A Light unto My Path* (Trafford Publishing 2013) 92-101

[71] Note: The word "grows" is a biological word, the idea a living organism. The church is pictured as a *living organism* – the union of various parts [members] of a living being, of a dynamic body. This may seem stange to speak of a building in biological terms – a building that grows. The point is that more and more parts, more and more believers are brought and fitted into the building as each day passes. The building grows and grows and shall continue to grow until the Lord Jesus Christ returns.

[72] Spiritual organism is wherein each member in the body of Christ seeks to faithfully and obediently fulfill the spiritual gift God has given you.

[73] Ray Steadman, *Body Life,* revised edition (Thomas Nelson Publishers 1995) 18

CHAPTER ELEVEN: EVANGELIZE OR FOSSILIZE

[74] Rick Renner, *Dressed to Kill* (Tulsa OK: Published by Harrison House, New Edition 2007) 392

CHAPTER TWELVE: GOD'S WAY OR NO WAY

[75] Francis Schaeffer, *The Mark of a Christian,* 2nd edition (Dowers Grove, Il:InterVarsity, 2006) 29

CHAPTER THIRTEEN: BE SILENT NO MORE

[76] Richard Dawkins, *The God Delusion* (New York: Houghton Mifflin, 2008) 51

[77] Jonathan Leeman, *Reverberation: How God's Word Brings Light, Freedom, and Action to His People* (Chicago, IL.: Moody Press Publishers, 2011), 87-88.

[78] A. W. Tozier, *The Pursuit of God* (Camp Hill, PA: Christian Publications, Inc. 1972) 80-81

[79] Barna Group, *Reviving Evangelism* (Alpha USA 2018) 5

[80] Ibid. 9

[81] Ibid. 9

Printed in the United States
By Bookmasters